HUMANITARIANISM FROM BELOW

Humanitarianism from Below

FAITH, WELFARE, AND THE ROLE OF
CASAS DE MIGRANTES IN MEXICO

Alejandro Olayo-Méndez

NEW YORK UNIVERSITY PRESS
New York

NEW YORK UNIVERSITY PRESS
New York
www.nyupress.org

© 2025 by New York University
All rights reserved

Please contact the Library of Congress for Cataloging-in-Publication data.

ISBN: 9781479825615 (hardback)
ISBN: 9781479825622 (paperback)
ISBN: 9781479825646 (library ebook)
ISBN: 9781479825639 (consumer ebook)

The manufacturer's authorized representative in the EU for product safety is Mare Nostrum Group B.V., Mauritskade 21D, 1091 GC Amsterdam, The Netherlands. Email: gpsr@mare-nostrum.co.uk.

Manufactured in the United States of America

10 9 8 7 6 5 4 3 2 1

Also available as an ebook

To Mamá Chanita, Lina, and Li,
for everything you gave me in life.

Para Mamá Chanita, Lina, y Li,
por todo lo que me dieron en la vida.

CONTENTS

Introduction

Neither virtue nor foresight can effectively shield individuals from the fragility of the human body in a hostile world. Communities, in contrast, can do much to protect their members. They can guard, insure, inoculate, and nurse. They can supply work, food, shelter, and defense. The group can protect—or at least sustain—its members in ways unavailable to most people, because of its greater resources. But should they do so? If the answer is yes, who should receive the benefit of communal protection? And what should they be protected against?
—Lynn Hollen Lees

He Did Not Die Alone

Everything went completely quiet. The silence was striking in comparison to the blasting music often played through the speakers during the day. When I came down from the volunteers' room to investigate the silence, there was no one around on the patio. I heard a whisper coming from the dormitory; upon entering, I saw migrants gathered in a circle. In the center of the circle, in a recliner, there was a body covered with a white sheet, and a candle flickered next to him. A man had died and migrants were already praying. The setting exuded mixed feelings, solidarity, and anxiety at the same time.

There were around forty-five migrants that day at the *casa del migrante*. Everybody remained quiet and prayed in the room until Mexican authorities came to take the body away. Once the body was put in a van, migrants accompanied the car as though in a procession until they reached the exit door. They could not go further since this shelter, which was in the city of Saltillo in northern Mexico, was a "closed shelter," where migrants could not go out. Migrants kept singing and praying for a while, even after the body left the shelter. Later that night, a Mass was held. Padre Toño, the shelter's director, said, "At least he did not die like a dog on the street, alone and with no one to take care of him."

Rubén, a fifty-eight-year-old Honduran migrant, had died in a chair while watching television, surrounded by many other fellow migrants who, like him, were on the road to the United States.[1] He had been at the shelter for over four months after several failed attempts to cross the border. He was sick and his family in Honduras did not have money to help him get back home. He refused to return home through the removal process of Mexican migration authorities. As he was too ill to fend for himself, several volunteers took turns taking care of him; migrants staying at the shelter sometimes helped to move him from place to place, until the day when his body finally gave up.

Casas de migrantes (migrant shelters) might be perceived as "pockets of safety" scattered throughout Mexican territory.[2] These organizations offer humanitarian assistance to people on the move along migration routes and in border cities in Mexico. But they do not operate in a vacuum—and neither do they own all the resources that are made available to migrants in distress. Rubén's story illuminates how *casas de migrantes* and their residents have to stretch themselves occasionally to serve migrants' needs. Rubén had stayed at the shelter for several months. A daily routine of feeding, bathing, changing diapers, and moving him from place to place was part of the ritual surrounding his care. On his last day, additional mobilization of resources was needed. Arranging a burial, notifying the local state of his death, contacting the Honduran consul, and finding the family were actions that needed to be taken as the dominoes fell. My presence at this event reminded me that shelters operate in a dense context and engage with a number of different actors: the local community, the government, international nongovernmental organizations (INGOs), researchers, and other actors.

Migrants, asylum seekers, refugees, internally displaced persons (IDPs), and other persons in contexts of mobility face many challenges while trying to cross Mexico on their way to the United States.[3] Vulnerability, precariousness, uncertainty, creativity, and resilience appear at different moments in migrants' journeys. In the background of narratives and research about migration in Mexico, *casas de migrantes* emerge not only as places attempting to address migrants' precariousness, but also as places that international organizations like the Red Cross, the United Nations High Commissioner for Refugees (UNHCR), the International Organization for Migration (IOM), the International Rescue Committee (IRC), and Doctors Without Borders (Médecins Sans Frontières, or MSF), among others, seek to partner with because migrants gather there. Researchers also seek out shelters because of the convenience of finding migrants willing to share their stories, or the opportunity to collect information and observe dynamics that unfold along migration routes. Yet while many migrants are aware of the existence and support of migrant shelters along the way, and researchers and international organizations use them to facilitate finding and engaging with them, the analysis of their role in the Mexican humanitarian ecosystem has been fragmented and remains underdeveloped.

This book offers a deeper analysis and understanding of this crucial yet underexamined aspect of international migration: the role played by *casas de migrantes* in the migration process in Mexico. It argues that *casas de migrantes* emerge as an important type of what I call "humanitarianism from below"; they function as an informal welfare system for migrants, asylum seekers, refugees, deportees, and IDPs in Mexico and perform a critical intermediary role in the humanitarian architecture of migration. The volume engages in debates about humanitarianism and challenges traditional understandings of what counts as humanitarian aid. It provides an in-depth discussion of the role of migrant shelters, revealing the tension between security and insecurity along migrant routes, and examining how migrant shelters emerge as critical brokers of aid that are part of the humanitarian ecosystem in Mexico. It also reviews the underexplored role of faith-based humanitarian organizations in Mexico, whose engagement with migrants is generally perceived more as "charity work" than professional humanitarian work, though I make the case for classifying it as the latter. Finally, the book analyzes the tension between welfare and containment prevalent in humanitarian settings. Thus, it contributes to a deeper understanding of the role of humanitarian actors in the migration process, the interactions between migrants and *casas de migrantes*, and three concurrent and self-reinforcing dynamics: poverty, violence, and care (humanitarian aid). The guiding questions the book seeks to answer are, What are *casas de migrantes?* What has facilitated their emergence and development? And what is their role and what impact do they have on the migration process in Mexico?

Dynamics and Actors along Migration Routes in Mexico

Mexico is a country of origin, transit, destination, and return of migrants, asylum seekers, refugees, deportees, and IDPs. While it has long been known as an emigration country, in the past three decades, the country has also become an important transit country for US-bound migrants from Central America, mostly from Guatemala, El Salvador, and Honduras, due to push-pull economic factors, family reunification arrangements, emerging patterns of displacement due to increasing levels of violence, and climate change shocks.[4] Furthermore, Mexico has also become a new immigrant destination as more migrants and people seeking refugee status are unable to enter the United States. Haitians, Venezuelans, Cubans, and Africans from different countries, as well as people from other nationalities, now have a significant presence in border towns, cities where refugees have been resettled, and all along migrant routes through Mexico.[5]

According to official and unofficial data, the number of migrants (mostly Central Americans) passing through Mexico on their way to the United States ranges from 150,000 to 450,000 a year.[6] Migration patterns in Mexico also need to account for the number of Mexicans deported from the United States who are returning to the country with diverse social circumstances and needs, who are not included in the data above. According to statistics from the US Department of Homeland Security, the number of deported Mexicans remained relatively steady at around 230,000 annually between 2016 and 2020.[7]

Different events and US exclusionary programs and policies have complicated migration patterns in Mexico. In late 2018 and early 2019, migrant caravans consisting mostly of Central American migrants moving en masse across Mexico, brought criticism from the US government and put pressure on the Mexican government and society to address their mobilization.[8] Increasing numbers of asylum seekers and migrants were left stranded at border towns in Mexico as a result of programs and policies like the Migrant Protection Protocols, or "Remain in Mexico" program, which sent people seeking asylum in the United States to wait in Mexico for their administrative procedures,[9] and Title 42, an order issued by the US Centers for Disease Control and Prevention (CDC) during the COVID-19 pandemic that prevents the entrance into the United States of certain persons from countries where a communicable disease exists.[10] Stranded migrants in northern Mexico contributed to an increase in irregular crossings into the United States.[11] During the fiscal year 2022, the US Border Patrol detained slightly over two million migrants along the United States' southern border.[12] Moreover, the increasing numbers of IDPs in Mexico cannot be overlooked within the migration patterns in Mexico, as by the end of 2021, close to 850,000 persons remained internally displaced due to violence. Internally displaced persons, like refugees, are nationals fleeing violence and persecution, but have not crossed an international border.[13]

In the last two decades, the main routes used by migrants have seen increases in violence, risk, and cost. These changes have resulted from stricter immigration policies, an increase in border control and militarization—in both Mexico and the United States—and a rise in criminal activity along migratory routes.[14] The increase in immigration control relates to the Mexican government's efforts to present Mexico as a modern country that is able to maintain order and control its migration flows.[15] These efforts have been reinforced through changes in Mexican migration laws and framed within the National Development Plan 2013–2018, a document that established the national objectives, strategies, and priorities that should govern the actions of the government during president Enrique Peña Nieto's administration, and the subsequent policies implemented by the Mexican government in the administration of president Andrés Manuel López Obrador since 2018.[16]

Since the mid-2000s, there has been a perceptible and visible increase of violence in Mexico. This rise in violence is due to several factors, including the war on drugs, turf battles among drug cartels, firearms trafficked from the United States, and the effects of government policies and enforcement—in regard to drug crime—among other structural factors like poverty and corruption among politicians, police, and military entities.[17] The increase in criminal activity against migrants is partially due to an overlap between the migratory routes and the routes used by drug traffickers and criminal gangs, since occasionally, drug traffickers and migrants use the same main or secondary roads to move through the country. Similar rises in violence, kidnapping, and risk have been seen at the border cities where Mexicans arrive after deportation, consistent with a general increase of violence in Mexico.[18] In the last decade, kidnapping and extortion of migrants have become a source of easy income and cash flow for criminal groups and government authorities. Cash transfer organizations like Western Union, Elektra, and Banco Azteca, among others, struggle to monitor accounts that receive large amounts of money on daily basis which has fueled a 'political economy' that sees migrants as commodities, and which generates more than 50 million dollars annually.[19]

As a result of the violence and the precarious conditions for the migrants during their journeys or after deportation, humanitarian aid organizations—shelters, soup kitchens, and human rights organizations—managed by local NGOs have emerged to assist and advocate for migrants and deportees. Many of these local humanitarian organizations are faith-based, while a few are NGOs with no particular faith affiliation. The assistance they provide consists of food, shelter, medical care, legal assistance, educational instruction on human rights and health—especially AIDS prevention—and information about the risks and dangers on the route. In addition, there are other places along the route that provide food and medical care, but not shelter. Generally, services are free of charge for migrants.[20] While these organizations can be distinguished as *albergues* (shelters), *comedores* (soup kitchens), and *centros de atención* (attention centers), they are commonly known as *casas de migrantes* (migrant shelters) or simply as *albergues* (shelters).[21] The differences among these organizations consist mostly of the types of services they are able to provide to migrants, deportees, and, most recently, asylum seekers. A shelter usually offers overnight stays for migrants, while soup kitchens offer food and healthcare during specific times, but no overnight stays, and attention centers offer only information and emergency assistance.

In 2022 there were more than 150 such groups and NGOs supporting migrants, deportees, internally displaced persons, asylum seekers, and refugees in Mexico. The core mission of many of these *casas de migrantes* is to care for vulnerable migrants and refugees, as well as to advocate for their human rights. These groups often emerge as local initiatives.

Sometimes they flourish, grow, and expand their services; other times these organizations struggle to remain open to provide basic services. The number of shelters has grown since the late 1980s. They have increased not only in numbers, but also in the services provided, which have required adjustments due to the changing profiles of the migrants over the years. Some migrants hear about the shelters before starting their journeys, while others learn about them along the way. Migrants recognize the helpfulness of these humanitarian spaces and use them as resources, as long as it is convenient for their trajectory or when they are in dire need. While staying in these temporary safe spaces, the migrants consider their next moves forward, which may sometimes include either returning to their country of origin or remaining in Mexico.

In this book, to give variety to the prose, I refer to these groups and organizations as *casas de migrantes*, *albergues*, migrant shelters, or simply shelters. As noted above, the *casas de migrantes* offer a combination of humanitarian aid consisting of food, shelter, first aid, and educational instruction both in human rights and in practical matters of health and safety.[22] Slowly, *casas de migrantes* and other humanitarian groups have gained prominence and have impacted the Mexican political landscape. For instance, Father Alejandro Solalinde, director of the shelter Hermanos en el Camino (Brothers along the Road) and Norma Romero, leader of Las Patronas (a group of volunteer women providing assistance to migrants), received the Mexican Human Rights National Award in 2012 and 2013, respectively. Other shelters have received state awards for their work among migrants, including FM4 Paso Libre (FM4 Free Transit), a shelter in Guadalajara in western Mexico; Casa de la Caridad Hogar del Migrante (Charity House, Home for the Migrant) in San Luis Potosí, in central Mexico; and Posada Belén (Belen Shelter) in Saltillo, in northern Mexico. In addition, some shelters, like La 72 in Tenosique, Tabasco, have become prominent advocates for refugees arriving from Central American countries. Due to their significance in the migration process in Mexico, some *casas de migrantes* have forged alliances and partnerships with international humanitarian organizations.

Migration research has largely focused on origin or destination contexts, neglecting the study of the journey itself. Yet the migration process includes not only points of origin and arrival, but the factors and interactions that lead to migration and influence its course.[23] Within the analysis of actors and structures that sustain, facilitate, and control migration, the focus has been mostly on social relations, collectives, social networks, and the formation of social and symbolic capital.[24] More recently, concepts like the "migration industry," which commonly refers to individuals, organizations, and other actors who provide services that facilitate and sustain international migration, have tried to capture the ways in which intermediate actors shape and structure migration patterns.[25] As more empirical evidence has been gathered, it has become clearer that the conceptualization of the migration industry, as it stands now, does not fully analyze the complete range of actors who play key roles in migration processes, such as humanitarian groups and organizations providing aid outside emergency settings.[26] While Carpi and Fiddian-Qasmiyeh (2020), Pallister-Wilkins (2022), and Carruth (2021) have explored different approaches to humanitarian work from local perspectives and migration governance, the role of local humanitarian actors and the relationship between humanitarian aid and migration has remained underexplored in the existing migration studies literature.

In the case of Mexico, migration scholars have documented and analyzed the experiences of Central Americans crossing the country, as well as the experiences of deported Mexicans arriving at cities along the border with the United States. Among others, Vogt (2018) and Brigden (2018) analyze the violence and exploitation migrants experience, as well as the ways these experiences shape their journeys; Silva Quiroz (2014) looks at the ways migration policies have affected the journeys of Central Americans; and Sládková (2010) conducts a psychosocial analysis of the journeys of Honduran migrants to the United States. Examining the border between Mexico and the United States, Sanchez (2014), Martínez (2013), and Slack (2019) document the experiences of migrants at the crossing point, explaining the interplay between violence, smuggling, and deportation contexts. These studies provide significant insights into the journeys of migrants and migration dynamics in Mexico. Still, their focus remains mostly on the migrants' experiences, political aspects of the migration process, or specific geographical regions. Furthermore, several of these studies have collected data and conducted participant observations at different *casas de migrantes*, but with the growing number of shelters providing aid, few scholars have looked more deeply into the roles these humanitarian spaces play as intermediaries in the migration process in Mexico.[27] This book takes a deeper look at the humanitarian ecosystem that has emerged in Mexico, which plays a critical role in the migration system and operates with the inherent tensions and challenges of humanitarian work.

Humanitarianism: Forgetting the "Local"

The emergence of humanitarianism is often linked to the Battle of Solferino and the cofounder of the Red Cross, Henry Dunant.[28] In his book *A Memory of Solferino*, Dunant offers a detailed account of the raging battle at the town of Solferino, in northern Italy in 1859, part of the second Italian War of Independence, and also describes the atrocities on the battlefield after the fighting, the effort to care for the wounded in the small town of Castiglione, and the plan that gave rise to the Red Cross.[29] The account of the battle and its consequences is a grueling cry for help and the pointed desire to respond to that plea:

> The stillness of the night was broken by groans, by stifled sighs of anguish and suffering. Heart-rending voices kept calling for help. Who could ever describe the agonies of that fearful night. . . . When the sun came up on the twenty-fifth, it disclosed the most dreadful sights imaginable. Bodies of men and horses covered the battlefield; corpses were strewn over roads, ditches, ravines, thickets, and fields; the approaches of Solferino were literally thick with dead. The fields were devastated, wheat and corn lying flat on the ground, fences broken, orchards ruined; here and there were pools of blood. The villages were deserted and bore the scars left by musket shots, bombs, rockets, grenades, and shells. . . . The town was completely transformed into a vast improvised hospital for French and Austrians. . . . The towns people gave all the blankets, linens and mattresses they could spare. The hospital of Castiglione, the Church, the San Luigi monastery and barracks, the Capuchin Church, the police barracks, the Churches of San Maggiore, San Guisseppe, and Santa Rosalia, were all filled with wounded men. . . . Although every house had become an infirmary, and each household had plenty to do in taking care of the wounded officers . . . I succeeded, by the Sunday morning, in getting together a certain number of people who helped as best they could with the efforts made to aid the wounded. It was not a matter of amputations or

operations of any kind. But, food, and above all drink, had to be taken around to men dying of hunger and thirst; then their wounds could be dressed and their bleeding, muddy, vermin-covered bodies washed. . . . Before long a group of volunteer helpers was formed. The Lombard women went first to those who cried the loudest. . . . The women entered the churches, and went from one man to another with jars and canteens full of pure water. . . . Their gentleness and kindness, their tearful and compassionate looks, and their attentive care helped revive a little courage among the patients.[30]

Henry Dunant received the Noble Peace Prize in 1901 as recognition for his humanitarian efforts and his plan to create national relief societies, made up of volunteers, trained in peacetime to provide neutral and impartial help to relieve suffering in times of war. These national societies could make relief efforts more sustainable and organized.[31] However, in the excitement surrounding his idea and the pressing need for aid in wartime, local efforts took a back seat in history. Dunant played a critical role in rallying and organizing the townspeople. Local communities were one of the first responders offering relief and support in a time of crisis. But as humanitarianism evolved, the critical role of local communities, rather than of those foreign actors who came to offer help from abroad, became overlooked and undervalued.

Two centuries ago, people started using the concept of humanitarianism to characterize lifesaving relief actions and to pay attention to the underlying causes of suffering. By the beginning of the nineteenth century, the notion of humanitarianism gradually entered into everyday vocabulary. Yet the distinction between humanitarianism and previous forms of charity, compassion, and philanthropy remained unclear. Thus, early understandings of humanitarianism included both international and domestic action, characterizing them as distinct interventions. However, humanitarianism slowly became associated with compassion across boundaries, due in large part to the creation of the International Committee of the Red Cross in 1863.[32]

Other examples of contemporary humanitarians include people like William Wilberforce, who helped stop the slave trade in the late eighteenth century, Florence Nightingale, who introduced female nurses into the military and served as an inspiration for the classical principle of neutrality in humanitarian work, Englantyne Jebb, founder of Save the Children, Dr. Bob Pierce, founder of World Vision International, and Bernard Kouchner, cofounder of Médecins Sans Frontières (Doctors Without Borders) and Médecins du Monde (Doctors of the World). In varied ways and contexts, these humanitarians helped to reshape society's views to be more inclusive of the helpless and wounded. They pressured states to extend their obligations to populations in distress and provided the foundation for the current structure of care for strangers. Their contributions show that it is possible to respond to suffering in a manner more robust than mourning.[33]

Humanitarianism evolved and now generally includes three key dimensions: a global and transnational reach expressed in assistance beyond borders, a general belief that such transnational action is related in some way to a transcendent or higher morality, and the organization and governance of activities designed to protect and improve humanity regardless of race, political affiliation, or nationality.[34] Humanitarianism today has become increasingly public, hierarchical, and institutionalized.[35] It is commonly associated with international nongovernmental organizations like the United Nations High Commissioner for Refugees (UNHCR), MSF (Doctors without Borders), or the Red Cross. Due to its international and institutional nature, current humanitarian work can be characterized as "humanitarianism from above." However, we know that solidarity and the desire to alleviate suffering are dimensions of the ethos of civil society.[36] If the idea of community has any meaning for the work of humanitarianism, it must include "the mutual obligations, and moral responsibilities felt among its members."[37] This desire to alleviate the suffering of others drives secular and religious movements and organizations and goes beyond the responsibilities of legal and political institutions. This book argues that migrant shelters challenge traditional understandings of what counts as humanitarian aid. Thus, in contrast to "humanitarianism from above," humanitarian work in Mexico, operating mainly through the *casas de migrantes*, is best understood as a type of humanitarian assistance that I theorize as "humanitarianism from below." This type of humanitarianism is deeply humane and local, and exists within formal and informal organizational structures. Humanitarianism from below is also self-sustained and adaptable, and often identifies with a faith-based affiliation. As we will see, this distinct type of humanitarianism plays a key brokerage role in Mexico's migration process, and is anything but neutral.

Understanding humanitarian work in Mexico requires considering the social processes from which it emerges because the context dictates much of its modus operandi. Despite its limitations, humanitarianism from below challenges the classical humanitarian principles of neutrality and impartiality. It does so by showing a spirit of solidarity that results in advocacy. The grassroots humanitarian work in Mexico demands that local actors take sides—specifically, the side of the most vulnerable. Some shelters are places of confrontation and advocacy, while others facilitate alliances with key actors to achieve their goals. Over time, these humanitarian groups have gained prominence, impacted the political landscape, and inevitably become part of Mexico's growing humanitarian ecosystem and migration management structure.

A Note on Method

Eighteen months of ethnographic research provide the backbone of data in this book. The stories and analysis here emerged from conversations and interviews collected while I lived in migrant shelters along migrant routes between 2014 and 2016, with additional visits in 2018, 2019, 2020, and 2022. During that time, I collected data in several geographical regions in south, central, and northern Mexico. I traveled along migrant routes from south to north several times to understand the dynamics generated by the movement of migrants and their encounters with humanitarian actors.[38] Later, I had longer stays at three shelters (one in each geographical region) and visited other shelters nearby. In 2023 I spent another eight months visiting *casas de migrantes* and collecting data along the US-Mexico border. During that time, I conducted interviews at the eight US ports of entry able to receive asylum seekers, from Matamoros in Tamaulipas to Tijuana in Baja California Norte.[39] In total, I lived and volunteered at sixteen migrant shelters along migratory routes in Mexico, collected data at another nineteen shelters and two migrant camps at border cities, and visited another fifteen migrant shelters close to where I conducted research.

Migrants' interviews focused on their experiences along the journey and how they perceived and engaged migrant shelters. In 2023 interviews focused more not only on the journey and its challenges but also on migrants' digital practices and the ways they collected and used information in their decision-making process. Interviews with shelter directors, several staff members and volunteers, and stakeholders focused on shelters' day-to-day operations and life, collaborations and relationships with other actors, challenges with changes in policies and migration patterns, and understanding of their mission and work. Aside from formal interviews, my fieldwork consisted of participant observation of everyday life at shelters. Often, I assisted with intake procedures and orientation, received and sorted donations, helped to prepare and serve meals, and coordinated the distribution of clothes and shoes. Due to my social work background, I was able to assist with some psychosocial activities and with some crisis interventions. I also provided some pastoral accompaniment because I am also a Jesuit Catholic priest.

Data include important events like the migrant caravans of late 2018, the impact of exclusionary programs and policies like the Migrant Protection Protocols (MPP), or "Remain in Mexico" program, implemented by the United States in early 2019, and the Title 42 policy used during the pandemic, which remained in place for thirty-eight months, as well as some of the effects of the COVID-19 pandemic, and the rollout of the CBP One app.[40] Including these events allows the book to be close to the current scenarios in the migration process in Mexico. From a methodological perspective, I considered the fieldwork as an extended field site and approached it using an adapted mobile methodology.[41] The result is an overview of the role of shelters as migrants move through or return to the country, as well as a deeper understanding of the work and challenges of migrant shelters across different regions in Mexico.

As suggested above, research on migration has greatly limited the field of inquiry to mainly "departure" and "arrival" places, leaving aside the spaces in between.[42] In his proposal for multi-site fieldwork, Marcus (1995) insists that researchers must not be limited to geography or location but must follow connections, associations, and relationships.[43] Other scholars have averred that one can follow migration journeys,[44] study dynamics in migratory corridors and global pathways,[45] or focus on social processes and relations.[46] Researchers of irregular forms of migration have frequently focused on "transit areas," understanding them not as fixed sites, but rather as areas where migrants "arrive intending to continue their journey as soon as possible to a further destination."[47]

However, some scholars insist on exploring field locations beyond fixed or multiple settings. They argue for considering the site as an "extended" field, constituted by several brief in-depth studies on specific aspects of migrants' lives in different places.[48] Collecting data in an extended field site allows an understanding of how migration journeys are shaped not only by single moments or spaces, but also by what occurs along the way. Furthermore, seeing the field as an extended site helps us understand how external migration dynamics play out all along migratory routes.

In this book, I approach the migrant routes and border cities in Mexico as an "extended field site." While dictated to some extent by the cargo train system, these routes are not completely fixed. They vary due to immigration controls, level of crime or violence, migrants' economic resources, and migrants' decisions. Considering border cities as part of this "extended field site" is critical, as they are ports of entry, as in the case of cities in southern Mexico, or dead ends, as in the case of those at the northern border of Mexico. This understanding of migrant routes and border cities in Mexico as an extended field site allows us to see how similar dynamics, like violence and migration enforcement, look in different regions or how common actors, such as migrant shelters or international organizations, influence migration journeys as a whole.

Mobility is a critical dynamic along migrant routes in Mexico. Migrants often are on their way north, sometimes caught in a revolving door of enforcement at the southern border, other times looking for ways to reach the border with the United States, even when they become stranded along migration routes. Hence, the need to look at the extended field site through the lens of a "mobile methodology."[49] This methodology looks closely at the world of everyday life practices and emphasizes its mobile nature through the experiences of moving subjects. A mobile approach to migration emphasizes the role of the journey and challenges the "rootedness" or "sedentary bias" that scholars have criticized in migration studies.[50] The mobile methodology requires the researcher to both be in motion in the field to understand the movement of the subject of study itself, and remain in place at various transit points to observe the subject in motion and to understand its dynamics.[51] Movement not only modifies migrants' perceptions of the people and places they encounter but also changes those who engage with migrants on a daily basis.

Understanding both migrants' journeys and the dynamics that emerge as they move through migrant routes is critical to obtain a more complete picture of migration dynamics in Mexico. Thus, I used an adapted version of a mobile methodology in the field by choosing strategic points to collect data and conduct field observations.[52] When I started research for this project, most of the data available had been collected at different points in the states of Tapachula, Oaxaca, and Veracruz, and some border cities with the United States. With the idea of an "extended field site" in mind, I collected data while traveling from the southern border to the northern border of Mexico several times while using public transportation and volunteering at different migrant shelters for different periods. Some journeys included visits to Guatemala, Honduras, and the United States. During the journeys, I closely observed the interactions between migrants and humanitarian organizations. Moving across the whole Mexican territory helped to illuminate the extension of the field and how interactions between migrants and *casas de migrantes* change. Later, I chose three migrant shelters along the Gulf of Mexico routes, where I had longer stays volunteering and observing the dynamics unfolding as migrants passed through the shelters. In this way, I tried first to be part of the motion and later to observe the movement. Different insights came out of this approach. I noticed that when in movement the focus was more on migrants' journeys and experiences, while the stays at the shelters allowed for more opportunity to observe not only interactions between migrants and *casas de migrantes*, but also how shelters engage with other actors and shape migration processes.

While the methodological approach involved moving from place to place and understanding how geography, movement, and the local sociopolitical context influenced the work of *casas de migrantes*, it also required balancing different identities (volunteer, researcher, social worker, and priest) and the impact they have on migrants' perspectives of the shelter, as well as the work of the shelter and their permanent staff.

In managing different identities, I constantly reflected on my positionality and how it shaped my understanding of shelters' work and life.

Book Structure

Chapter 1, "The Changing Patterns of Migration in Mexico and Its Violent Context," argues that a full picture of migration patterns cannot be reduced to those moving north. A more comprehensive understanding of migration patterns in Mexico needs to consider Mexican deportees from the United States and the increasing number of asylum seekers and internally displaced persons waiting at Mexican border cities and other parts of the country. The chapter discusses emerging needs and contexts along migrant routes and border cities as migrants or asylum seekers become stranded or remain in limbo due to the changing political landscape. The backdrop for this discussion is the generalized context of increasing violence in Mexico. The chapter offers profiles of the many migrants who move, return to, or become stranded in Mexico and highlights the violent context in which they move.

Through the narratives of shelter directors, migrants' accounts, and documents that have registered the work of these places, chapter 2, "Humanitarianism from Below," discusses what *casas de migrantes* are, how they function, and their importance in the migration processes in Mexico. The later part of the chapter delves more deeply into the concept of "humanitarianism from below," arguing that this distinct form of humanitarianism is deeply humane and local, contains formal or informal organizational structures, is self-sustained and adaptable, and often has a faith-based affiliation, and that this form of humanitarianism plays a critical role in Mexico's migration process and is anything but neutral. The chapter highlights how humanitarian groups emerged from one formal shelter that opened in the city of Tijuana in northern Mexico back in 1987 and gradually expanded into a loose network of over 150 shelters and soup kitchens that offered some form of assistance to migrants, asylum seekers, refugees, internally displaced persons, and deportees by 2022. A glimpse into the daily life of migrant shelters and how they operate illustrates why migrants with few resources or vulnerable deportees quickly learn that the shelters exist to support them with an array of services.

The emergence of humanitarian assistance in Mexico has historical roots and influences from migration experiences in Mexico. Chapter 3, "Fertile Ground," presents the elements that have given rise to the work of migrant shelters, especially its faith-based nature. It also addresses the tension between humanitarianism from below and humanitarianism from above, where one appears as "charity" and the other as proper humanitarian work. The emergence of migrant shelters is not spontaneous. While there are different experiences throughout the world of humanitarian assistance offered to migrants by faith-based organizations (FBOs), this chapter discusses how the Mexican case is unique regarding the number of shelters in the country, the length of time they have been providing services, and the relationships they develop to continue their work. The chapter analyzes the elements that have made it possible for the shelters to emerge and sustain their work despite their limited resources and institutional fragility.

Chapter 4, "An Informal Welfare System along Migration Routes," argues that while migrant shelters may seem scattered throughout Mexico, they do not operate in a vacuum. Shelters function in a dense humanitarian ecosystem that includes different actors: the local community, religious leaders, the government, international NGOs, and others. This chapter argues that humanitarian spaces aiding migrants in Mexico have become an informal social welfare system for Central American migrants, as well as an outsourced welfare system for deported Mexicans.

Chapter 5, "Brokers of Aid," emphasizes that these humanitarian organizations are not defined only by their humanitarian work; they are also framed and understood by their brokerage role, which refers to the different relationships shelters have with other actors to gather resources and aid the migrant population. While providing services and exercising brokerage roles, migrant shelters simultaneously exercise dynamics of facilitation, control, and care. An analysis of shelters as brokers of aid and as an informal welfare system provides a different angle for understanding the role of humanitarian actors as migration intermediaries. This is distinct from a political-economy approach and expands discussions on the so-called "migration industry."

Due to their local nature, *casas de migrantes* across Mexico differ significantly in size, services, and capacity. Chapter 6, "Between Welfare and Containment," examines the internal dynamics of migrant shelters and discusses the tension between welfare and containment that is ever present in humanitarian work. The narratives of migrants and shelter directors show that, in practice, the line between a migrant shelter and a detention center can be blurred. The chapter analyzes the experiences of both migrants and humanitarian workers regarding this tension. This discussion contributes to the view of humanitarian work in Mexico as both welfare and containment.

The last chapter, "Contestation, Alliance, and Institutionalization," analyzes why geographical location determines the emergence of *casas de migrantes* as places of contestation, alliance, or institutionalization in the migration process. It also argues that while shelters share some best practices, it is impossible to have a single model for a migrant shelter across the country. Shelters' styles correspond with their locations, leadership, and contexts. The chapter illustrates how shelters in southern, central, and northern Mexico shape their work in different ways. The various examples of migrant shelters across the country show that the relationship to the federal and local governments, the local community's size, and the timing of migrants' journeys determine the ways shelters operate. Furthermore, the chapter shows how, inevitably, *casas de migrantes* become part of the humanitarian governance of migration in Mexico.

The conclusion brings the reader to the present moment, including narrating how migrant shelters coped with the COVID-19 pandemic. It highlights the diversity of migrant populations that move through Mexico and the different ways shelters keep adapting and facing the challenges of providing aid in the current political and social climates. While recalling the humanitarian goal of easing the suffering of others, the conclusion stresses the motivations people have to engage in this work and the tensions they feel with the communities surrounding these places. It emphasizes the book's contribution to understanding the dynamics of "humanitarianism from below," and how it has emerged in the Mexican context.

1

The Changing Patterns of Migration in Mexico and Its Violent Context

Migrants often have mixed motivations for attempting to reach the United States; these range from the desire to leave poverty and improve their livelihoods to family reunification to flight from violence. Initially, scholarship about migration patterns and dynamics in Mexico concentrated on the US-Mexico border regions and focused on Mexican migration to the United States. While there are reports that Mexican migration to the United States has reached its lowest point in years, current migration patterns in Mexico include people from a wide range of nationalities attempting to reach the United States and an increasing number of asylum seekers and refugees.

Central Americans remain the largest group moving irregularly through Mexico. However, according to statistics from the Mexican government from 2019 until 2022, the number of Venezuelans crossing Mexico has grown exponentially.[1] Irregular migrants are classified as those who are entering, transiting, staying, and/or working in Mexico without the necessary authorization or documents required by immigration regulations. According to data from the Instituto Nacional de Migración (INM, Mexico's National Migration Institute), in recent years, there has been an increase in the number of irregular migrants from other nationalities.[2] In 2016 Mexican migration authorities detained over 17,000 Haitians. Between 2016 and 2018, an average of 3,000 African nationals—mostly from Cameroon, Congo, Ethiopia, and Eritrea—have attempted to cross Mexico irregularly. During those same years, close to 5,500 migrants from Asian countries—mostly India, Bangladesh, and Nepal—tried to cross Mexico without authorization.[3] Interviews with irregular migrants from Congo, India, and Bangladesh at detention centers in Mexico indicate the existence of smuggling networks that use migration routes starting in South America.[4] Mexican migration authorities detained 183,000 irregular migrants in 2019 and

187,000 in 2021. The impact of COVID-19 on migration patterns was felt in 2020, with Mexican migration authorities reporting that detentions of migrants dropped to 87,000. In 2022 the Mexican government reported having 441,409 irregular migrants in the country. By August 2023, the number of irregular migrants crossing Mexico had already surpassed 400,000. The main countries of origin were Venezuela, Honduras, Guatemala, Cuba, Nicaragua, and Colombia, with increasing numbers of nationals from Haiti, Brazil, and Ecuador. As of 2022, there was still a steady and visible presence of nationals from Asian countries like China and Uzbekistan and some African countries like Senegal and Mauritius.[5]

In the case of refugees and asylum seekers, the number of applications for refugee status has had an upward trend since 2010. Records from UNHCR and COMAR (Mexican Commission for Refugee Assistance) indicate that between 2014 and 2021, the number of asylum claims registered in Mexico jumped from 2,137 to close to 131,000. In 2022 the number of applications decreased slightly, to 118,756. From those applications, the number of those people recognized as refugees in Mexico jumped from nearly 3,000 in 2015 to close to 23,000 in 2022.[6] There are cases in which migrants do not apply for refugee status but still receive other forms of complementary legal protection, such as visitor cards for humanitarian reasons, which are granted when people have been victims of violent crimes in Mexico. This temporary form of protection allows migrants to stay in Mexico legally. It confers permission to move through the country but not permission to work. In 2021 and 2022 the Mexican government issued over 87,000 and 131,000 of these cards, with 40 percent granted to women.[7] Still, many irregular migrants seeking to file their claim to refugee status in the United States try to cross Mexico. The presence of irregular migrants from other countries and the increasing number of asylum seekers have added to the complexities of the US-Mexico border.[8]

Migration dynamics in Mexico cannot be properly understood without a consideration of the number of deported Mexicans arriving at different towns at the border between Mexico and the United States, and the more recent surge of internally displaced persons (IDPs) from different Mexican states. According to statistics from the US Department of Homeland Security and the Mexican government, an average of 230,000 Mexicans were deported each year from the United States between 2015 and 2022. Regarding IDPs, UNHCR has reported that close to 831,500 Mexican people have been displaced from their hometowns due to increasing violence.[9] Displaced Mexicans join many other migrants and asylum seekers in northern Mexico in the hope of applying for asylum in the United States.

Casas de migrantes deal not only with the shifting numbers of migrants seeking their support, but also with migrants' different profiles and legal statuses. These differences call for different types of accompaniment and support. Migrant shelters with larger staffs or longer trajectories are capable of adjusting some services, such as offering legal information about the asylum process or having a psychologist or social worker on staff who can run psychosocial activities and provide emotional support for migrants in crisis. Smaller shelters or shelters where migrants pass through quickly may be content with providing basic assistance. Still, they may alert migrants that shelters in other cities have more specialized services.

Migration Routes

Within Mexico, there are well-known and frequently traveled routes that irregular migrants follow on their way to the United States. Mappings of those routes often coincide with the infrastructure of freight trains that run from the southern end of Mexico to the northern end, as well as with the road infrastructure.[10] Over the years, these routes have been used, developed, and maintained by networks of Salvadorans, Guatemalans, and, most recently, Honduran, Haitian, and Venezuelan migrants.[11] Figure 1.1 shows these routes and also indicates the main cities to which Mexicans are deported from the United States. In some of those border cities to which Mexicans are deported, migrants seeking asylum in the United States have set up camps while they wait to file asylum claims. Some of the camps emerged due to the application of the Migrant Protection Protocols and Title 42, which, as noted earlier, sent asylum seekers who entered the United States through the southern border back to Mexico to wait for their administrative proceedings or prevented them from entering the United States to claim asylum.

Irregular Central American migrants and migrants of other origins are especially visible and vulnerable along migratory routes because they

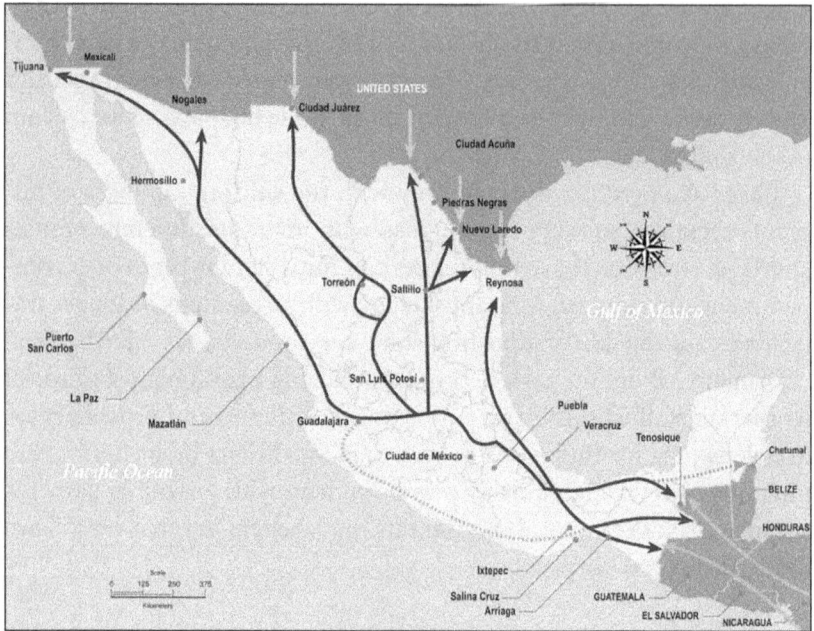

Figure 1.1. Mainland routes used by migrants from Central America and other countries. Source: Map adapted from Casillas (2006).

often use the cargo train system to travel through Mexico (see figure 1.1).[12] An increase in violence, extortion, kidnapping, mutilation, death, and accidents adds to the already physically exhausting experience of traveling on top of freight trains and, more recently, walking and using public transportation through secondary roads.[13] The increase in violence was primarily due to the so-called "war on drugs" declared in 2006 during former president Felipe Calderón's mandate, as well as the rise of other criminal actors with particular agendas.[14] Furthermore, other social and political factors have contributed to a generalized climate of violent events, including the disappearance of forty-three teacher trainees in the state of Guerrero in 2014 and the increasing number of *feminicidios* (female killings) in different states.[15] Recently, and with more frequency, migrants have decided to move in caravans as a form of protection from violence.[16] While the strategy works in the short term, it raises the question of how long communities and humanitarian organizations throughout Mexico can support large numbers of migrants at once. Further, how will both Mexico and the United States respond to these movements?

In Mexico, there are main and secondary migration routes. These may be differentiated according to functional distinctions such as long or short, safe, economical, alternative, or any possible combination. Migrants or smugglers may use parts of a main route and then get to other parts of the country through secondary paths, choosing their approaches based on a series of factors ranging from preference to the prevalence of criminal activity to the positioning of migration control. Often, migrants may take diversions, only to return to the original pathway once migration control or the threat of criminal gangs has been averted.[17] For example, if part of a main route has a new migration control checkpoint, a secondary road may be temporarily used. Other groups may use these routes for different purposes. Thus, migrant trajectories may overlap with drug trafficking routes and/or those regularly used by the general public.

Overland paths are the most used and freight trains have been the most frequently chosen mode of transportation by migrants with the fewest resources, though in recent years, walking long distances and increased use of local transportation have become more common as riding the cargo train has become more difficult.[18] Land routes are narrow in the southeast because of Mexico's geography, but they diversify from central Mexico onward, mainly due to the railway infrastructure. These may be activated or deactivated depending on a variety of factors mentioned earlier. However, despite the discussion about new migration routes in Mexico, migrants use the existing infrastructure to move through the country; "migrants do not make their own routes, they make existing ones their own."[19]

Migration Patterns in Mexico

Central American Migrants

From a historical perspective, Central American movement within the region has been constant. Internal migration movements characterized the region from the colonial expansion in the nineteenth century until the 1970s.[20] Usually, labor market opportunities drove these migration patterns.[21] In the second half of the 1970s and throughout the 1980s, armed conflicts in the region led to the displacement of many of its residents. The vast majority remained internally displaced, but some found asylum opportunities in the United States, Canada, and Europe. After the conflicts ended, many of those who had been displaced returned, but others stayed in the countries where they had taken refuge. This to some extent was the pivotal moment of social network formation.[22] Currently, 20 percent of Central American migration still occurs within the region, while the rest goes toward other countries.[23]

In recent years, the main destination for Central Americans has become the United States. According to data from the US Census Bureau's 2010 and 2019 American Community Surveys, by 2019, there were 3.8 million Central Americans (documented and undocumented) living in the United States.[24] Over the past five decades, Central American immigrants' share of the total immigrant population in the United States grew from less than 1 percent in 1960 to almost 8 percent in 2011. Since 2000, the number of undocumented entries from Central America to the United States has more than doubled.[25]

Push and pull factors, increasing violence, and the possibility of sending remittances continue to be significant factors guiding Central Americans' decision making about whether or not to migrate to the United States.[26] Additionally, climate shocks have increased food insecurity in the region.[27] For some Central Americans, particularly Guatemalans, Salvadorans, and Nicaraguans, migrating may be easier since they have a longer history of social networks. For others, like Hondurans, the situation is more complicated since their migratory patterns developed later on.[28] In any case, crossing Mexico has become a key step for migrants.[29] Calculating the number of irregular migrants moving through Mexico—especially those from Central America—poses a challenge, and obtaining an exact number would be difficult. Numbers that are available often come from a composite of three sources: records from detentions by Mexican migration authorities, records from detentions by US migration authorities at the southern border of the United States (which assumes that a certain number of irregular migrants are able to cross Mexico), and estimates of the growth of the undocumented population living in the United States (this assumes that many other migrants are able to cross Mexico and successfully enter the United States). It is important to note regarding records from detentions that statistics do not distinguish whether a migrant has been detained more than once in a year.[30]

On average, between 2015 and 2019 there were close to 135,000 detentions of migrants in Mexican territory—most of them from Central American countries. Even though official statistics of the number of detentions decreased by 2020, at the beginning of the COVID-19 pandemic, migrants detained in Mexico increased to slightly over 185,000 in 2021 and reached nearly 389,000 in 2022.[31] These figures do not include the number of migrants who successfully crossed the Mexican border without being detained. Similarly, statistics from Homeland Security indicate that between 2015 and 2019, an average of slightly over 465,000 migrants from Central America were detained at the border between Mexico and the United States.[32] Variations in the increase and decrease of detentions correspond to changes in the labor market and migration policies.[33] In 2020 US migration authorities at the southern border reported 113,588 encounters with migrants from Central American countries, representing a significant decrease from the previous years, due to the pandemic. Numbers surged in 2021, with 798,413 encounters with Central Americans at the US southern border reported by the US Customs and Border Protection. The fiscal year 2022 saw record numbers, as migration authorities recorded 2,379,000 encounters with migrants from all nationalities, including Venezuelans, Cubans, Nicaraguans, Haitians, Colombians, and Ukrainians. From these record numbers, nationals from Guatemala, Honduras, and El Salvador accounted for close to 546,000 encounters, and nationals from Mexico accounted for slightly over 823,000 encounters. In past years, it has been estimated that between 150,000 and 400,000 migrants aiming to enter the United States travel through Mexico yearly.[34]

Deported Mexicans

As noted earlier, to better understand migration dynamics in Mexico, we need to consider the number of deported Mexicans returning to their country. Between 2011 and 2022, an average of 293,000 Mexicans were deported from the United States. What we generally call deportations has two administrative modalities, removals and voluntary returns, with legal consequences attached to each of them. On the one hand, "removal" is a term used by the US government instead of "deportation." It is often accompanied by a period of detention, either in a jail or a detention center, depending on the case.[35] On the other hand, a voluntary return refers to those departures not based on a removal order (deportation) and often do not have legal consequences. The voluntary return is exercised at the discretion of US Customs and Border Protection. However, as migration policies have hardened, there has been an increase in removals and a corresponding decrease in voluntary returns.

These terms have legal implications. As opposed to the more neutral connotation of the term "return," the label "removal" has criminal consequences attached to it. This shift in labels reflects what Juliet P. Stumpf, a legal scholar at Lewis and Clark Law School, calls "crimmigration," which refers to a current trend in immigration law that blurs the boundaries between immigration law and criminal law.[36] In practice, this means attaching both criminal consequences to immigration violations and immigration consequences to criminal conditions. A surge in enforcement has led to an increase in the criminalization of migrants, as well as the professionalization of smuggling, creating a vicious cycle. Furthermore, the number of deportations and increasing internal enforcement in the United States create an environment of fear and insecurity, which has been characterized as "legal violence."[37]

Furthermore, American migration authorities use several deportation practices that frequently put deported Mexicans at risk of being kidnapped, extorted, and/or killed. These practices include repatriating migrants to cities with high levels of drug-related violence and criminal activity; returning migrants in the middle of the night, when services and migrant shelters are closed; using "lateral deportation," in which migrants detained in one sector are deported to a far distant city, which constrains their ability to contact any social network and is especially dangerous for women, who may be separated from travel companions; and failing to return migrants' belongings, meaning that migrants may return to their country without any money or identification.[38]

Within Mexico, regardless of the final outcome of their migration trajectories, a good number of migrants transit with the intention to reach the United States and many deported Mexicans return to border towns with different needs and intentions for their next steps after deportation. Compound statistics of detentions in Mexico, detentions at the southern border of the United States, as well as deportations and removals from the United States provide an idea of the volume of irregular migrants and deported Mexicans who move through Mexico. These statistics show also that migration patterns are multidirectional, and these patterns often change due to contextual circumstances, policy changes, and enforcement practices.

These migrants and deportees are economically stratified, which means that some migrants may have more resources available for their migration trajectories or upon return, which decreases their vulnerability.[39] In reality, not all Central American migrants or Mexican deportees need support. Thus, only those migrants and deportees who have the fewest resources or the highest needs use the humanitarian support that has emerged in Mexico. Still, it is estimated that around thirty thousand migrants and deportees use the services of at least one migrant shelter during their migration trajectories each year.[40]

The figure of thirty thousand migrants a year may represent less than 10 percent of the total number of migrants and deportees moving through Mexico. However, depending on their own resources, humanitarian organizations must exercise great effort to provide adequate services to these migrants and deportees consistently. Furthermore, the interactions between migrants and deportees and humanitarian organizations reveal that while migrants may receive care and aid, other forms of facilitation and control exist at the same time.

Refugees, Asylum Seekers, IDPs, and the Emergence of Mixed Migration Movements

Migration patterns in Mexico are dynamic. Through decades there have been changes in populations seeking refuge or moving through Mexico. Civil wars in Guatemala brought an influx of refugees to southern Mexico during the 1980s. During the 1990s, the deepening of civil conflicts in Central America combined with punishing economic conditions led to an increasing number of migrants embarking north, hoping to reach the United States. In further years, the flow of migrants was augmented as people were fleeing "unofficial" violence in their home countries generated by gang activity and drug trafficking.[41] The migrant caravans of the late 2010s added another chapter to the migration patterns through Mexico.[42] The changes in migration configurations have not only been about nationalities; there has been a shift from young male migrants to more women migrants as well as family units and unaccompanied minors.

As of 2023, an increasing number of IDPs and asylum seekers made it necessary to address their presence in Mexico and at the border between Mexico and the United States. Four reasons, among others, help to explain the upward trend: First, social violence—especially gang- and cartel-related violence—has increased in past years, displacing a growing number of people. Second, governments in Central America and Mexico have been unable to protect their citizens from these criminal organizations. Third, humanitarian organizations in Mexico have started to accompany and represent people applying for refugee status. And fourth, there have been climate shocks that have fostered food insecurity in different parts of Central America.

Until 2016, in Mexico, around 90 percent of the applications for refugee status were from people from Central America. In 2017, in addition to Central Americans, an increasing number of people from Venezuela applied for refugee status to stay in Mexico. These numbers have increased significantly, reaching close to 130,000 applications for refugee status in 2021 and 111,257 in 2022. In those two years, Haitians, Cubans, and Venezuelans were among the largest groups of applicants.

Furthermore, an increasing number of migrants are stranded along Mexico's northern border while waiting to file for asylum in the United States. Due to border dynamics and migration patterns, it is extremely difficult to determine how many people are waiting at the Mexican border at any given time and how long they remain at the border. However, US Customs and Border Protection data indicate that, in September 2023 alone, American authorities encountered close to forty-eight thousand migrants in different sectors along the US-Mexico border.[43] This means that people crossing irregularly the Mexican northern border into the United States spend some time waiting at the border. This number does not include migrants waiting in Mexico to get an appointment to file for asylum in the United States through the CBP One app. The growing presence of migrants, asylum seekers, refugees, and people in diverse contexts of mobility has contributed to the emergence of mixed migration movements, which refers to the different profiles, motivations, legal statuses, and vulnerabilities of migrants moving along migration routes.[44]

Internal displacement is an important rising issue in Mexico, which impacts migration dynamics. Many IDPs from Mexico continue to arrive at the border between Mexico and the United States in search of protection from violence and social conflict. By the end of 2020, Mexico had 357,000 IDPs who were fleeing conflict and violence. In 2021 the number of internal displacements increased to 831,490.[45] While the Mexican Commission for the Defense and Protection of Human Rights collects comprehensive data on internal displacement, official data on internal displacement in Mexico remain limited, as internal displacement data are aggregated in the registry of victims of human rights violations managed by the Executive Commission for Attention to Victims. Moreover, in 2022 the Mexican government started to monitor internal displacement through the National Survey of Victimization and Perception of Public Safety (ENVIPE), managed by the National Institute of Statistics and Geography (INEGI).[46]

The different profiles of people in contexts of mobility make it clear that migration patterns in Mexico are dynamic. They include not only movement toward the United States, but also toward the south, particularly due to deportations from the United States to Mexico and deportations from Mexico to different countries in Central America. A complete picture of migration patterns in Mexico must include people recognized as refugees settling in Mexico, and those migrants from Central America and other countries who may consider Mexico as a final destination. Poverty, violence, and harsh migration policies increase the vulnerability of these groups, which may need support or protection at different stages of their migration journeys. Migrant shelters face the challenges of addressing the needs of people on the move with different legal statuses, reasons for migrating, and expectations. Also, depending on their location along migrant trails, *casas de migrantes* may see different numbers of migrants. In southern Mexico, shelters will either see larger numbers of asylum seekers and migrants passing quickly in their attempt to reach the United States as soon as possible, or serve stranded migrants as moving through Mexico becomes increasingly tricky. Shelters in southern or central Mexico will not see deportees or IDPs because Mexican nationals can reach the Mexico-US border freely or because the United States often deports Mexicans to the border with Mexico. Sudden changes in migration patterns test migrant shelters to adjust their services quickly, which is not always an easy task due to limited staff and resources.

Fixed Borders, Mobile Borders, and the Increasing Number of Detention Centers

Detection, detention, and deportation strategies are some of the most visible forms of internal enforcement today.[47] Migration controls and surveillance in Mexico occur in two ways: at fixed places, such as those located at the geographical borders of the country or at different fixed points along main roads, as well as through the use of mobile units that are able to set up temporary checkpoints at any time in different parts of the country.

Fixed Checkpoints of Enforcement

Mapping migrant trajectories allows for the identification of likely fixed points where migration controls operate. Migrants' narratives often describe how they sometimes go around checkpoints at the border with Guatemala to avoid encountering migration authorities or being detained. Other times, narratives describe getting off the train to circumvent a checkpoint after passing the town of Palenque in southern Mexico, or having to walk around the checkpoint of Playas de Catazajá, which is also near Palenque, with the same purpose of avoiding migration authorities. Further along the route through the Gulf, migrants referred to the need to be aware of a checkpoint near Chontalpa, which was located right before the town of Coatzacoalcos. Migrants entering through the state of Chiapas and traveling along the Pacific route mentioned a checkpoint around the town of Pijijiapan, where they often experienced aggressive migration raids. These migration control checkpoints are located either near the train tracks or along main roads. In one way or another, migrants tend to become aware of them by word of mouth or information gathered at migrant shelters.

At these fixed points of control, migration officers or members of the National Guard board commercial buses and request identification from

Figure 1.2. Member of the National Guard checking documents on a commercial bus along an interstate road in southern Mexico. Photograph by Alejandro Olayo-Méndez.

passengers, questioning them about the purpose of their travels. Those who are unable to provide identification are detained. Migration controls are not only focused on buses, and may include private cars and people moving on foot or bicycle. Twice, I witnessed this process as I was riding the bus from the shelter in Tenosique to the one in the town of Palenque. "Good morning," said the migration officer. "Please have your official identifications at hand." The officer walked along the bus looking from one side to another. It was clear that he was looking for particular profiles, as he passed by me without even looking. The officer asked five men and two women to get off the bus. We continued the journey without them. Figure 1.2 displays one of these instances.

Mobile Checkpoints of Enforcement

The other important form of migration control in Mexico appears in the form of mobile migration control units that are able to be stationed anywhere along the main roads or the train tracks. The Mexican government enabled 120 provisional-mobile stations in fourteen states during 2016.[48] By law, police groups can perform surveillance and migration control checks. Hence, different states in Mexico have migration, military, and other police officials patrolling main roads, train tracks, ports, and coastlines. Since 2001, there has been an increase in the number of police and military actors along the southern border due to the security approach taken in the region after the terrorist attacks of 9/11. Federal police, migration officials, army and navy personnel, and state and local police are among the actors who patrol the region. While programs like the Merida Initiative and the Programa de la Frontera Sur, which include partnerships between the US and Mexican governments to fight organized crime and other types of violence to create strong border structures, have aimed to foster development and security in the region, in practice they try to decrease irregular migration coming from Central America and to control drug cartels and trafficking organizations.[49]

The dynamic of these mobile units often requires screening and questioning passengers in vehicles or on public transportation. Along different migration routes, there are mobile checkpoints run by federal police, by members of the army, and by migration authorities. Some of the strategies used for policing are X-ray screening and vehicle searches.

Furthermore, any of these authorities can question people transiting within the region. Migration officers, as well as federal police, can ask for some form of identification. If targeting bus travel, migration officers and federal police stop and board the vehicles at different mobile checkpoints. They screen the travelers on the bus, and if they perceive someone to be of a different nationality, they ask for identification and an explanation of the trip's purpose.

Migration controls along train tracks often involve detaining the train in different places to verify that no irregular migrants are riding on top. The existence of these mobile units demands migrants' complete alertness and attentiveness to any information that can be gathered along the way. The last hurdle a migrant wants, deep into Mexican territory, is to be caught by mobile units of migration control. Figure 1.3 depicts a mobile unit with migration authorities and a vehicle from the federal police stationed along one of the main interstate roads along the southern border in Mexico.

Increase in Detentions

In addition to the increasing number of detentions in southern Mexico, control practices operate throughout the country. Accompanying these practices is the emergence of many detention centers in Mexico. Some scholars have described the migration routes in Mexico as *la ruta del encierro* (the route of confinement), a description that comes from the increasing number of detention centers that have appeared all over the country.[50] In 2000 there were twenty-five *estaciones migratorias* (detention centers) in Mexico, and they were located in Mexico City, Sinaloa, Chihuahua, and Tamaulipas. Of these locations, five centers are in the latter two cities, which are in northern Mexico. The other twenty were in southern states, including Guerrero, Oaxaca, Tabasco, Chiapas, and Veracruz. The fact that most detention centers were in southern Mexico indicated the country's intention to contain irregular migration patterns coming from the south. By 2005, the number had increased to fifty-two detention centers, still mostly located in southern Mexico. The number decreased slightly to forty-eight by 2007, due to irregularities in the management of the detention centers that were brought to light by the CNDH (Mexico Human Rights National Commission).[51] By the end

Figure 1.3. Checkpoint along an interstate road in southern Mexico. On the left is a vehicle from INM (Instituto Nacional de Migración) and on the right, two federal police vehicles. Photograph by Alejandro Olayo-Méndez.

of 2016, there were thirty-two detention centers and twenty-six substations nationwide. Except for one, every state in Mexico has at least one detention center.[52] In 2022 the number of detention centers in Mexico remained the same, with the addition of one additional substation. These changes in the number of detention centers, which cover almost all national territory, and their refinement in size and operation reflect the evolution of migration policies and the trend to manage migration patterns throughout the country.

Detention centers can hold irregular migrants for up to fifteen working days. They can provide food, shelter, and special accommodations for particular groups (women, minors, families), and can offer access to medical assistance, psychological services, and legal services, including access to consular services in some cases. By contrast, substations Type A can hold migrants for forty-eight hours, and substations Type B up to seven days, depending on the number of migrants detained. Often, migrants are transported from substations to detention centers, where they remain until the Mexican government arranges for their removal from the country, which needs to happen within the fifteen working days migrants can be held in detention, as mentioned above. Figure 1.4 shows the location of the detention centers and the substations across Mexico as of 2016; by 2023, there had not been significant changes to these locations. After a fire at one of the migration detention centers, where several migrants died, there have been changes in how the Mexican government administers these facilities. By the end of 2023, most Type A facilities remain suspended.

Militarization as Migration Management: La Guardia Nacional (National Guard)

As noted earlier, by the end of January 2019, the US Department of Homeland Security announced the implementation of the Migrant

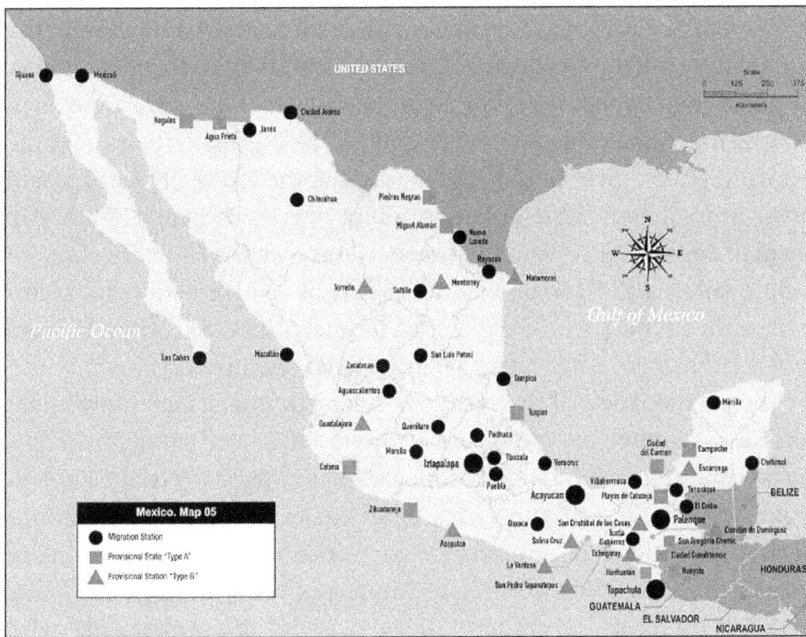

Figure 1.4. *Estaciones migratorias* (migration stations/detention centers) in Mexico in 2016. Source: INM (Instituto Nacional de Migración).

Protection Protocols (MPP), or "Remain in Mexico" program, indi-
cating that it would ask some asylum seekers arriving at the United
States' southern border to remain in Mexico while their applications
were processed. In June 2019, the Mexican and American governments
reached an agreement to avert the imposition of tariffs on Mexican
goods imported into the United States, which included a provision to
manage migration through Mexico. The Mexican president, Andrés
Manuel López Obrador, agreed to deploy the recently created Mexican
National Guard to combat irregular migration, accepted the expansion
of the Migrant Protection Protocols along the US-Mexico border, and
committed to increase collaboration with the United States to disrupt
migrant-smuggling networks. By the end of September 2019, the Mexican government had deployed twenty-five thousand members of the
National Guard to support migration enforcement. Ten thousand were
deployed to crossing points at the southern border, and fifteen thousand at the border between Mexico and the United States. Troops from
the National Guard were also deployed along common migration routes
throughout the country.[53]

The Mexico National Guard is a police force created to address the
increasing violence in Mexico. It responds directly to the federal government, and its function is to support state and local governments in
addressing violence and crime.[54] One of the biggest criticisms of the
Mexican government in this regard was that the National Guard would
bring in members of the different military forces and collaborate with
them in addressing violence. In practice, this means a "militarization" of
public safety. The National Guard is a mix of civilian police and members of the military who are prepared to work with civil society, but also
to use lethal force while facing enemies from organized crime.[55]

The participation of the National Guard in migration enforcement
has been a source of contention, as there have been numerous complaints about how it has been participating in migration control operations. There have been complaints about abuses and arbitrary detentions
against migrants. Furthermore, the participation of the National Guard
means that migration control in Mexico is being militarized.[56] The
Mexican president has argued that the presence of the National Guard
supporting migration enforcement is a matter of national security and
interest. Furthermore, he affirmed that controlling migration made it

necessary for Mexico to become a "safe third country"—that is, providing recognized asylum seekers, refugees, and other people in need of international protection with a lawful stay in a country other than the country where they are applying for refugee status.[57] The presence of the National Guard has added an extra layer of migration control along migration routes. It has also contributed to militarization as a form of migration management, which seems to be a trend in different parts of the world.[58]

The Return

As we have seen, in discussions of migration control and surveillance, most of the attention is generally given to those moving north—in other words, to irregular migrants moving through the corridor to the United States. The work of many organizations that advocate for the rights of irregular migrants and asylum seekers reinforces this trend. As has been made clear, attention to deportees, both Mexican and Central American, is underdeveloped and the effectiveness of governmental programs for deported Mexicans who are returned to dangerous cities at the northern border of Mexico remains weak.

Deported Mexicans are often returned through various cities along the US-Mexico border. As we have seen, they frequently are returned without money or identification, and to places where they have limited possibilities for trying to contact their networks. Criminal groups in border cities, sometimes in collusion with commercial bus companies and even local police, prey on deportees. These criminal groups may kidnap deported Mexicans for ransom, or extort them in cases where they want to return to the United States.

Due to the increasing number of Mexicans returning voluntarily or after deportation from the United States, the Mexican government developed a strategy called "Somos Mexicanos" (We are Mexicans). This strategy aims to facilitate services and reintegration opportunities for Mexican nationals who return voluntarily from the United States or those who are deported. In other words, the program's goal is to make the repatriation process safe, orderly, humane, and respectful of the returnee. The strategy has opened eleven reception centers across the northern border states and another reception center in Mexico City.

The program also offers information regarding other resources that are available to support social reintegration after deportation, communication with the consulate in case deportees want to file claims against foreign authorities, medical and psychological assistance, local and international phone calls, information about local shelters, support for transportation to the place of origin, or repatriation documents that may temporarily serve as an official ID.[59] More recently, the Mexican government created, within the Instituto Nacional de Migración, the Department of Repatriation with Dignity (Dirección de Repatriación Digna) to coordinate the services offered to Mexicans returning voluntarily or being deported from the United States.[60]

However, the process of return varies across border cities. Larger cities have better reception centers and more resources available to support deportees. In practice, the Mexican government "receives" the deportees and scrutinizes them to ensure that they are of their stated nationalities. The next step consists of registering deportees and providing them with documents that serve as identification. Yet many local police officers do not recognize the documents, and few banks or wire transfer companies accept them as a valid form of identification, which is problematic especially because IDs are essential in Mexican territory for most financial transactions. When no large reception center exists, deportees are dropped at the international port of entry by American border authorities.[61] In these cases, there is often confusion over what the next step is. While the government provides some immediate assistance at points of entry, there is no long-term or even medium-term assistance. The government instead pushes a policy of "returning to the place of origin" or "the place where the person could be useful" and pressures deportees to move quickly to the towns where they were born or where they have family members. In other words, there is no support from Mexican authorities to help migrants move to another border town. Figure 1.5 shows deported Mexicans arriving to the INM Reception Center in Reynosa, Tamaulipas.

The repatriation program demonstrates that migration controls also exist for returning patterns of migration. But deportees are not the only population the Mexican government caters to; Mexican authorities have developed good reception programs for Mexican migrants living in the United States who return to their country for vacation. The program, called Bienvenido a Casa Paisano (Welcome Home, Conational) and

Figure 1.5. Deported Mexicans arriving at the INM Reception Center in Reynosa, Tamaulipas, waiting to be registered by the Mexican government. Photograph by Alejandro Olayo-Méndez.

sponsored by the Mexican government, has developed a series of recommendations for returning migrants visiting the country that help them navigate dangerous routes through Mexico.[62] Federal police will occasionally escort caravans of returning Mexicans during the Christmas and summer vacation periods. Additionally, a new program has emerged called Amigo Centroamericano (Central American Friend). This program tends to Central Americans residing in the United States who travel through Mexico on their way to their home countries in Central America.[63]

Programs for the reception of deported migrants and programs supporting documented migrants (Mexicans and Central Americans) living in the United States attest that migration patterns in Mexico also move south. At the same time, these programs reveal how returning migrants are treated differently depending on their status and potential contributions to the country. For Mexican and Central American nationals with visas and legal status in the United States, a red carpet is rolled out, protection is offered, and multiple services are laid out. For deportees, however, limited resources are available, and there is always pressure to remove them from the border. While programs have been developed to tend this population, their effectiveness still needs to be improved. These programs also highlight that migrants with legal status in the United States are perceived as worthy or as "heroes," as the Mexican government calls them, because they may be able to contribute to their country even when abroad. In contrast, deportees are perceived as failures, receive little support, and are also treated inconsistently because of deportation.[64]

Fixed border controls, mobile border practices, increasing detention centers, repatriation programs, and assistance for visitors residing elsewhere are evidence of a process of border internalization and different expressions of migration management. It is evident that the management and control of migrant populations in Mexico do not occur solely at the geographical and political borders of the country. Rather, management and control, which are features of the US-Mexico border, emerge and move through different routes and in various directions throughout the Mexican territory.[65]

Heavy migration controls along migration routes force migrants to find ways to avoid or escape migration authorities. Migrants' narratives often refer to experiences of being surveilled, chased, and even injured when running away from migration enforcement authorities. *Casas de migrantes* offer sanctuary from migration authorities, as by Mexican migration law, authorities cannot conduct inspections at places where humanitarian assistance is provided, but often the *casas de migrantes* have to tend to injuries and accompany migrants in legal proceedings to file claims of human rights violations and incidents of violence at the hands of governmental authorities. This circumstance points to the multiple and various services that shelters need to provide for migrants.

The Constant Threat of Violence

As we have seen, the increase in criminal activity throughout Mexican territory is partially due to the overlap between the migratory routes and the routes used by drug traffickers and criminal gangs, since occasionally, drug traffickers and migrants use the same main or secondary roads to move through the country. Similar increases in violence and risk have been seen at the border cities where Mexicans arrive after deportation or where asylum seekers and other migrants have become stranded.[66]

In its 2016–2022 annual reports, REDODEM, a network of migrant shelters, documented the different types of violence that migrants experience during their journeys. It offered regional comparisons showing that the southern region of Mexico continues to record high levels of violence against migrants, especially in the states of Chiapas, Veracruz, Oaxaca, and Tabasco. States like Guanajuato, Jalisco, Estado de Mexico, and Querétaro (located in the central and western regions) are seeing upward trends in violence. The most common types of violence along the journey are robbery, beatings, extortion, kidnapping, and abuse from migration or police officers. Among the perpetrators of violence are criminal gangs, various local and federal authorities, migration authorities, and smugglers. Ethnographic narratives from Vogt (2018) and Brigden (2018) confirm these findings and reports, as they analyze the violence and exploitation that migrants experience and the ways these experiences shape their journeys.

Sanchez (2014, 2017), Sanchez and Zhang (2017), Martínez (2013), De León (2015), and Slack (2019) document the experiences of migrants at the crossing point, explaining the interplay between violence, smuggling, and deportation contexts. Sanchez (2017) indicates that physical violence, sexual assault, homicide, labor trafficking, extortion, and kidnapping are some of the most common abuses that occur along migrant trails and at the US-Mexico border. There is also a correlation between migrant deaths and environmental exposure.[67] However, the dynamics of violence at the border are more complex and nuanced than a simple correlation with clandestine cross-border migration. Violence takes specific forms in specific markets and is not random in nature.[68]

Nevertheless, kidnapping of migrants and asylum seekers is of considerable concern at the border: "Kidnapping acts are most often described as those carried out by crews who rob smugglers of the migrants they transport. These actors, known in the region as 'bajadores,' retain migrants until a ransom fee from their friends or families is secured. Migrants report being subjected to emotional abuse, intimidation, beatings, sexual abuse, and torture."[69] Kidnapping has a large impact on the dynamics of violence in Mexico. Here it is not only the impact and effect it has for particular people, but also the financial gains and implications for different actors, who range from organized crime to migration officials.

The experiences of direct violence against migrants, deportees, refugees, and asylum seekers lead to two revelations: First, direct instances of violence reinforce and increase migrants' vulnerabilities and precariousness as they move through Mexico or return to the country. Beatings, rapes, extortion, or threats have physical and emotional effects on migrants and deportees. Second, as concrete expressions of violence become a common experience of the migration process, they become "everyday violence."[70] In everyday violence, violent acts become normal, expected, and assumed; violence becomes "terror as usual."

In the case of migrants journeying through Mexico, violence is incorporated as part of the journey and internalized as part of internal migration dynamics. Migrants are aware that something may happen to them along the journey; in their narratives, violence is the norm and an uneventful journey is considered to be lucky. Thus, the effects of direct violence against migrants appeared in the forms of their elongated journeys, strandedness, emotional and physical harm, and a permanent sense of insecurity.

Nevertheless, violence cannot be limited to experiences at the micro-level. Any analysis of violence needs to consider how it also emerges as a structural force that finds expression at the macro-level. Structural violence is embodied in those social, political, and economic mechanisms and dynamics that either create or reinforce inequality and continued marginalization of people. The structural forces present in the migration process range from endemic poverty experienced by migrants as they reside in their countries, insecurity and fear as they move through or return to Mexico, increased vulnerability along migration routes, and the failure of the government to protect citizens, migrants, and humanitarian workers. Violence along migration routes is not only real but is also a permanent threat to the general population in Mexico. For migrants moving through Mexico, identifying perpetrators of crimes and human rights violations remains difficult, as migrants are often on the move, or are unable to distinguish criminal groups or police enforcement bodies.

This situation often negates any possibility of obtaining justice. This fail-ure to protect or serve justice for migrants should be understood as legal violence, a form of structural violence. Humanitarian assistance to mi-grants and deportees emerges in response to migrants' vulnerability and the violence that they experience. Humanitarian organizations aim to ease migrants' suffering and to serve as a safe place where they can rest. Yet humanitarian actors themselves are not immune to generalized vio-lence; they are also victims and targets of criminal groups. In this way, violence is linked to both poverty and humanitarian assistance.

Violence against migrants also needs to be seen in a larger context of increasing violence in the region (Central America and Mexico). While Central America is characterized by social violence and gov-ernments' inability to provide security for their citizens, in Mexico, there are "violent pluralities" exercising violence to preserve their par-ticular agendas.[71] In this context, violence against migrants becomes a by-product of larger violent patterns present in the country. Thus, violence also emerges as an external dynamic in the migration process, which affects migration journeys. Migration patterns shift as violence increases and migrants seek routes that may appear less dangerous. In response, criminal activity appears in other areas as new groups prey on migrants.

Within this violent landscape, *casas de migrantes* have emerged as "pockets of safety" to assist and advocate for migrants, asylum seekers, refugees, IDPs, and deportees. They shield migrants from danger, but they operate in the same violent context that migrants have to navigate. These "pockets of safety" are sometimes compromised by this context, and dangers infiltrate migrant shelters. Slowly, these humanitarian groups have gained prominence and have impacted the Mexican po-litical landscape as well as the bordering practices that appear all over migration routes and Mexican borders.

Migrant Shelters

Migrants who are poor or lack active networks are often more vulner-able. While the migration literature tends to assume that poor migrants move less frequently and less further away,[72] data show that in spite of meager resources at their disposal, poor migrants do move. Those with few resources or limited access to their networks rely on other resources to cope with the more challenging events during their journeys, but they still embark on long journeys. And one of the resources they rely upon is the support offered by humanitarian organizations along Mexico's migratory routes.

Initially, migrant shelters appeared at the northern border to aid migrants crossing into the United States. Records indicate that the first formal shelter appeared in the city of Tijuana and started operations in the late 1980s.[73] By the end of 2020, there were more than 150 humanitarian organizations aiding migrants, deportees, and asylum seekers and refugees. Additionally, there are six human rights centers that advocate for migrant rights, among other causes. These organizations do not offer direct assistance, but partner with migrant shelters to advocate for migrants' rights. Figure 1.6 shows the distribution of *casas de migrantes* as of 2020, with a clear concentration of organizations working in central and southern Mexico, but with a continuing presence in the north.

While most shelters and soup kitchens have operated along the migratory routes defined by the freight train system in Mexico, some have appeared on secondary routes and in urban areas that previously did not have a significant migratory presence. This change comes as a response to the increased border control and violence, which has forced migrants to shift their journeys toward more isolated areas.[74] For many years, they tended mostly to deported Mexicans from the United States.[75] However, migration patterns can change rapidly in Mexico. During 2016, some of the northern shelters tended to a significant number of Haitians, Congolese, and other African migrants who sought to file for refugee status in the United States.[76] The presence of mothers with children, unaccompanied minors, the migrant caravans, the Migrant Protection Protocols, and the recent surge of asylum seekers at the border between Mexico and the United States have presented different challenges for *casas de migrantes*. COVID-19, the implementation of Title 42, and the requirement to use the CBP One app to seek asylum in the United States led to a significant stranded population, largely concentrated along the northern Mexican border but also present at different points along the migration routes in Mexico. For humanitarian organizations in Mexico, change and adaptation were the norm, even before the pandemic.

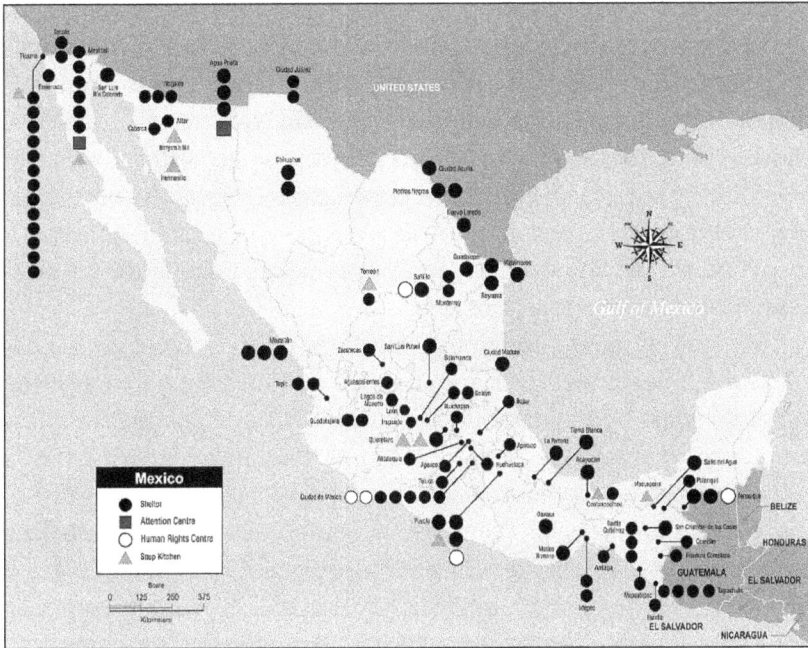

Figure 1.6. *Casas de migrantes* and other organizations aiding migrants in Mexico as of March 2020. Sources: Adaptation from Li Ng 2020.

Humanitarian organizations serving migrants in Mexico therefore need to continuously evolve. Initially, most shelters and soup kitchens offered ad hoc humanitarian aid. As the needs of migrants and the socio-political circumstances changed, the services that the shelters and kitchens provided also developed, and educational functions were added.[77] Other specialized services included programs to facilitate phone calls to places of origin and reception of money transfer services.[78]

Shelters report an increase in requests for help from LGBTQI+ migrants, as well as an increase in legal support and representation for people applying for refugee status. Regulations and facilities have been adjusted as necessary to ensure the safety and fair treatment of these diverse populations. Despite efforts and some progress, safety and fair treatment of diverse populations and even women remain elusive in many *casas de migrantes*. Transphobia, homophobia, and sexism still persist even within these presumably "safe" spaces.[79] Another population that has been identified is "migrants in a train situation" (*migrantes*

en situación de tren), as *casas de migrantes* staff refer to them. This popu
lation consists mostly of migrants who did not reach their final destination; sometimes they ride up and down on trains along the route or
remain in the locality. Many of them have substance abuse problems,
show trauma from some type of violence committed against them, and
are poor.[80] Others who failed in their attempts to cross the border remain at the outskirts of border towns and live in deplorable and unsani-
tary conditions.[81] Many of these migrants eventually find their way to
casas de migrantes in search of help.

The work of humanitarian organizations in Mexico not only illustrates the link between humanitarian aid and migration, but also the
variety of ways humanitarian assistance is delivered and the ways this
assistance changes according to changing migratory patterns. While
discussing the origins of humanitarianism, Wilson and Brown write,
"Faced with the suffering of others, humanitarians maintain that their
ethical response arises from emotions: compassion, sympathy (in the
nineteenth century), and more recently, empathy."[82] The ethos of many
of these shelters in Mexico is rooted in these humanitarian sentiments
and concerns.

An Evolving Situation

Migration patterns in Mexico changed rapidly beginning at the end of
2018. While Central American migration is not new in Mexico, intense
media coverage of migrant caravans from late 2018 to early 2019 put the
issue in sharp focus in both Mexico and the United States. The migrant
caravans, or "migrant exodus," as migrants call it, were a combination
of opportunity and a strategy to protect themselves from violence,
smugglers' fees, and corrupt officials. Their members were generally
poorer than migrants who pay smugglers. The caravans also included
an increasing number of families and unaccompanied minors, which
transformed the face of migration patterns through Mexico.

The political responses to the influx of Central Americans varied as
the situation became more and more politicized. The Mexican government approached caravans with adversarial, protective, and controlling
practices. By the end of January 2019, the US Department of Homeland

Security implemented the Migrant Protection Protocols. The program started in Tijuana/San Diego, Mexicali/Calexico, and then Ciudad Juárez/El Paso by mid-March; later, Nuevo Laredo/Laredo was added. By mid-September 2019, estimates indicated that sixty thousand asylum seekers were waiting in those cities for their claims to be processed in the United States. Due to economic pressures, the Mexican government toughened its implementation of migration policies and deployed close to six thousand members of the Mexican National Guard to manage migration flows at the southern Mexican border.

In a way, this move fulfilled Trump's campaign promise that Mexico would pay for the border wall between the United States and Mexico. Essentially, Mexico *became* the wall. Nevertheless, migrants' and asylum seekers' journeys are still evolving just as much as migration and asylum policies are changing. For example, the Trump administration announced that it would deny asylum protections to migrants traveling by land who wanted to enter the United States from the Mexican border. The US Supreme Court confirmed this stance on September 11, 2019, which allowed the Trump administration to bar most Central American migrants from seeking asylum in the United States, while the legal fight played out in the courts.

According to data from the US Department of Homeland Security, during the implementation of the Migrant Protection Protocols, approximately sixty-eight thousand individuals were enrolled in the program and sent back to Mexico to wait there while their asylum applications were processed. The Biden administration terminated MPP in June 2021. However, legal battles and inductions kept the program in place until June 30, 2022, when the US Supreme Court held that the Biden administration's termination of MPP did not violate the Immigration Nationality Act and that the secretary of homeland security could terminate the program.[83]

The COVID-19 pandemic and the application of Title 42 marked the years from March 2020 until May 2023. The effects of travel restrictions and rapid expulsions of migrants and asylum seekers led to a dire situation along the US-Mexico border. Repelled migrants overwhelmed shelters and created informal camps at the border, where uncertainty, distress, misinformation, and an increasing vulnerability due to insecurity were the norm. A system of expulsion and exclusion characterized these years. Title 42 remained in place until May 2023 as an exclusionary policy that put people in harm's way at the border.[84]

The presence of people seeking asylum in the United States and having to wait in Mexico presents a number of humanitarian challenges for the Mexican and US governments. First, since January 2023, migrants seeking asylum in the United States must use an app to request an appointment at any qualified port of entry; often, they must also wait in Mexico for several months before their hearings with migration authorities. Additionally, many migrants and asylum seekers lack the necessary information about how to present their cases to migration authorities in the United States.

Second, Mexican authorities lacked a defined and sustainable model to receive and support migrants expelled during the implementation of MPP and Title 42. The Mexican government sponsors migrant shelters in Ciudad Juárez, Tijuana, and Mexicali border cities. Still, these shelters do not consider the medium- and long-term needs of people waiting a long time before presenting themselves on different court dates in the United States or the impact of expulsions under Title 42. The International Organization for Migration (IOM) and UNHCR run different programs to support Mexico in dealing with the constant influx of migrants at the border. By the end of 2022, the efforts remained insufficient.

Third, migrant shelters across Mexico scramble to offer differentiated services because they receive a mixed migrant population. Lack of information, safety, and mental health are some of the main concerns for the migrant and asylum seeker populations. Shelters in border cities are often exposed to the generalized levels of violence in Mexico. Thus, some shelters do not allow migrants to go outside. Idleness becomes one of the main issues, as there are not enough staff or programmed activities. Children, women, and men face the challenge of spending entire days without activities other than taking their meals and the contributions they can make at the migrant shelter.

Finally, tensions have emerged among humanitarian workers, migration authorities, and the Mexican National Guard. These tensions have led to threats directed at some shelters in the northern region of Mexico and abuse from authorities against migrants and asylum seekers, on top of the generalized violence that exists at border cities.

Conclusion

The analysis of the migration patterns and dynamics in Mexico cannot be limited to the dynamics emerging along political and geographical lines. In practice, the whole Mexican territory has become a "border zone" or a "vertical border" for those who intend to enter the United States or return to Mexican territory after deportation. Mexican migration policies, their enforcement, and the different regional agreements between the United States and Mexico have fostered the emergence of this "vertical border."[85] In a way, the United States has externalized its southern border and Mexico has become a forceful guardian of it. This has led to border mobility and control practices appearing all along migration routes in Mexico, reshaping our understanding of the border.

Migration patterns have diversified and are no longer limited to Mexicans. They include migrants from Central America and the Caribbean—especially Haiti—and occasionally extra-continental migrants from African or Asian countries. This dynamic has constructed a migration system that is not limited to Mexico and Central America, but has extended to the Darién Gap, which is a tropical forest region in Panama currently used by many migrants coming from Haiti, Venezuela, other nationals from South America, and extra-continental migrants from Africa and Asia.[86] Furthermore, migration patterns include a return direction that brings back deportees, while the presence of IDPs, asylum seekers, and refugees enhances the diversity and complexity of migration patterns that move through Mexico. The *éxodo migrante* (migrant exodus), as participants of the migrant caravans call themselves, is a sign of patterns that have existed for a while. As much as migrants, deportees, and asylum seekers try to reach the United States, not everybody makes it. Some migrants unable to reach their intended destination may return to their places of origin, others decide to stay in Mexico in border towns like Tijuana, Ciudad Juárez, or Matamoros, some may never quite establish themselves and end up homeless, and some may die or disappear along the way or as they attempt to cross the border.

In response to the different migration patterns, border control practices, surveillance, and detention have appeared all over Mexico. These everyday practices reshape not only geographical border dynamics, but also the way migrants move through Mexico. Often the result is increased vulnerability as migrants are forced to move in even more clandestine ways. These control practices have an effect on people's lives, as well as their social interactions. As resilient as many migrants are, every journey or deportation takes a toll on the individual.

Violence is always an omnipresent threat that reshapes migrants' journeys and migrant trails at different points along the routes, as well as border dynamics. Violence also impacts how state and non-state actors operate or support migrants; in many cases, violence and abuse are committed by authorities. While robberies, beatings, and injuries are common experiences in migrants' and deportees' journeys, being kidnapped at any point along the journey seems to be one of the biggest concerns for migrant advocates and migrants themselves. Indolence and a lack of interest from the authorities, as well as fear of retaliation from perpetrators, lead to underreporting of these types of events.

Continuous changes in policy and implementation make the migration routes in Mexico an evolving reality. There is uncertainty at all levels about how things may unfold. Migrants, asylum seekers, humanitarian workers, and communities in general suffer the consequences of exclusionary immigration policies and immense political pressures, raising ethical concerns regarding the vulnerability and needs of mobile populations.

The emergence of humanitarian organizations has added another significant actor in the migration dynamics along migration routes. While migrant shelters serve distinct populations at different points along the journey, there is no doubt that they are safety nets for migrants, protecting them from violence, serving as respites where migrants can recharge to continue their journeys, or simply being a place where they can pause and ponder their next steps.

2

Humanitarianism from Below

The rice was chirping on the frying pan, the smell of freshly cooked beans filled the room, and several women were washing plastic bottles outside the kitchen. A couple of hours later, we were packing rice with beans in plastic bags and tying refilled water bottles so migrants could grab them while the train was moving. By three in the afternoon, we had put bags and bottles in several produce containers and carried them to the train tracks, where we were waiting for the train to pass through the town.

For over twenty years, a group of women known as Las Patronas has been offering relief to migrants who ride a cargo train called "La Bestia." This train runs on a transit system that connects southern, central, and northern Mexico and has been a mode of transportation for poor migrants attempting to reach the United States for many years. The number of people riding the train has changed through the years, but Las Patronas' desire to help them has not. On the busiest days, the women have cooked three hundred meals and put them in plastic bags, filled a similar number of plastic bottles with water, and carried the packages to the train tracks, where they tossed that food and water to migrants riding on top of the cargo train as it passes through the small town of Guadalupe (La Patrona) in the state of Veracruz.

Norma, the leader of Las Patronas, recalled the first time she experienced the urge to support migrants: "As the freight train was passing, they kept shouting at us from the top of the wagons, 'Give us the bread! Give us the bread! We are hungry!' The clamor was such that we could not do otherwise. We threw them the bread we were carrying." Since then, they have devised different ways to support them. "In the beginning, it was difficult to manage. We started cooking in our own houses. We cooked as much as possible, but often we did not have enough for the people riding the train. But we could not do otherwise," said Norma.

As the group grew, Las Patronas' capacity to cook more meals also increased. For a while, the group resisted becoming a nongovernmental organization (NGO) because it wanted to preserve its original spirit and motivation. "We do not want to lose the spirit of this work, which is seeing God suffering in these poor migrants. If we become an NGO, we will have other things to do, and we will not focus on helping these migrants," Norma explained. Las Patronas reversed their original decision and finally became an NGO in 2015 because the status would facilitate the reception of donations, allow the group to collaborate on projects that could strengthen its work and acquire crucial funding. Since then, it has been able to grow, establishing a soup kitchen and a small shelter to aid injured migrants. It has also become a prominent advocacy group for migrants in Mexico.

Humanitarian assistance in Mexico has become a very complex ecosystem in which *casas de migrantes* are the backbone. Just as the freight train system has structured some of the migration routes in Mexico, *casas de migrantes* have similarly shaped and driven migration journeys because many have emerged close to the train tracks. Through the narratives of shelter directors, migrants' accounts, and documents that have registered the work of these places, this chapter describes the dynamics of life within *casas de migrantes*, and introduces the notion of "humanitarianism from below." It argues that in contrast to classical approaches to humanitarianism that emphasize neutrality and independence, this distinct form of humanitarian assistance is still deeply rooted in compassion, empathy, and concern for the other, but also engages in advocacy and brokering. A glimpse into the daily life of migrant shelters illustrates the key brokerage role *casas de migrantes* play in the migration process in Mexico. This discussion also explains why migrants with few resources or vulnerable deportees quickly learn that *casas de migrantes* exist to support them with an array of services.

Casas de Migrantes

Casa Sutuj, a shelter in Arriaga, Chiapas, in southern Mexico, is open twenty-four hours a day, seven days a week to receive migrants who seek refuge while they mull over whether to wait for cargo trains or use public transportation to enter deep into Mexican territory on their way to the United States.[1] "Migrants usually stay overnight or maximum two nights. Here they really try to move quickly," one volunteer told me when I visited the shelter. Further along the migratory route, in the town of Coatzacoalcos, Veracruz, there is Casa Serrano, a small shelter on the outskirts of the city. In this shelter, twenty bunk beds, three showers, four toilets, and a small kitchenette are the only necessities available for migrants. A beaten-up notebook serves as a registration tool, and a fragile metal fence serves as a gate. Between twenty and forty migrants come to this place daily in search of safety in a city that is deemed dangerous and violent.

Further north, about 210 miles from the border with the United States, migrants find Casa Requena. This shelter, located in the state of Coahuila, allows migrants to stay as long as they need, either recovering physically or waiting for the right moment to continue their journey north. The last time I visited the shelter, an average of ninety migrants stayed there over a period of two weeks. This *casa del migrante* has a long history of serving migrants in northern Mexico. It has also developed services for members of the LGBTQI+ population and formed partnerships with the local community and international organizations like the United Nations High Commissioner for Refugees (UNHCR).

As mentioned earlier, these migrant-serving spaces are known by many different names: *casas de migrantes, albergues para migrantes, comedores para migrantes*, migrant shelters, or simply shelters. No matter what they are called, migrant shelters are local organizations (formal and informal) that provide humanitarian aid to migrants, deportees, asylum seekers, IDPs, and refugees in distress along migrant routes and in border cities in Mexico. Often, these spaces have a faith-based nature, and while they are officially directed by priests, pastors, or nuns, there is a strong presence of laywomen leading their efforts on the ground. Through the years, migrant shelters have developed an uncanny ability to adjust their services to the changing profiles of migrants moving through or returning to Mexico. However, due to their local nature, *casas de migrantes* vary in size, infrastructure, services, and internal regulations. Figure 2.1 presents images from three different shelters that illustrate these differences. In practice, shelters function as brokers of aid and have emerged as an informal welfare system that supports vulnerable migrants, asylum seekers, deportees, and refugees across the

Figure 2.1. *From left to right*: Dining area at a *casa del migrante* in Palenque, Chiapas; exterior of a migrant shelter in Coatzacoalcos, Veracruz; interior of a migrant shelter in the city of Tijuana, in northern Mexico. Photographs by Alejandro Olayo-Méndez.

country.[2] Understanding the history, ethos, and dynamics of migrant shelters, and their relationships with other actors provides a more comprehensive perspective of evolving humanitarian architecture in Mexico.

As we have seen, *casas de migrantes* offer a combination of humanitarian aid, consisting of food, shelter, first aid, communication, educational instruction (both in human rights and in practical matters of health and safety), and spiritual support.[3] Shelters that have grown and become more professionalized offer legal services, reception of cash transfers, and the capacity for more extended stays. This differentiation of services may be less clear since shelters may offer all, some, or a variety of combinations of services, depending on diverse factors like locality, leadership, alliances, and available resources. Services are mostly free of charge; it is rare for a shelter to charge small fees for its services. Places that do are often less established or lack the support of more established faith-based organizations.

In general, migrants using shelters are those who have fewer resources to migrate or those needing services due to their vulnerability or because of particular emergencies during their journeys. Fray Rubén, the director of Casa Rojche, noted that migrants arrive at shelters for different reasons: "At this shelter, the migrants who arrive are those who truly need services and help. . . . It could be because they ran out of money or because they were robbed, or because they were victims of a crime or maybe because the smuggler abandoned them and they need some help." Furthermore, migrants quickly learn that shelters exist to support them with an array of services. They also seek support at these places because there is a certain level of trust that support will be offered because of their faith ethos or plainly because they have not many other options other than sleeping or staying on the streets, which carries its own risks. If the cargo train, public transport, or walking have been mobility forms for poor migrants, shelters have emerged as oases or stepping stones along the migrant trails because of their ability to aid migrants as they sort out their journeys.[4]

Shelters frequently finance their efforts with the sponsorship of faith-based organizations, the support of local communities, and occasionally international grants for specific projects to serve the needs of migrants. Limited staff and the presence of local volunteers are often the norms, especially in small towns. However, shelters in big cities or with well-developed networks have larger teams to run the shelter and attract volunteers of all kinds. Casa Rojche, a shelter in southern Mexico, has a pipeline of international volunteers who commit to working there for several months or even a year. Casa Sutuj, in San Luis Potosí, has developed partnerships with local organizations, schools, and colleges that run different kinds of programs to accompany migrants. Casa Cuc, a shelter in Guadalajara, has more than 150 volunteers—mostly from colleges in the city that support the running of daily operations. The shelter at Reynosa, in northern Mexico, runs its operation with the support of parish groups, neighbors, and collaborations with the state government. These examples illustrate how *casas de migrantes* may vary in size, infrastructure, services, and internal regulations due to their local nature.

Migrant shelters have emerged as a type of humanitarianism that, as noted, I call "humanitarianism from below," which moves away from classical principles of humanitarian work like neutrality. To understand this kind of humanitarianism, we must consider the social processes from which it emerges. As these shelters respond to their contexts and adjust to the changing needs of the people they serve, they also face challenges, such as insufficient funding to offer more services, targeted violence, and changing migration policies. Despite its limitations, this humanitarianism from below challenges the classical humanitarian principles of neutrality and impartiality by exhibiting a spirit of solidarity that moves into advocacy. Often, humanitarian work at the ground level demands that actors take sides—more specifically, the side of the most vulnerable. Some of these shelters become places of confrontation (with the government, other parts of the local community, or enforcement authorities) and advocacy, while others become places where alliances with other actors are key.

How Migrant Shelters Start

Since 2014, Salto de Agua, in the state of Chiapas in southern Mexico, has emerged as a significant stop for irregular migrants entering Mexico. The town grew in importance mainly because migrants experienced difficulties riding the train. Without this option for transportation, they had no choice but to walk close to fifty miles between Palenque and Salto de Agua, hoping to avoid migration authorities and criminal gangs. During interviews in late 2014, migrants mentioned this town but did not provide many details. They mentioned that the train passed through it, but they were more concerned with avoiding migration authorities than anything else. However, analysis of migration trajectories and interviews at that time revealed a pattern: migrants arrived in the town on foot and often found themselves needing support but had nowhere reliable to go. Rafael, a Honduran migrant, recalled, "I was so exhausted that I knocked on the door of a house and plainly asked for some food." By March 2015, other migrants mentioned that the parish priest permitted them to sleep in the church, but those interviews did not provide further details about their stays. In interviews conducted through the end of October 2015, migrants began to mention the presence of a nun and a priest who provided help with the collaboration of the community. Rubén, a Honduran migrant, described his journey: "We arrived on foot because there is no other way to get there if you want to avoid migration authorities, but now a nun and a priest are helping in the church. Also, the townspeople come to support us." In February 2016, the bishop of Chiapas announced plans to build a shelter in Salto de Agua. Later that year, he reported that construction had started.[5] The construction of this shelter was not the result of a sudden decision to aid migrants; instead, it was part of a longer process that reveals the ways humanitarian aid to migrants has emerged in Mexico. By 2018, the migrant shelter was running and offering shelter and basic health services to migrants moving along the migration routes.

The genesis of this shelter in southern Mexico is similar to the beginning of many other places that offer humanitarian aid to migrants in Mexico and could be summarized in this way: Communities provide ad hoc help to migrants in distress, often in the form of food and occasional shelter. As the presence or precariousness of migrants increases, a threshold is reached, and the local community organizes to provide aid. The provision of aid moves to a more consistent and coordinated effort. Usually, it is at this stage that soup kitchens appear. Often the community uses the infrastructure that is available to them, mostly from churches. At a later stage, shelters emerge as other needs are identified. While a process of institutionalization becomes evident, it is important to underscore that the beginning of these efforts is often the local community. Furthermore, in most cases, the local community continues to support migrant shelters, either offering material support or serving as volunteers at the shelters.

The way humanitarian aid has been made available to vulnerable migrants, deportees, asylum seekers, IDPs, and refugees makes the Mexican case unique, as there are no other migration routes where local humanitarian assistance has been offered to the extent and level of coordination that exist in Mexico. Furthermore, this bottom-up type of aid emerges not in the presence of international actors—at least initially— and aid agencies, but rather in cultural and historical experiences that allow the process to start, develop, and remain at the local level.

The Emergence of Humanitarian Assistance in Mexico

The Catholic Church of Mexico has a long history of supporting migrants and refugees through different parish groups or organizations. Archival material shows that by 1957, the Catholic Church in Mexico was running programs serving labor migrants who were part of the Bracero Program, which allowed millions of Mexican men to work legally in the United States on short-term labor contracts.[6] The program brought more than four million braceros (physical laborers) to work in US agriculture. The program was designed to address the national labor shortage during World War II.[7] During the 1980s, projects emerged to serve refugees from Central America. These operated mainly in Mexico's southernmost state of Chiapas.[8] In 1983 the bishop of Tijuana, a city that borders the United States, asked the Scalabrinians—a Catholic religious order specialized in ministering to migrants—to assess the situation of migration at the border, to conduct a feasibility study, and to consider opening a shelter for migrants in the city.[9] As a result of that study, Casa del Migrante en Tijuana (Migrant Shelter in Tijuana) opened its doors in 1987.[10] It is difficult to precisely date the moment *casas de migrantes* begin providing services, because many offer support in informal ways before their official establishment as formal shelters.[11] As far as has been documented, the number of *casas de migrantes* and *comedores* (soup kitchens) grew from one in 1987 to over 120 by 2020.

During the early 2000s, the ecclesiastical leaders of the Catholic Church in Mexico pushed for the creation of a national network of shelters serving migrants, which became the Dimensión Pastoral de la Movilidad Humana (DPMH, or Pastoral Dimension of Human Mobility).[12] The network sought to articulate and support the efforts of shelters already serving migrant populations along migrant routes, to establish contacts with other NGOs around the world working with migrants, and to foster relationships with governmental and international agencies on issues related to migration.[13] The structures of the humanitarian aid network were consolidated in 2006.[14] The network kept growing and served as a platform for some of the strongest shelters that gained importance as advocates for migrants' human rights. Other figures, such as Father Pedro Pantoja, founder of the *casa del migrante* in Saltillo; Sister Dolores Palencia from the shelter in Tierra Blanca Veracruz; and Sister Leticia Gutiérrez, a Scalabrinian Missionary and the network's executive secretary, were instrumental in the development and success of the network. By 2023, the network continued operating, hosting an annual national meeting to discuss trends in migration patterns, best practices, and advocacy strategies.

The number of shelters actively serving migrants or deportees grew from one single official shelter in 1987 to thirty-two in 2005. Figure 2.2 shows the locations of these shelters.[15] At that time, all of them were sponsored and managed by faith-based organizations—mostly the Catholic Church. Until 2005, most shelter locations were concentrated along the border between Mexico and the United States. Anecdotal evidence

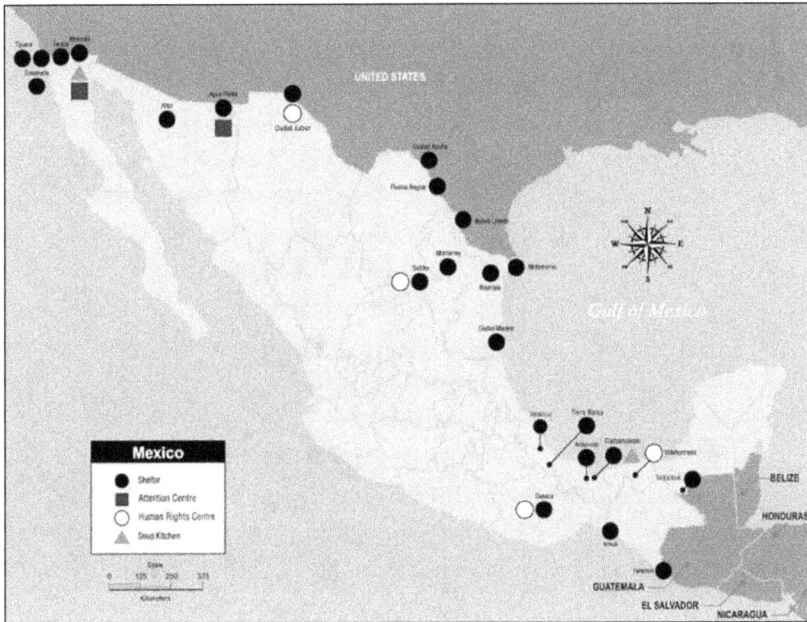

Figure 2.2. *Casas de migrantes* in Mexico until 2005. Source: Adaptation from DPMH 2012.

suggests that most of them focused their work on tending to Mexican migrants who were attempting to cross the border. However, the presence of shelters in southern Mexico indicates that some migration patterns from Central America were already present.[16] Between 2006 and 2009, nineteen shelters joined the DPMH, bringing the total to fifty-one organizations providing humanitarian aid and legal counsel to migrants.[17] Figure 2.3 illustrates the geographical distribution of these shelters, which had now shifted toward the southern border of Mexico and includes some shelters in central Mexico and others in the Pacific region. By that time, shelters were clearly providing humanitarian assistance to transit migrants from Central American countries.[18]

The political context in which migrant shelters emerged and developed has changed through the years. Until the mid-1990s, Mexico had not expressed much interest in legislation around migration issues. This position changed with time, as the need to protect Mexicans living and working in the United States and engage those Mexican nationals living

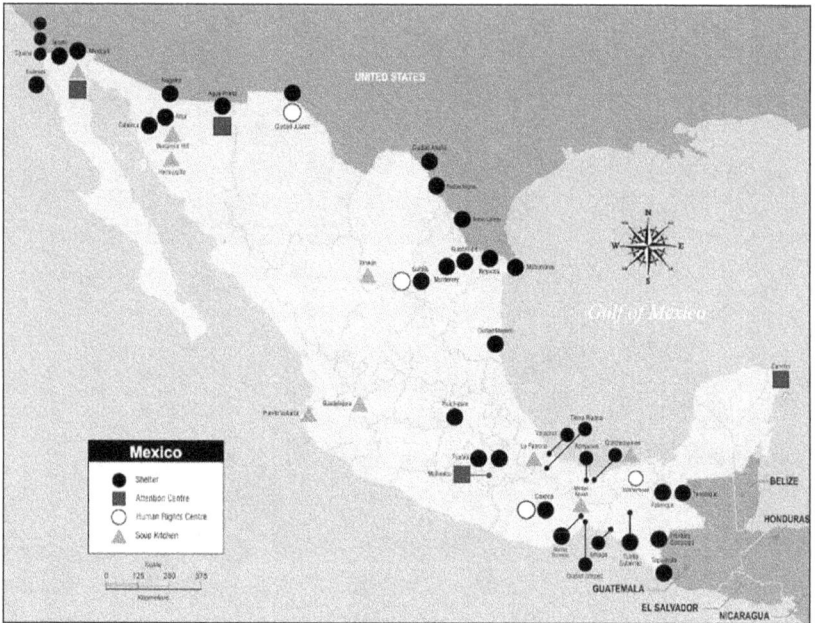

Figure 2.3. *Casas de migrantes* in Mexico until 2009. Source: Adaptation from DPMH 2012.

abroad has become a priority for the country.[19] This process led Mexico to take a more explicit stance on transit migration and immigration into the country. However, the events of 9/11 impacted bilateral security cooperation between Mexico and the United States, as US migration policies became more restrictive and focused on security, which in turn politicized transit migration in Mexico.[20]

One of the main reforms regarding migration was made in 2008, when changes to the Ley General de Población (General Population Law) were made. One of the reforms decriminalized irregular migration. In practice, this meant that migrants entering, transiting, or staying in the country without a visa or official authorization were not committing a criminal offense. However, changes in the law did not translate into practice, and abuse by authorities toward migrants continued. Additionally, as we have seen, violence against migrants intensified across the country.

In June 2009, the Mexican National Commission for Human Rights (CNDH) published the *Informe Especial sobre los Casos de Secuestro en contra de Migrantes* (Special Report on the Kidnapping of Migrants) to document the growing trend of kidnapping and abuse perpetrated against migrants.[21] In the report, violence appeared more clearly as a dynamic that influenced the migration process: "Because of their undocumented status, migrants traveling through Mexico have long been subject to abuse by criminal groups. . . . In recent years, the expansion of organized criminal groups in Mexico has added one additional layer of danger to the trip."[22] Despite the report from the CNDH, it was not until August 25, 2010, when the massacre of seventy-two migrants in San Fernando, Tamaulipas, was discovered, that the issue was brought to international attention.

These events fostered the emergence of more shelters along migratory routes. By the end of 2012, the DPMH included forty-seven shelters, twelve soup kitchens, and four attention centers for migrants, as well as six human rights centers advocating for migrants' rights.[23] Figure 2.4 shows the distribution of shelters at that point. This distribution was shaped by the changes in migratory patterns that responded to the changing patterns of control and violence in Mexico.[24]

The massacre of migrants in San Fernando and the work of humanitarian organizations led to more changes in the migration laws. The 2011 Migration Law explicitly recognized Mexico as a country of origin, transit, return, and destination for migration (Article 2), and it further reaffirmed the decriminalization of migration (Article 2). The law also recognized Mexico's obligation to guarantee migrants' rights as outlined in the Constitution and international treaties, regardless of a migrant's immigration status. It ensured the protection of unaccompanied minors and adolescents, pregnant women, and older adults in migration detention centers and during migration control operations.[25]

This version of migration law in Mexico formally recognized local groups and NGOs providing humanitarian aid and advocating for migrants' rights and contains two articles that are crucial for the way humanitarian assistance for migrants has developed in Mexico. Article 72 states that the Mexican Department of State will create agreements with federal entities, state governments, and local municipalities to devise actions to support the work of humanitarian actors who assist migrants. Furthermore, Article 76 states that INM cannot conduct operations or demand documentation in places where humanitarian organizations or

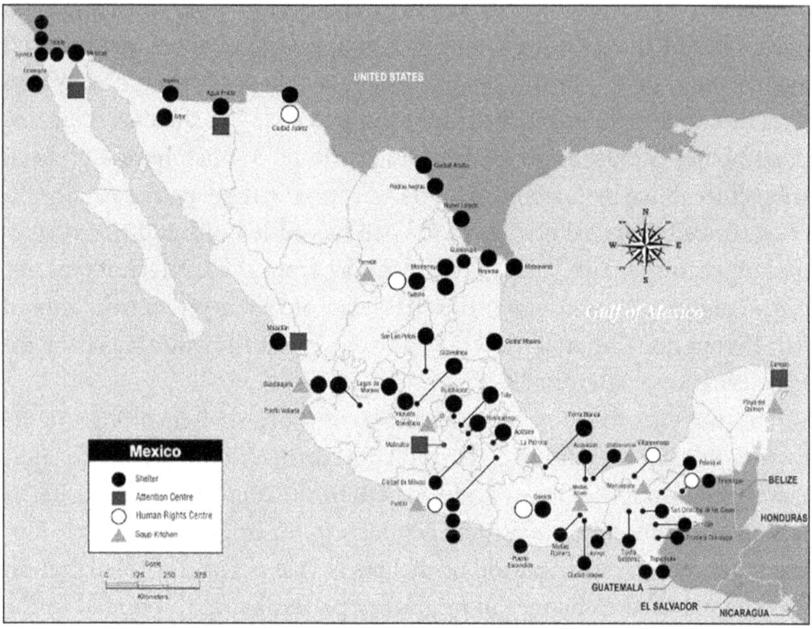

Figure 2.4. *Casas de migrantes* and other organizations aiding migrants in Mexico until 2012. Source: Adaptation from DPMH 2012.

people provide shelter or humanitarian assistance to migrants.[26] These changes reflect a movement toward a human rights approach in the migration laws. With this move, Mexico presents itself as an advanced nation in the international community. In practice, the government has left the responsibility of providing care for migrants and deportees to citizens and nongovernmental organizations.

By 2017, seventy-eight faith-based and non-confessional humanitarian actors provided direct services to migrants, deportees, and asylum seekers. Additionally, five human rights centers and at least six different networks pushed advocacy efforts. Figure 2.5 depicts the distribution of *casas de migrantes* at that point.

In March 2020, Li Ng, a senior economist at the BBVA Research Center in Mexico, mapped some of the main shelters assisting migrants, asylum seekers, refugees, IDPs, and deportees in Mexico. Figure 1.6 depicts an adaptation of that exercise, which includes additional data I collected. The map shows 122 organizations working in the whole country at that time. Ng noted that it is almost impossible to compile an exhaustive list of all the organizations that provide humanitarian assistance to migrants in Mexico. This is due mainly to the organizational differences in capacity and formality. Also, some *comedores* (soup kitchens) or *casas de migrantes* will provide services to other vulnerable populations, like homeless people. This situation complicates the definition of a migrant shelter.

By the end of 2022, the humanitarian architecture in Mexico had become even more complex. Several cities, especially those at Mexico's northern and southern borders, have many organizations tending to migrants' needs in many different ways. A study conducted by El Colegio de la Frontera Norte (COLEF), a premier university and migration research center in Mexico, mapped ninety organizations working along the northern Mexican border.[27] The same study identified thirty-one organizations operating in different capacities to offer various services to migrants. In 2021 and 2022, during visits to Ciudad Juárez, across El

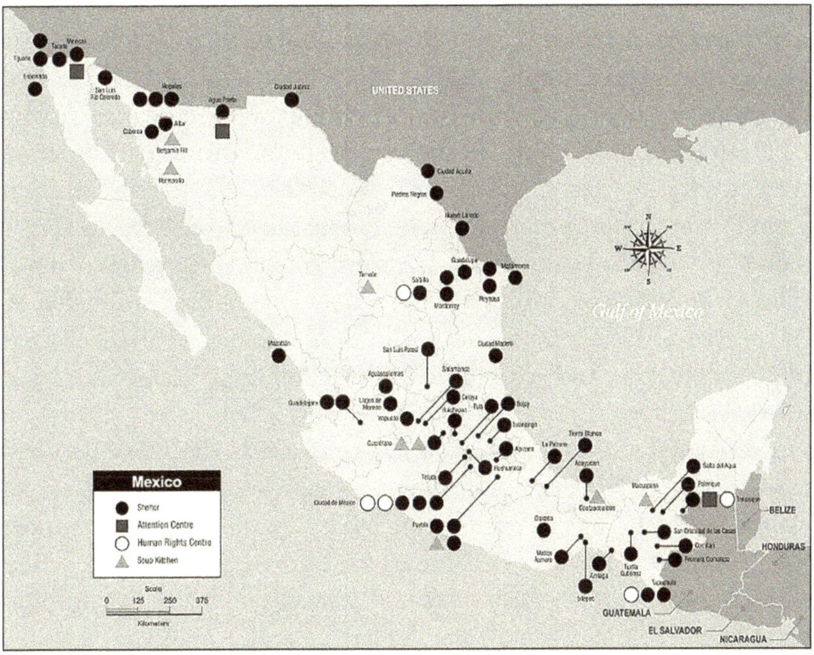

Figure 2.5. *Casas de migrantes* and other organizations aiding migrants in Mexico until 2017. Source: Adaptation from DPMH 2012.

Paso, Texas, and during conversations with local government authorities and staff from migrant shelters, I ascertained that thirty-two organizations spread throughout the city tend to the needs of different migrant groups.

These numbers and the diversity of organizations serving migrants along Mexican borders reinforce the idea that it is difficult to delimit the scope of work of migrant shelters. Nevertheless, understanding the origins and ways of operating of these humanitarian organizations helps with analyzing the dynamics of the migration system in Mexico.

Everyday Life

Every day, around 7:00 a.m., you would hear a familiar voice saying, "¡Compañeros, a levantarse! ¡Compañeros, a levantarse! Hay que hacer el aseo." (Companions, get up! Companions, get up! We have to clean up.) This was the voice of Fray Rodrigo every morning at Casa Rojche. Slowly after that wake-up call, the shelter and its occupants began to arise. You would hear some children crying, and the women's dormitory began to buzz. Men started to pile up the mats that they slept on. Some migrants began to clean up toilets, while others cleaned the showers. Others collected trash from the patio, while some set up tables in the dining room. Still others swept the dirt floor that led to the entrance. By 7:30 a.m., the shelter was clean, and people began to gather and line up near the kitchen; breakfast would be served at 8:00 a.m. Breakfast consisted of tea, some rice and beans, and two tortillas for each person. Milk was reserved for the children at the shelter. As they finished their breakfast, one by one, each migrant washed their plastic plate, cup, and spoon in a bucket containing greasy water and a little bit of soap.

Every day, there were some new migrants among the crowd who had arrived overnight. Hence, soon after breakfast, some volunteers would ask the new migrants to come to the office for registration. They often would join other groups of migrants who had just arrived at the shelter and were waiting to be processed. All migrants at the shelter seem to be tired and sweaty upon arrival, probably because many of them had walked fifty-eight kilometers from the Guatemalan border to the shelter. Volunteers usually run the intake, which consists of briefly discussing the shelter's rules and providing recommendations for the road. Then, one by one, each migrant goes through a short interview to collect general information, take a picture, and answer an assessment to determine whether they qualify for asylum. To remain at the shelter, they needed to agree to the interview and show a form of identification.

The rest of the morning often has a usual pace; some migrants go out to the small town where the shelter is located in search of work. Other migrants, especially those who had been traveling, seek shade at the shelter to rest. Migrants ask for shoes, backpacks, or some clothes—valuable commodities since the shelter does not receive many donations of this kind. By 1:30 p.m., Fray Rodrigo regularly gathers another group of volunteers to clean up again, and at 2:00 p.m., lunch is served. The rest of the afternoon is usually uneventful, with migrants coming and going at will. Some of them would wait to make a free, three-minute telephone call offered by the Red Cross. Others played cards most of the day or otherwise passed the time.

Supper would be offered by 8:00 p.m., accompanied by the previous ritual of cleaning up the shelter half an hour before. At 9:30 p.m., everybody gathers in a circle at the patio. It is unpredictable how many migrants will be assembled, as some groups had left the shelter during the day to continue their journeys to the United States. While they gather on the patio, some instructions about sleeping arrangements are given, a short prayer is offered, and a moment of silence for reflection is taken. Then, women and children are dismissed first to their dormitory, and then the men move to their dormitory. Lights are out by 10:00 p.m., but some conversations could still be overheard. The next day, Fray Rodrigo's familiar voice would wake everybody up again with the same morning call: "¡Compañeros, a levantarse! ¡Compañeros, a levantarse! Hay que hacer el aseo."

Food, shelter, first aid, and other services—such as Internet access, phone calls, or reception of cash transfers—are pull factors that migrants consider when interacting with *casas de migrantes*. However, shelters' internal rules, policies, and treatment of migrants also influence the migration process, evoking considerations of structure-agency.[28]

The most significant rules at the shelters are those that allow migrants to go out of the shelter or mandate that they remain in the shelter during their stays. These rules create "open" and "closed" shelters. Open shelters are those that allow migrants to go out during the day as needed, but they must return by curfew. Closed shelters, by contrast, do not allow migrants to go out at all. In these shelters, once a migrant arrives, they cannot leave until they decide to continue their journey. Representing a middle ground, some shelters cease operations at some point during the morning and resume activities in the afternoon. In these cases, migrants remain outside the shelter during the day and can return in the evening.

Shelters insist on treating migrants as people, not as criminals. The benefits of an open-door policy are that some migrants can rest at the shelter if needed, while others can go out to town either to try to find jobs or to *charolear* (panhandle) and gather some money to continue their journeys. The director of one of the shelters with an open-door policy stated that they do not want to create a prison-like environment. By contrast, when questioned about their closed-door policies, shelter directors often point to safety as the main reason for not allowing migrants to go out, because the dangers surrounding *casas de migrantes* are real. Additionally, keeping migrants enclosed avoids creating trouble in the local communities. However, making migrants spend the day outside the shelters does foster mobility and pushes them to resume their journeys as soon as possible. On the one hand, because they could be apprehended by migration authorities or detained by police, migrants decide to move quickly from particular towns or resume their journeys more rapidly if they do not have the option to remain at the shelter. In the cases of shelters at the border with the United States, their rules encourage deported Mexicans to seek jobs that could allow them to remain in the city or support them in deciding to move quickly from that town or city at the border.

Shelters regularly post their rules and regulations in visible places. Policies commonly cover topics like the permitted length of stay, services provided, and basic rules that contribute to a good internal environment (no drugs, no alcohol, no fights). Migrants must agree to these rules if they want to receive services. If a rule is broken, the migrant who did so may be asked to leave the shelter, or may be permanently banned from that shelter or others along the way.

As migration journeys become more elongated or migrants and asylum seekers—willingly or unwillingly—find themselves stranded, it is common to see changes in some of the people at the shelters. People staying at the shelter longer than they had hoped often experience in-creasing idleness and uncertainty, which inevitably takes a toll on their mental health. For this reason, Doctors Without Borders (MSF), an in-ternational humanitarian agency, provides mental health support at dif-ferent points along migrant routes in Mexico; caregivers have indicated that depression, anxiety, and compound trauma are prevalent among migrants and asylum seekers who have sought their services.

Financing

One of the biggest challenges shelters face is how to finance their opera-tions. "No NGO serving migrants is self-sufficient and certainly none of them generates profit or any economic resource."[29] This means that shelters must find ways to support themselves and their operations. Interviews and archival research showed that the primary sources for a shelter's operation are social support from local communities (in goods and/or money), private donations, and grants from national and international organizations. Those shelters led by clergy members or religious orders also contribute financially by providing staff members who do not require a salary. Here it is necessary to consider the time and work volunteers provide, which offsets the financial hardship that shelters could face.

Shelters also have to seek and apply for grants from national and in-ternational organizations; in the search for this funding, several results emerge. One is the appearance of specific projects at the shelters, which in turn contributes to the development of services. Second, looking for grants and meeting the requirements of agencies (creating proposals, managing a budget, and reporting) require certain levels of profession-alization and capacity that have been developed at the shelters. Finally, shelters create different alliances and partnerships with other actors (both international NGOs and governmental agencies) that allow them to grow and continue providing services.

Services

Humanitarian actors in Mexico have grown in number and in the variety of services provided to migrants. Initially, most *casas de migrantes*, soup kitchens, and attention centers offered basic humanitarian aid consisting of shelter, food, and first aid, or some combination of these. As the needs of migrants and the context changed, the services provided evolved, and educational programs were added. In collaboration with other organizations, shelters offer instruction most commonly on health education (mainly AIDS prevention), human rights awareness, and information on the hazards and dangerous areas along migrant routes.[30] With changes in US policy and enforcement, some shelters, in collaboration with legal organizations, have started offering information about the asylum and immigration process in the United States.

The type of services offered by *casas del migrante* may be considered of a basic order when they offer food, shelter, clothing, cleaning facilities (showers), communication services (phone calls or Internet), and information regarding human rights, asylum, and tips for the journey, as well as spiritual support (since many of the shelters are faith-based). Services are of a secondary order when the shelter offers medical services, juridical assistance, reception of cash transfers, and connections with governmental authorities to facilitate returns to the place of origin. Finally, services of the third order may include formal workshops on different topics (human rights, the asylum process) and legal representation to file claims for human rights violations and crimes perpetrated by governmental authorities and accompaniment for those seeking asylum. Advocacy efforts and collaboration for migrants' human rights are also part of this level of services.[31] The differentiation of services may not be entirely clear since shelters may offer all, some, or various combinations of services depending on diverse factors like locality, leadership, alliances, and available resources.

Information

Migrants benefit from receiving information as they try to make decisions about moving forward, so shelters have put particular emphasis on providing helpful tips and strategies. The information provided ranges from basic geographical orientation to pocket maps that include the main train routes and estimated departure and arrival times of transportation, contact numbers for the human rights agency in Mexico (CNDH), and the contact details of various consulates in Mexico—mainly those of El Salvador, Guatemala, and Honduras. Several versions of these maps have

Figure 2.6. Migrants looking at a map at Casa Rojche. The map shows the migration routes in Mexico, along with key information such as the location of different cities, migrant shelters, and distances between various points. Photograph by Alejandro Olayo-Méndez.

been created through the years, adapted to include and reflect the reality of the time they were produced. Many of these maps have been produced in collaboration with the United Nations, the Red Cross, the International Organization for Migration (IOM), MSF, Jesuit Service to Migrants, and other NGOs. Most shelters also post a map in their facilities that indicates the different routes and locations of shelters throughout the country. Figure 2.6 shows migrants looking at a map at Casa Rojche.

Communication

Some shelters have programs that allow migrants to make phone calls to their places of origin. Occasionally, shelters will have computers and Internet services that migrants can use to communicate—often through Facebook. This service is crucial for migrants because it allows them to stay in touch with family or members of their networks as they make decisions to move forward, stay put, or even return to their home countries. By 2023, smartphones had become a necessity as migration patterns had changed. Many migrants rely on WhatsApp and Facebook to communicate with family members and look for and exchange information during their journeys. These changes and emerging needs have required *casas de migrantes* to have more electrical outlets, Internet access, and device procedures and systems so people can charge their phones and access Wi-Fi connections. With these needs, associated costs have increased, which is always a burden for low-resource organizations. Figure 2.7 illustrates some of these emerging needs.

Reception of Cash Transfers

In some places, money transfer services have been established. Two considerations arise with this service: First, migrants cannot receive cash transfers unless they hold valid passports to show to Western Union or similar companies. Among 220 interviews conducted with migrants along migrant routes, only one person was carrying a passport; this fact suggests that many migrants do not carry official documents aside from their national identification cards, which makes it difficult for them to receive cash transfers directly. Second, these services are free of charge at the shelter. In cases when migrants cannot receive cash transfers because they do not carry a passport, volunteer staff receive the cash transfers. This practice allows migrants to avoid paying other intermediaries to cash the transfers for them. However, even this practice has its limits, as there are legal limits on the amount of money people can receive monthly through cash transfers, as well as risks associated with going to cash money.

Legal Assistance

As violence has increased and migrants' profiles have changed, providing legal assistance in some shelters has become critical. Shelters may file claims for violations of human rights or crimes committed by governmental authorities. In some cases, these crimes are typified as "grave" crimes, which gives migrants the possibility of receiving regularizations for humanitarian reasons. Neither the *Ley de Migración* nor its regulations

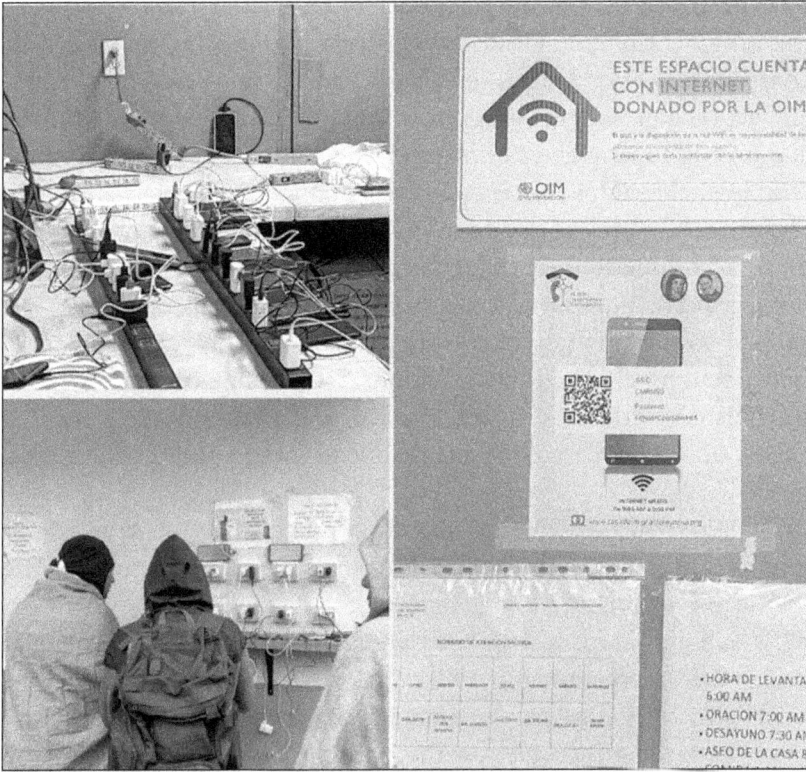

Figure 2.7. Mobile cell phone charging stations and Wi-Fi passwords are shown at three migrant shelters on the northern border of Mexico. Photographs by Alejandro Olayo-Méndez.

define a "grave" crime, making it difficult for authorities to apply the law consistently. As migrants' profiles continue to change, a growing number of asylum seekers have arrived at the shelters. Shelters, in turn, have partnered with other NGOs or found volunteers with legal backgrounds who can accompany asylum seekers while filing for refugee status. Because migrants have to wait long periods of time (up to forty-five working days), some shelters have become de facto refugee camps.

Psychosocial Support and Mental Health Services

Migration routes in Mexico offer a dynamic interplay of deprivation, predation, violence, and migration control. In a July 2022 report, the

IOM described the US-Mexico border as the "deadliest land crossing in the world."[32] Compound traumatic events during migration journeys contribute to poor mental health outcomes among migrants. Anxiety, depression, somatic symptoms, drug- and alcohol-use disorders, and post-traumatic stress disorder (PTSD) are some of the most common mental health issues encountered among migrants in transit.[33] In recent years, more shelters have tried to respond to these needs. They do so according to their capacities and ability to network with other organizations. Thus, while some shelters train their staff on psychological first-aid techniques, others hire psychologists or social workers to implement psychosocial interventions. Other migrant shelters establish alliances with organizations like Doctors without Borders, the Red Cross, or academic institutions that send interns to provide mental health services.

Shelter services shape the migration process because they permit migrants to elongate their journeys or become stagnant when waiting to establish communication with a contact at the intended destination. Also, migrants may consider different paths when hearing of particular dangers along common migration routes. Additionally, because of the availability of legal assistance, migrants may change their migratory status while at the shelters because they recognize that they have a rightful claim to refugee protection and apply for it. Other times, migrants may be granted a stay for humanitarian reasons, particularly if they were victims of violent crimes.

The Changing Nature of *Casas de Migrantes*

When you work in migrant shelters, you cannot help but notice how the profile of migrants changes. At some point, we started receiving women and had to have a room especially for them. In the beginning, we were able to fit twenty women and children. We also started to receive transgender and LGBTIQ people, and we created a safe space for them. In the last ten years, the needs have changed. Now you have more women; you have unaccompanied teenagers; you have the LGBTIQ; we are seeing more families coming through;

and more people seeking refugee status. All of them with a
vast array of needs because of their circumstances.
—Fray Rubén, director of Casa Rojche

A critical trait of *casas de migrantes* has been their ability to shape and
reshape their services according to the changing needs of a highly mobile
migrant population with a wide range of profiles. *Casas de migrantes*
have faced challenges and limitations as they navigate changing contexts, but they have also evolved and adjusted their services to better
fit the new profiles of migrants. They strive to adjust their regulations
and facilities to ensure diverse populations' security and fair treatment.[34]
These specializations are signs of the growing complexities in the migration processes in Mexico and the proliferation of places offering aid of
the first and second orders that allow emerging humanitarian actors to
fill particular gaps within this informal welfare system.

Adjustments to internal regulations could be subtle, like relaxing the
rules to allow for longer stays or permitting an additional phone call in
shelters that offer that service. Other changes may be more significant,
like creating playgrounds for children when the shelters saw a surge of
women traveling with children in 2014. The biggest and most successful
shelters have created projects to receive unaccompanied minors, receive
LGBTQI+ migrants, serve a growing number of people seeking refugee
status by providing alternatives to detention, or develop programs to
allow deportees to settle and integrate into border towns.

Shelters located at both borders (north and south of Mexico) must
react more quickly and adapt more effectively to serve migrant populations. The shelter's director in the city of Matamoros, which is at the
border with the United States, explained how they had adjusted services over the twenty-eight years the shelter has been in operation: "The
context and circumstances have changed, migration is not a standard
thing. In the '80s, we had the braceros; then Central Americans came
through. That stopped because of the changes in policy and '*Plan Frontera Sur.*' Then, five or six years ago, we started to receive massive deportations from the United States." He said that making necessary changes
in response to migrants' different needs required extra effort and think-
ing beyond the static or fixed nature of a shelter: "Now, because fewer

people come to the house, we go out and try to locate them wherever they are. That is the reason we opened the reception center at the bus station, to serve deportees. We offer basic things, a phone call, food, and provide information. We assess the situation, and if needed, we take migrants to the shelter to stay overnight. But this is like a circle; every time a new reality or need emerges, we have to learn and sometimes get training to deal with the new reality properly." He noted that

the implementation of the Migration Protection Protocols or "Remain in Mexico" policy in the early part of 2019 brought new changes as more extended stays were needed. Now, rather than having a staff to prepare food, we allow people to use the kitchen at different times, and we only provide produce for migrants to cook. That way, Central Americans can cook food that makes them feel better. The same is for Africans, Brazilians, and Haitians. We noticed that we were wasting less food. This has been a good change. The coronavirus pandemic threw us another challenge as we need to be very careful in settings where we cannot have too much social distancing.

Shelters at the southern border also deal with changes that challenge them not only to be more flexible and to develop programs that may meet emerging needs, but also to be more attentive to emerging forms of violence. The shelter's coordinator in Tapachula, close to the border with Guatemala, reflected, "Every year, we have different situations. This year we have many people fleeing violence, but with them also arrive some that are criminals. Some people arrive at the shelter pretending to be migrants, but in the end, they are just preying on people." She also noted that the shelter has received more people fleeing violence and poverty in their countries in the past two years: "Either they cannot work, or they simply cannot live in peace." Listening to migrants' stories helps shelters identify the needs of those migrants, as well as changes to be made. For example, they have identified an increasing number of people fleeing due to gang violence. The shelter director in Tapachula explained, "We received fathers and mothers fleeing with their children because gangs are trying to enlist them, and if they do not flee, they will be killed. First, we had teenage girls with their mothers. Now, we have mothers with children—boys and girls—fleeing their countries because the gangs have already killed some of their children. Since people started to request asylum, we had to be more flexible with their stays and help them to find another place to stay more long-term."

The delicate balance between running the shelter's day-to-day operations and understanding the needs that emerge from that operation triggers the start of new projects. In other words, humanitarian NGOs have to be self-reflexive. While data were collected for this book, Casa Rojche started a project for unaccompanied minors. Fray Rubén indicated that the project emerged because they noticed a rise in the number of unaccompanied teenage migrants at the shelters. Unable to continue the journey because of a lack of resources or contacts, teenage migrants sometimes remain at the shelter for longer periods of time. Furthermore, they may get into trouble with the local population or become recruitment targets of criminal gangs operating in the area for different reasons. Fray Rubén explained,

> I think migrants have the desire to get to *El Norte* [the United States] to work. I will call that more "survival resistance," because you find very poor people with nothing, and still, they embark on the journey. Thus, it is unsurprising that some migrants occasionally steal, work with smugglers, or take on casual work. They do anything to achieve their goal. But sometimes you find unaccompanied minors. We identified a teenager, probably fourteen years old, who was recruited by a gang operating by the train tracks. They wanted to get information about the number of migrants in the shelter. The teenager used to come to the shelter often, and we learned he was conveying information to the gang. He probably made three hundred pesos [fifteen US dollars] for three or four information exchanges. But this money was enough for him to survive. . . . From the experience with that teenager, we decided to start the project with unaccompanied minors.

The experiences of those operating shelters in Mexico confirm that migration processes are dynamic. While some shelters have grown, developed, and evolved, others have struggled to continue providing services and much-needed safety for migrants. "Humanitarian ecology is a lively and fecund ecosystem that springs to life whenever crisis hits."[35] I believe that it is also an ecosystem that must adapt to a constantly changing environment to survive.

Analysis of humanitarian work in Mexico widens the boundaries and the understanding of humanitarianism in at least three ways. First, in Mexico, there is no official acknowledgment that a humanitarian crisis exists.[36] Thus there is limited intervention or direct/primary participation of international NGOs.[37] In the absence of a full intervention by international humanitarian actors, what has emerged is what, as discussed, I am calling a "humanitarianism from below" that offers a humanitarian response to migrants and asylum seekers transiting through Mexico on their way to the United States or those who have just been deported from the United States, regardless of their legal status.[38] Political interests frame the position that mobility through Mexico is not a crisis. The Mexican government prides itself on the "human rights" approach of its migration law and enforcement and the United States faces divergent opinions on migration—one that sees migration as a threat or risk to security and another that calls for more compassionate immigration policies and better treatment of migrants. Furthermore, migration patterns in Mexico have usually been labeled "economic migration," and the emergence of mixed flows (people with different motivations for migrating, legal statuses, and protection needs) has made it even more difficult to consider migration through Mexico as a crisis in spite of the vulnerability and dangers migrants, asylum seekers, refugees, and IDPs endure.

Second, the case of humanitarian organizations along migration routes in Mexico demonstrates how local experiences can overshadow the presumed standard approach of global, transnational, and international actors delivering humanitarian aid. In Mexico, the transnationals (migrants en route to the United States or deportees) are the primary recipients of humanitarian assistance, while it is local people providing the aid.

Third, the common secular notion of humanitarianism leaves out the role of many faith-based organizations.[39] In the case of Mexico, the faith-based nature of many humanitarian actors is a key part of the dynamic that has allowed this humanitarianism from below to emerge and grow.

Understanding Humanitarianism from Below

Humanitarian work has evolved over the decades, but since the end of the Cold War, humanitarianism has grown in scope, scale, and significance.

As humanitarian work flourished, the principles of humanity, neutrality, impartiality, and independence emerged as its pillars.[40] The second half of the twentieth century saw a number of armed conflicts and emergencies arising in various ways and circumstances. To account for the violence and the humanitarian response, the term "complex humanitarian emergency" was devised to describe "emergencies created by displacements of people and other collateral suffering occasioned by armed conflict in which sides and territories were unclear, and in which the primary parties were not (or at least not all) recognizable states."[41] Two critical elements of a complex humanitarian emergency are who and when someone determines that a particular pattern of mobility or forced migration becomes a humanitarian crisis or a crisis migration.[42] In the case of Mexico, as noted, there has been a reluctance by the Mexican and US governments to officially label migration movements and patterns a humanitarian crisis, no matter the suffering involved.

The language used to characterize humanitarianism reveals the politics of determining where and when a humanitarian intervention is needed. Labels matter. The United Nations and powerful countries have used selective language when referring to a crisis, avoiding using terms such as "genocide," as in Rwanda, to evade the humanitarian duty to intervene.[43] In 2021 UNHCR used the term "Venezuelans displaced abroad" to refer to the increasing number of Venezuelans leaving their home country. In 2022 UNHCR started using terms like "people in refugee-like situations" and "other people in need of international protection." These language changes attempted to address emerging scenarios but stopped short of naming them an "emergency" or a "humanitarian crisis."[44] Hence, some critical situations may arise where there will be no international relief actors, or their presence becomes discretionary. In spite of the language used to describe a particular situation of displacement, humanitarian support is provided, often through local actors, in circumstances that do not necessarily fit a static definition of an emergency.[45]

Humanitarian action often involves two sets of aid-providing actors: international and local. International actors include UN humanitarian agencies, the International Committee of the Red Cross, and other international actors like MSF or Oxfam. This "international community" is primarily based in North America and Europe with multiple operations in different locations, commonly in conflict-affected areas in the Global South. Local actors include government agencies of states experiencing different kinds of violence, local NGOs, volunteer associations, and other forms of "civil society." There is diversity among these actors, but their geographical focus remains one of the most significant differences, with "internationals" largely operating in a range of locations around the world where humanitarian assistance is needed and "locals" working within national borders alone.[46] Furthermore, there is a tendency to see international actors as the experts and owners of the know-how. In contrast, local actors are often seen as less developed or as providing a form of charity or solidarity.

However, local organizations often appear at the front line of contexts of displacement. Emergencies not only attract international relief organizations, but also give rise to the participation of local NGOs to deliver emergency assistance, to advocate for human rights, and to foster development that allows for sustainable growth.[47] Humanitarian workers on the ground have clearly stated that human suffering takes precedence no matter the type of emergency or circumstance. As noted, in Mexico, migratory movements have not been labeled a "humanitarian crisis," even as significant levels of distress, violence, and suffering exist for the people involved. Without an official crisis, international relief organizations like the United Nations, UNHCR, or Doctors Without Borders (MSF) can assist in only curtailed ways. As a result, local actors have been the primary source of relief assistance. Their work has been ongoing for more than thirty years.

Classical approaches do not see humanitarianism as characterized by a long-term economic development plan, the promotion of democracy, or advocacy for human rights. The primary focus is on an immediate response to "sudden, unpredictable, and short-term explosions of suffering."[48] Nevertheless, in his analysis and critique of humanitarianism, Rieff asserts that "there is humanitarianism as caring in Rwanda; humanitarianism as emancipation, as in Afghanistan after the fall of the Taliban; humanitarianism as liberation, as in the case of humanitarian support for rebels of southern Sudan; and humanitarianism as counterinsurgency, as it was in Vietnam and may yet be again in Afghanistan. All are possible; all have been true at times over the past four decades."[49]

While these words come in the context of how the media have portrayed humanitarian interventions to the general public, they also reflect that, in practice, there is no objective definition of humanitarian action; it may be motivated, oriented, practiced, and interpreted in different ways. "Humanitarianism from below," as I am describing it here, is a distinct form of humanitarianism, which is profoundly humane and local, contains formal or informal organizational structures, is self-sustained and adaptable, and often has a faith-based affiliation. It results from immediate and present needs, and constitutes a responsive intervention to a particular place and time.

While some strands of humanitarianism acknowledge that it is almost impossible for humanitarian NGOs to stay away from politics, they still advocate for humanitarian organizations to adhere as much as possible to the principles of humanity, impartiality, neutrality, and independence. A contrasting position holds that it is not desirable to separate humanitarianism from politics. NGOs' work and operations cannot be apolitical; their actions have political consequences.[50] Since humanitarian organizations in Mexico emerge from a bottom-up process, it is difficult to see them operating purely within the classical humanitarian principles. Indeed, the *casas y comedores para migrantes* (shelters and soup kitchens for migrants) are humanitarian and act in solidarity with migrants; few remain neutral and impartial.

Analysis of humanitarianism in practice might usefully emphasize voluntarism and altruism. It might stress adhesion to classical humanitarian principles—even with internal contradictions—or assess assistance based on outcomes and lessons learned. Different strands of humanitarianism have always existed.[51] Michael Barnett explains that "we live in a world of humanitarianisms, not humanitarianism."[52] Overall, the various approaches to humanitarianism converge on the notion of giving a compassionate response to those suffering in precarious situations.[53] An understanding of humanitarianism from below helps to support an expanded notion of humanitarianism, embracing the idea that humanitarian work needs to attend to the immediate relief of suffering and intend to address factors that cause the suffering in the first place. Due to Mexico's particularities and the contours of its migration process, the type of humanitarianism from below offered to migrants in Mexico remains deeply humanitarian while simultaneously evolving in other directions to promote human rights and advocate for different migration policies.

Humanitarianism and Local Ethos

Attention to bottom-up experiences of humanitarian work and the role of local communities in the work of international humanitarian agencies has gained prominence in recent years.[54] In her book *Humanitarian Borders* (2022), Polly Pallister-Wilkins describes "grassroots humanitarianism" as a response from "grassroots" actors to the failures of state actors and traditional humanitarian organizations to protect migrants and refugees. She observes that many actors and perspectives are involved in humanitarian borderwork. These actors refer to their work in different ways: "humanitarianism; aid provision; helping; volunteering; on-the-ground presence; stepping in; stepping-up; being human; activism; solidarity; and accompanying. This range illuminates the complexity of people and practices included under the umbrella of grassroots humanitarianism."[55] Pallister-Wilkins explains that this form of humanitarianism has been operating longer than the more organized, official, and visible efforts to provide aid to migrants, refugees, and other populations in contexts of mobility.

While Pallister-Wilkins explores the experiences of humanitarian workers in the Mediterranean from Calais to Lesbos, Lauren Carruth, in her book *Love and Liberation* (2021), discusses another example of local humanitarian work. She describes how local communities in the Horn of Africa get involved in humanitarian work through association with international humanitarian agencies. Carruth emphasizes how "humanitarian modes of power and knowledge remain exclusionary and harmful even through contemporary efforts to 'localize aid.'"[56] Simultaneously, she describes how local humanitarian workers in the Somali region have reconfigured global humanitarianism into *samafal*, which is a local way to enact humanitarian assistance that is more than providing food, water, medicine, training opportunities, or even jobs in the aid industry. *Samafal* provides ways in which Somalis care for each other, repair their physical and political bodies, and organize basic governmental services at the margins of the Ethiopian state.[57]

The Refugee Hosts Project, led by Elena Fiddian-Qasmiyeh, a migration scholar at the University of Central London, has provided insights into what she calls refugee-refugee humanitarianism, which focuses on the role of local communities, civil society groups, established refugee communities, and faith-based organizations in supporting refugees in the Middle East.[58] The project has examined the experiences of providing, seeking, receiving, and being excluded from different forms of support. The emphasis is on inquiring how local groups or organizations respond to displacement, which provides significant knowledge for those working in humanitarian and development policy and practice. Fiddian-Qasmiyeh and her team also argue that different humanitarian and development groups need to support local communities better rather than unintentionally undermine them.

These three examples offer analyses of bottom-up processes and local experiences of humanitarianism. *Casas de migrantes* illustrate a different experience, where there is no official recognition of a humanitarian crisis, as in the Mediterranean, the Somali region, or the Middle East. While Pallister-Wilkins recognizes that volunteers with privileges and often from the Global North are the ones giving identity to the notion of grassroots humanitarianism, Carruth acknowledges that locals in Somalia appropriate a global humanitarian system already in place, and Fiddian-Qasmiyeh and her team call for recognizing and valuing local refugee-refugee experiences as humanitarian work, the humanitarianism from below operating in Mexico is primarily offered by local communities of Mexican nationals and creates its own humanitarian interventions and services.

The work of *casas de migrantes* is deeply humanitarian because it sees and recognizes those who are vulnerable and distressed. The first concern of humanitarian actors in Mexico is to provide direct aid and alleviate the distress they observe. Humanitarian work in Mexico often begins informally long before an organization is legally constituted and formalized as an NGO. The process of formalization can often vary according to leadership, resources, and context. Casa Rojche, a shelter in southern Mexico, started operations in the 1990s. Las Patronas, a humanitarian group in Veracruz, celebrated its twentieth anniversary in 2014 and decided to become a formal NGO in 2015.

As noted earlier, the first shelter in Mexico began operations in 1987 in Tijuana, a border town with the United States. The shelter started operations with minimal infrastructure and financial support. The shelter's director describes its beginning this way: "In 1987, while doing the due diligence, we saw a house and a church that could allow us to work. The local church gave us moral support, but no money to run the place. However, we had the freedom to do the work, to shape it in the best possible way. Later, we had to become a legal NGO to gather more funds to sustain this work." As shelters become more established, they are able to expand services to migrant populations. The director of a shelter in Oaxaca explains the origins of the shelter in this way: "Twelve years, in February, it will be twelve years since we started providing humanitarian assistance. Shelter, food, and medical care. Later on, we have been adding more activities as part of our regular operation."

While discussing the origins and evolution of *casas de migrantes*, the director of Casa Cuc—a shelter in the city of Guadalajara, in western Mexico—expressed in the best possible way the humanitarian and local nature of these places:

> That is the beauty of these humanitarian spaces. Their histories and origins bring different capacities and perspectives to serve and bring justice to migrants in need. But they emerge from the ground, from the field. Then, they grow and start moving forward, with some becoming more professionalized. In Mexico, humanitarian aid emerges from the local base, unlike in other contexts where international agencies provide aid.

Adaptability

As we have seen, migrant shelters operate in a context of high uncertainty and change. "We have seen Central Americans, Haitians, Mexicans, Ukrainians; today it is the Venezuelans. We will see what the new season will bring. Somehow, we will find a way to manage and respond as we have done it in the past," explained a shelter director during a visit to Ciudad Juárez in 2023. Applications of contingency theory to the analysis of humanitarian work assert that "the quality of humanitarian assistance is contingent upon the complexities of the situation in which it is given and the network of other actors involved. . . . Humanitarian action must be adjusted to take account of the contingencies or vicissitudes posed by different types of disaster, countries and cultures, and diversity among aid recipients."[59] This approach emphasizes situational awareness. In practice, shelters react to new realities or changes in migration patterns. With limited capacities, they meet the emergent need. However, questions emerge around the standards, quality of aid, and sustainability. Often short on staff and with basic training to provide assistance or meet humanitarian standards, shelters see adaptation as a risk rather than a strength. Furthermore, some changes reinforce inclusion and/or exclusion dynamics and heighten unequal power relationships present in the shelters.[60] Analysis of shelters' ability to adapt needs to be approached from a humanitarian practice approach, as well as an understanding of humanitarian governing and bordering practices.

Change at the shelters often arises because of shifts in migration patterns; it could be a change in migrants' profiles, which leads to creating new spaces or regulations; it could also be a change in migration policy, which may lead to the need to change the allowed length of stay, the need for information about forms of regularization in Mexico, the development of integration programs, or the search for work opportunities for migrants. In some cases, shelters' ability to change may lead to reinforcing bordering practices of control. In migration research, "bordering practices" are activities associated with control over people's mobility but are not necessarily implemented at territorial borders. Such practices can be intentional and unintentional, carried out by state and nonstate actors, including citizens, private security companies, and other actors engaged in borderwork. They may happen in everyday life and away from geographical and political borders.[61] In the case of *casas de migrantes*, bordering practices happen when border or migration policy enters a shelter's everyday life. Changes to registration processes, more explicit consent to adhere to shelters' rules and regulations with consequences, and alliances with international humanitarian actors that require information sharing are some examples not only of the adaptation practices shelters have but also of how practices of control take shape in the day-to-day operation of a shelter.

The Faith-Based Conundrum

"Humanitarianism from below" is several things at once: a feeling, a cluster of moral principles, a basis for ethical claims, and a call for action.[62] Even when contemporary humanitarianism appears to be secular, it often evokes sacred religious categories and legacies.[63] These ideas repeatedly appeared during interviews with the directors of local shelters. Describing how a concern for migrants' welfare emerged, the director of the shelter in Saltillo reflected,

> The Misioneras Catequistas de los Pobres started this shelter. . . . Later on, Father Pedro Pantoja arrived to join the team, and I started working here at that time. . . . I feel that there was an ethos or spirit in the work we were doing. At the center of everything was the desire to care for migrants and to serve them directly. At the same time, there was an effort to advocate for the human rights of migrants. Caring for migrants was essential, no matter social or political perceptions. Caring for them was the foremost important thing the staff at the shelter needed to remember.

Sor Teresa, a religious Catholic sister and the director of a shelter at Mexico's border with the United States, related the humble beginnings of the shelters that mainly serve deported Mexicans today. She explained that the shelter started operations in 2000 and used to accommodate migrants passing through the city:

> Migrants were all over the city, seeking help and begging. People fed them or gave them some clothes. . . . Members of the parish and volunteers got organized to accommodate and feed them. . . . They opened the church's basement and used the multipurpose rooms as dormitories. They had to improvise a dining area, toilets, and showers to meet the needs of the people. . . . That is the beginning of this shelter. People who, seeing the migrants' needs, got organized to build a space that could provide a more consistent and dignified service.

This experience shows how local people linked to religious groups organized themselves to support vulnerable migrant populations. Initially, they used the infrastructure available through their religious affiliations, with their work then evolving into more complex organizational structures.

A similar process took place at the southern border with Guatemala. Fray Rubén, director of a shelter in the state of Tabasco, recalled that migrants from Central America began passing through this town in the late 1990s when the railroad system's operation was handed to foreign companies. The rail system changed from transporting passengers to moving cargo at that point. Fray Rubén believed that because of this change, the freight train became a popular mode of transportation for poorer and more desperate migrants. At that time, migration authorities also opened an office in this small town, close to the Guatemalan border, and conducted raids in collaboration with local police. Fray Rubén described abuse by the police:

> They chased migrants all the time, even into the church. One day, authorities were conducting raids; when a migrant entered the church seeking protection, police entered the church and started beating up the migrant, who was holding onto the altar. There was a confrontation with police and migration authorities. After that, we started thinking more about the needs of these migrants.

Laqueur argues that narratives of suffering "constitute a claim to be recognized, to be regarded, to be noticed, to be seen as someone to whom the living have ethical obligations."[64] "Seeing" takes place in time and is not a matter of imagining a narrative. Seeing interrupts, challenges, and calls the other to action. Thus, *casas de migrantes* respond to the lived narratives of migrants' suffering. They emerge in local communities as a response to the compelling presence of migrants along migrant paths.

However, the work of *casas de migrantes* is often perceived by the humanitarian international community to be of lesser value or importance, in comparison to the work of international humanitarian organizations, because of their local nature or faith-based ethos.[65] Michael Barnett and Janice Gross Stein state that "people, organizations, and governments provide assistance every day, and most of the time, we consider these kinds of actions as the fulfillment of obligations and do not describe their actions as 'humanitarian.' . . . It is only when such assistance crosses a boundary that we tend to call it humanitarian."[66] In Mexico, aid does not cross the international border; the transnational passes through different towns and regions, leading to local responses that grow and develop in various capacities. The pleas of migrants lead to actions; migrants' presence in a particular town leads them to be seen and recognized. The beating of a migrant in a church triggers reflection on their needs. The dispersal of migrants throughout a city leads groups to look for them to tend to their needs.

What is referred to as humanitarianism today was once called charity. The idea that it is a moral obligation of the more fortunate to assist the less fortunate can be found in all the major world religions. The impulse to help may be understood as altruism, pity, solidarity, or compassion. Aiding others is so deeply rooted in human culture that it can be characterized as a basic human emotion, whether intrinsic or learned.[67] The humanitarian model and the way in which humanitarian aid has been made available to vulnerable migrants make the Mexican case a unique expression of humanitarianism.

As noted earlier, the role of local humanitarian groups has, until recently, not been generally incorporated into conceptualizations of humanitarianism and complex emergencies.[68] As an exception, Ian Christoplos argues that local humanitarian groups "are usually presented as either the seed of civil society and future democracy or as pawns and components of the predatory economic, political and military elites."[69] In spite of the increasing religious literacy of international organizations like the United Nations and international humanitarian actors, local and faith-based humanitarian organizations are frequently seen as being of lesser value than international ones, as the expert knowledge of INGOs is perceived to trump the value of practical knowledge.[70] Recognition of local humanitarian actors is often impeded by predominantly secular frameworks of international humanitarian organizations and the way humanitarian principles frame humanitarian assistance, especially the principle of neutrality and the risk of proselytization.[71] That is the case with humanitarian actors in Mexico, which are often categorized as "community experiences of protection to migrants"[72] or "migrant activism" of civil society actors.[73] Nevertheless, as we have seen, international organizations like the Red Cross, Doctors without Borders, and the United Nations Development Program often partner with different shelters to provide services.

Conclusion

Casas de migrantes have become vital in Mexico's growing and complex humanitarian architecture. Shelters grew in number and evolved in structures as they adapted to the changing migration patterns in Mexico. Their spirit and concern have remained close to the desire to alleviate the suffering of others, a desire emerging from moral concerns and the faith-based ethos embraced by many of them. The context, leadership, and links to faith-based communities have enhanced their initial agenda, leading them to diversify services, become advocacy groups, and enter into different alliances to provide more services.

The notion of humanitarianism from below typifies the kind of humanitarian work executed by migrant shelters, emphasizing the importance of locality, adaptability, and faith-based affiliation. It has emerged in Mexico because of the political complexities that avoid recognizing migration patterns there as a humanitarian crisis, preventing international humanitarian agencies' full intervention. UNHCR, UNICEF, IOM, the Red Cross, MSF, Save the Children, and other international humanitarian organizations instead join the humanitarian ecosystem in Mexico through specific projects, often establishing partnerships with migrant shelters. Humanitarianism from below thus emerges in contraposition to humanitarianism from above. It expands the notion of humanitarianism by recognizing that local humanitarian responses are not of lesser value than humanitarian work from international organizations. Local humanitarian responses may not have the sophistication or level of professionalization. However, they are always the first responders and often the ones who remain after the international organizations have departed because their mandates and agendas have changed.

As much as shelters emerge in Mexico to assist migrants in vulnerable situations and have an uncanny ability to adapt to contextual changes and new patterns in migrants' profiles, their humanitarian work also comes with an inherent tension between care/welfare and control. *Casas de migrantes* are not immune from exercising forms of control and power; some of these forms of control are merely organizational in nature. However, others create dynamics of inclusion/exclusion or reproduce what has been called "bordering practices." Indeed, as we will see in a later chapter, in this respect, the question that sometimes emerges in the analysis of shelters' role in Mexico is whether they are sometimes doing more harm than good.

Finally, secular frameworks of humanitarian agendas diminish the faith-based affiliation of many shelters. The concern of these approaches is that migrant shelters may not adhere to the principle of neutrality. However, in many cases, the faith-based affiliation and ethos of migrant shelters facilitate the sustainability of providing welfare and safety to migrants. Removing faith-based and local actors from the humanitarian landscape in Mexico could only increase the vulnerability and precariousness of people along migration routes. Thus, it is necessary to recognize that the role of *casas de migrantes* is essential, vital, and critical in the humanitarian architecture in Mexico. The next chapter presents and analyzes the context that fosters the emergence of faith-based organizations in Mexico as critical actors in the migration process.

3

Fertile Ground

We were tossing food to migrants riding the train as it was passing through the town of La Patrona in southern Mexico. Before that moment, there was a certain anticipation, excitement, and rush since we knew that the train passes quickly through the town. Looking at the train as it came closer, volunteers positioned themselves to throw out bags of food and hand out water bottles. The event lasted no more than two or three minutes as the train chugged by and we tossed the food and water to migrant riders. It was quite quick in contrast to all the preparation involved. The last thing I saw at that time was Norma, the leader of Las Patronas, putting her hand on her chest, blessing people, and waving goodbye to the train as it disappeared on the horizon. There was a sense of accomplishment as we looked around: no bags of food were left, and all the bottles of water were gone, the crates we had carried them in empty.

That evening, as we were conversing and debriefing about the experience, I asked Norma about her commitment to the project and her desire to serve migrants in distress. She recounted,

> It was late that night, probably one or two o'clock in the morning, when someone started to bang on the door. We were scared. But they started yelling, "We need help, we need help, someone has been wounded on the train." Hesitantly, we got up and opened the door. There were two migrants. My sister and I walked to the train tracks, which are like a quarter of a mile from the house. There the train had stopped [often migrants can activate the emergency brakes and make the train stop]. They told me there had been an attempted robbery, and one of the migrants had been badly wounded. Then in the middle of the night, with only the moonlight shining, several migrants grabbed the wounded migrant by both arms to bring him down from the top of the train. What I saw was "un Cristo Negro" [a Black Christ] covered in blood who was being brought down

from the top of the train. We took him home, cleaned him, and cared for his wounds. He stayed with us for several days. When he had recovered some strength, he left. That was it; I knew I needed to serve them. But it was at that moment, I knew that in helping them, I was helping Christ.

At that time, Las Patronas had been working for some time, cooking food and tossing it to migrants riding the cargo train on their way to the United States. It is not too difficult to understand why Norma saw "un Cristo Negro" being brought down from the train. The migrant was probably a Honduran migrant from the Garifuna ethnic group; the people in that group are of African descent. If he was badly wounded, the safest way to bring him down from the train would have been to stretch his arms to slide him down from the top of the train's wagon—an image reminiscent of Jesus Christ on the cross. For her, this was another significant moment deeply rooted in her Catholic faith, which propelled her to continue to serve and work for migrants. The experience was confirmation that she was doing the right thing and, in a way, what she was called to do. Her faith empowered her commitment, and it has lasted more than thirty years and has extended to include other people and projects.

One of the elements that gets lost in the description and analysis of the work of humanitarian groups in Mexico is the role faith has played in the emergence of these actors, how faith has influenced the ways these organizations approach their services to migrants, and how the role of faith or their faith-based identity has contributed to their somewhat successful work. As mentioned earlier, this neglect of the role of faith in humanitarian work is not new; it has been mentioned in different contexts by Ferris (2011), Ager, Fiddian-Qasmiyeh, and Ager (2015), Fiddian-Qasmiyeh and Pacitto (2016), Sezgin and Dijkzeul (2016), and Wilkinson (2018).

While there is no general agreement on how faith and religion are defined, often religion has been understood as referring to an "institutionalized system of beliefs and practices concerning the supernatural realm," and faith relates to "the human trust or belief in a transcendent reality."[1] To open up the scope to include a variety of actors, I use the term "faith" in referring to faith-based organizations and local faith actors instead of using terms like "religious organizations" or "religious actors," which would seemingly confine the definition only to groups that are directly and explicitly linked to religious institutions.[2]

The role of faith and the faith-based nature of most humanitarian groups in Mexico are unquestionable. It is because of the faith-based ethos, mostly Catholic, of these organizations and the long history of social movements in Mexico that the humanitarian work has flourished and remained along migration routes in different capacities. However, while acknowledged by different scholars, the faith element is usually either quickly downplayed or labeled as solidarity practices of civil society.[3] In the end, the role of the faith element is rarely analyzed in the migration process in Mexico.

Furthermore, while humanitarian assistance in Mexico emerged and continues, thanks to many faith-based organizations, there has been a process of secularization in which faith-based organizations have to be constituted into formal nongovernmental organizations to be able to operate and grow in services.[4] This has created a dual identity for many organizations tending to migrants in distress. The faith-based identity allows them to appeal to vulnerable migrants in need of services, to dialogue with religious authorities, and to collaborate with communities to sustain their immediate work. Their secular identity allows them to be part of other networks of NGOs and to seek resources outside faith-based networks. Nevertheless, the faith-based component is generally eclipsed by the emphasis on the role of civil society in humanitarian responses.

This chapter discusses the historical conditions and dynamics that serve as the basis for understanding why faith-based humanitarian organizations in Mexico emerged, flourished, and sustained their humanitarian work through decades. It discusses why faith matters in the humanitarian landscape in Mexico and why it is overlooked, as well as the contributions of the faith-based ethos of many *casas de migrantes*. It concludes with a consideration of why migrant shelters have developed a dual identity that allows them to navigate politics in religious and secular arenas.

A History of Social Commitment

The humanitarianism from below that exists in Mexico, with its local and faith-based emphasis, did not emerge out of thin air. Rather, it grew on a fertile ground that was prepared by the emergence of civic associations during the nineteenth century and the experience of becoming an emigration country in the twentieth century.

In his work *Democracy in Latin America*, Carlos A. Forment describes how Mexicans from all parts of the country organized themselves into more than four hundred civic and economic associations between 1826 and 1856.[5] Civic associations emerged in the form of development groups, mutual aid societies, and patriotic, ethnic, and artisan associations. People from different backgrounds and social classes played a central role in shaping their everyday practices. Their work ranged from basic welfare and assistance to entrepreneurial initiatives and civic engagement. These associations emerged with force before the US invasion and occupation of Mexico (1846–1848). Still, they regained momentum after the war until 1855. This momentum stopped with the Reformation period in Mexico. One of the main changes brought by the liberal reforms in Mexico was the Law on the Seizure of the Goods of Civil and Ecclesiastic Corporations. This meant expropriating land and properties owned by the Catholic Church and banning it from acquiring more real estate properties. The confiscations affected institutions like hospitals, schools, soup kitchens, and retirement homes operated by the Catholic clergy.[6] In turn, this affected how citizens engaged in supporting vulnerable populations, as volunteering and charity donations became more limited and were seen with suspicion. Records show that approximately 40 civic and economic associations were created between 1826 and 1840. After the war, 96 new associations emerged between 1848 and 1850, and another 102 from 1851 to 1855. Many more may have existed, but their work was not recorded.[7]

Two of the most significant kinds of associations in providing forms of welfare were community development groups and mutual aid societies. Community development groups, alone or in partnership with local officials, gathered citizens to build or repair some infrastructure (building bridges, clearing roads, dredging irrigation canals, constructing schools, and repairing hospitals) and offered welfare and medical relief to the sick and the poor. Mutual aid societies were organized locally and sustained by members of the group. The work of these associations was rooted in daily life in neighborhoods, parishes, work, and extended kinship networks. They went as far as providing unemployment and forms of medical assistance to members in distress, as well as burial costs and monthly stipends to widows and surviving children. The duration and size of voluntary groups varied considerably. Some only existed for short periods of time, but others lasted twenty years or more.[8]

Forment argues that during the nineteenth century, socio-moral practices played a vital role in the emergence of civic democracy and the welfare of vulnerable groups. He maintains that citizens in Mexico

- were capable of creating new and diverse types of associations in the public arena
- developed complex relationships and extensive and durable social networks based on a variety of ties (strong/weak; direct/indirect; local/regional/national)
- protected institutional autonomy from the external threats that came from groups at the top—the state, Church leaders, markets, or family clans, and
- used civic terminology in everyday life to make sense of each other.

These dynamics demonstrate that Mexicans have been capable of creating social movements that emerge from the ground, navigate the sociopolitical landscape, and tend to social and moral issues. Hence, humanitarian actors in Mexico not only are frequently faith-based in nature, but are also part of a history of organizations that have been integral to civil society and have played significant roles in the local, regional, and national sociopolitical landscape.

In other words, in Latin America, a sense of democracy emerged in civic, economic, and political associations; these associations developed strong ties among members at all levels. These groups, and their formal and informal networks, allowed members to move between the private and the public with ease and navigate authoritarian governments. As Forment explains, "Associative life was the most effective safeguard available to modern democracy against the threat of totalitarianism."[9] In rural and some urban areas, resistance in daily life became a key component of the independence movement at the beginning of the nineteenth century (1810–1821). Evident class distinctions, privileges, and inequality present at that time in Nueva España (New Spain was the name of the Spanish colony that later became Mexico) were some of the triggers for the independence movement from Spain. The years after 1821, when Mexico became an independent nation, were marked by political negotiations and social changes that emerged with the process of becoming a new nation. Political recognition, developing a constitution, and addressing inequalities became the most significant tasks. Civic and economic associations played essential roles in the development of the country between 1840 and 1846.[10] Community development groups emerged and formed partnerships with the local government to build an infrastructure and offer welfare and medical relief to the poor and the sick.[11] The twentieth century saw similar experiences during the Mexican Revolution, and more recently with experiences of social movements in the late 1960s, the Ejército Zapatista de Liberación Nacional (Zapatista Army of National Liberation, EZLN) movement in 1994, and the recent social movements focused on fighting for justice, as in the case of the kidnapping of forty-three teacher trainees in Guerrero and the attention paid to the increased violence in the country.

Hence, in Latin America and particularly in Mexico, local experiences and associations have played important roles in organizing people, developing ad hoc economic initiatives, fighting for justice, and providing relief and support to groups in distress. Many shelters providing aid to migrants emerged from and are sustained by these forms of association. But these shelters, rather than being just an alternative form of humanitarianism arising out of the mobilization of empathy, are rooted in larger traditions of social resistance and support for the vulnerable. These shelters and organizations advocating for migrants became an expression of civic engagement and public life.

Furthermore, historically, the Catholic Church has stepped up when "neither the state nor the local townships had the financial or administrative capacity to care for the destitute, which is why the Catholic Church, sometimes alone and sometimes in partnership with them, continued to play a significant role in [the public service] field."[12] Many migrant shelters play a dual role: they are simultaneously genuine local civil associations supporting vulnerable populations and communities

deeply rooted in their faith. In the nineteenth century this was understood as "civic Catholicism."[13] This dual role may allow them to navigate
both social politics and contexts.

The other element that has served as the bedrock for the emergence of
humanitarian groups in Mexico is the experience of emigration in Mexico. At the turn of the twentieth century, Mexico became a country of
emigrants to the United States. Bracero programs and economic shocks,
as well as the subordination of the Mexican economy to the economic
patterns of the United States, fostered a pattern of emigration. Direct
labor recruitment by private US corporations and the US government
played a critical role. The need for labor in the construction of the railroad in the United States as well as agricultural needs sent recruiters into
remote and rural areas in Mexico to recruit workers. Recruitment programs fostered by bilateral agreements between Mexico and the United
States to supply labor shortages during World War I and World War II
brought an influx of immigrant workers. Parallel to these recruitment
programs, irregular migration became a trend due to American farmers'
reluctance to recruit through the Bracero Program. This reluctance was
due to requirements that employers offer minimum safety assurances to
migrant workers. The demand for work in the United States and the desire of Mexican workers to work remained, even if that meant working
through irregular channels.[14]

The World War II-era Bracero Program brought close to 445,000
Mexican temporary workers to the United States. As the number of
Mexican immigrants increased, especially in the 1950s, the number of
unauthorized migrants apprehended by the US Border Patrol remained
almost equal to those numbers of Mexicans recruited through the Bracero Program. Irregular migration from Mexico continued throughout
the period. US farmers and ranchers opposed the program's requirement
that they provide adequate housing, sanitation, and disability insurance
to migrant workers, because these rules required them to cover the costs
of these safety provisions. In 1954 Operation Wetback, one of the most
aggressive enforcement operations in US history, was intended to force
employers to meet their labor needs through the Bracero Program. More
than one million apprehensions were made under the operation.[15] The
Bracero Program became the object of complaints by US labor unions

and religious groups, who denounced violations to pay guarantees for minimum wage and living conditions agreed upon by bilateral agreements with Mexico. The program was extended several times by the US Congress until 1964.

According to the Pew Research Center, the Mexican foreign-born population living in the United States grew from 768,000 in 1970 to 4.3 million in 1990, and from 8.7 million in 2000 to 11.2 million in 2017. These estimates include documented and undocumented Mexicans. While it is difficult to determine how strong the ties of these Mexicans are to their home country, there is no doubt that many of them still have links to different regions in Mexico. Narratives and stories among volunteers in *casas de migrantes* always mention a connection to people living in the United States. They may have a relative, a son, a niece, a daughter, or someone else close to them living in the United States. During my visit with Las Patronas in Veracruz, one of the women who belonged to the group explained, "I am helping these people because they are people in need. I have a son who migrated to the United States. I really hope that if one day he is hungry, someone will be kind enough to give him 'un taco'—that is why I do this." While traveling through Mexico and living in shelters, these words often emerged in conversations: "I have a son," "I have a daughter," "I have a nephew," or "My husband is there." Thus, migrant trails in Mexico are not only routes where migrants transit on their way to the United States, but also trails where the longing for someone who left on a migrant journey elicits acts of solidarity and care for those who are attempting to join other migrants in the United States.

But a sense of solidarity and a response to those in need come not only from volunteers on the Mexican side. The experience of emigration also has a reciprocity dynamic that elicits a sense of solidarity and responsibility toward others. Among the Mexican diaspora, hometown associations (HTAs) have been a great example of organization and solidarity with the homeland. By 2005, at least two thousand of these groups across the United States were working in various cities and states in Mexico—most prominently in Guanajuato, Zacatecas, Jalisco, Puebla, and Michoacán. HTAs are part of a trend in transnational social movements influenced by migration patterns and globalization. Their functions range from social exchange to political influence to support for small development goals in home communities, as well as church renovations and faith-based initiatives.[16]

Thus, the spirit of organization, solidarity, and commitment to vulnerable people has been present in Mexican society historically and in the experience of emigration. This is the fertile ground in which humanitarianism from below germinates to become a key actor in the humanitarian architecture of Mexico. Faith greatly influences the emergence of many shelters and how assistance is delivered to migrants. At the institutional level, the participation of the Catholic Church and other religious traditions has been vital. Just as civic associations are expressions of local communities, it is essential to understand the role of faith-based organizations aiding migrants as a bottom-up process often rooted in the local communities.

Christianity, especially the Catholic tradition, has a long history of addressing migration. Biblical foundations regarding immigration have always been present in Christian thought and reflection, especially the idea of welcoming the stranger and the virtue of hospitality.[17] Through the years, especially in the twentieth century, as migration has become a more complex phenomenon, the Church has taken clearer and stronger positions affirming the right to migrate and the reality of refugees. In 1952 Pope Pius XII issued the Apostolic Constitution *Exsul Familia*, the first official document of the Holy See to delineate the pastoral care of migrants globally and systematically.[18] It was during Vatican II, in the document *Gaudium et Spes* (GS), that the Church brought attention to the growing phenomenon of migration and its influence on life. There, the Church reaffirmed the right to migrate, the dignity of migrants, and the need to overcome inequalities in economic and social development, and to respond to the authentic needs of the human person.[19] At the same time, the Council recognized the right of public authorities to regulate the flow of migration.[20] By 1969, Paul VI had promulgated the instruction *De Pastorali Migratorum Cura* (DPMC), and by 1978 the Pontifical Commission for the Pastoral Care of Migration and Tourism released a letter entitled "The Church and Human Mobility."[21] Furthermore, when considering documents or statements regarding migration and refugees, we must highlight the message the pope offers yearly to commemorate the World Day of Migrants and Refugees. The message usually reflects on a particular theme related to migration or refugee issues.[22]

Years ago, the expression "irruption of the poor" started to appear in the theological world, opening new avenues for thought.[23] The concept helped people reflect on and speak of the God of Jesus Christ by giving voice to those living on our society's margins. Gustavo Gutiérrez, one of the first theologians to address the idea, argued that the "irruption of the poor" in history is of fundamental significance for our understanding of Christian theology because their presence became a "sign of the times."[24] This means that the realities that emerge in our world demand attention, reflection, and responses according to the values of the Gospel. Gioacchino Campese, CS, a theologian specializing in migration, proposes that the numbers of people in contexts of mobility and forced displacement speak of the "irruption of the migrant" in our world. He says that just as the "presence of the poor" is a sign of the times that needs to be taken into account, in the same way, the "presence of the migrant" (particularly "economic migrants") is a sign of the times that demands theological reflection, interpretation, and commitment to challenge this reality. Even more so because "theology not only 'thinks' about God, but commits to God's way and acts on God's word. It integrates conceptualization, commitment, and praxis."[25]

While approaching migration from a theological perspective, we must keep in mind what Robert J. Schreiter, a US theologian, affirms: "There does not exist 'the' theology of migration, but various 'theologies' of migration, and . . . this pluralism depends on both the methodological and thematic starting points of these reflections as well as their geographic and cultural context."[26] Theological reflection on migration has always had a very strong biblical foundation; the concept of the "alien" and the responsibilities toward her are strongly present in the Old Testament of the Christian Bible. More recently, the experiences of the migrant and the socio-pastoral responses to human mobility have moved to the center of reflection.[27]

While there is ample biblical and theological reflection on migration, the shelters keep their spiritual ethos thanks to the communities of faith that sustain many of these places. This experience of faith does not generally come from deep theological reflections or a deep understanding of dogmas. It comes from the raw and lived experience of the faith. It comes from the sense that in helping others, one is helping Christ. One of the elements that gets lost in considering the role of *casas de migrantes* is the importance of this lived experience of faith, which translates into a concrete commitment to aiding migrants, refugees, asylum seekers, IDPs, and deported Mexicans.

Faith Matters, and It Is Overlooked

A group of women tossing food to migrants along train tracks, a group of nuns going out with parishioners to look for migrants throughout the city to serve them, a priest opening a shelter after the police barge into a church while persecuting a migrant—these are not necessarily the standard images of official humanitarian assistance from a Western world perspective. In his book *A Bed for the Night*, David Rieff argued that "every concept of humanitarianism, like every concept of what it means to be fully human, has a history and, more important, a historical context that we ignore at our peril."[28] Understanding that the notion of humanitarianism emerges from a Western framework is crucial when we analyze why experiences of humanitarianism in other contexts, especially those emerging from the Global South, look different and operate differently.[29] While faith-based organizations in Mexico look different and may have difficulties adhering to the traditional principles of humanitarianism, this does not mean that they exist in conflict with the principles and rhetoric of more mainstream notions of humanitarian assistance. However, humanitarian organizations in Mexico are often seen as of lesser value because of their faith ethos and different levels of professionalization.

Fiddian-Qasmiyeh and Pacitto stated that "contemporary faith-based humanitarianism has often been constituted as an anomaly and/or potential threat, with the motivations and aims of such actors viewed with suspicion, and their activities often perceived as 'political' and 'ideological' rather than inspired by 'humanitarian' principles."[30] In practice, southern or local—especially faith-based—initiatives may not necessarily adhere to the mainstream model, which is why their role has not been highlighted in humanitarian studies. During the 2012 closing session of the United Nations High Commissioner for Refugees' Dialogue on Faith and Protection, António Guterres, the High Commissioner for Refugees, encouraged humanitarian NGOs to address more directly the religious needs and capacities of refugees and more effectively engage with the resources of faith communities in host countries:

> [There is] the need for humanitarian actors, including UNHCR, to deepen their understanding of religious traditions across faiths and to become more "faith literate": This means a better understanding not only of the central role of faith in the communities we work with, but more concretely of faith structures and networks, and of the different approaches needed for effectively engaging with different types of faith-based actors.[31]

Still, discussions of religion in the context of humanitarianism have become muted and arguably silenced.[32] In all, the lack of recognition of the role of faith in humanitarian contexts in the Global South is due to two dynamics: the way humanitarianism has been conceptualized and the understanding of the role of faith-based humanitarian organizations and local faith-based initiatives.

Northern Bias in the Conceptualization of Humanitarianism

Modern understanding of humanitarianism is embedded within northern practices and systems of knowledge. In a way, the Global North has appropriated the humanitarian label. While histories of the development of Western humanitarianism recognize the contribution of religion, as we saw earlier, Henry Dunant's account of the Battle of Solferino in 1859 called for the establishment of organizations mandated to address the relief of suffering in such contexts, emphasizing the need for neutrality in these circumstances, and the Red Cross and the Geneva Convention of 1864 resulted from these proposals.[33] The way humanitarianism developed in practice involved the emergence of NGOs based in the Global North, which has more secularized societies. These agencies serve populations in the Global South with more explicit and active religious affiliations. In these ways, policies, projects, and practices designed to address the needs of people in humanitarian contexts emerge from societies and mindsets with different degrees of secularism that may be suspicious of religion.[34] Hugo Slim argues that northern humanitarian NGOs form, to some extent, an oligopoly of assistance, where humanitarian action is "something they want everyone to value and enjoy but which only they are allowed to do."[35] At the same time, other authors consider this oligopoly a "relief elite."[36]

With the beginning of the professionalized aid industry after World War II, three assumptions regarding the role of faith and religion in humanitarian settings emerged among policy makers and practitioners: first, the expectation that societies will become more secular; second, that secular approaches offer the safest path to peace and stability because they guarantee neutrality; and third, that religious identities and structures will continue being forces of oppression and persecution.[37] However, much is debated concerning whether or not we live in a "postsecular" age, and whether religious belief and practice are more, or less, important for individuals and communities around the world.[38]

Most of the relief and assistance work provided by faith-based organizations (FBOs) is not officially recorded anywhere. Local churches and mosques provide necessary and tangible support to people in need in their communities. Soup kitchens organized by local religious groups or volunteers helping disaster victims are not recorded anywhere in the UN's statistics on humanitarian contributions.[39] Hence, there is an urgent need to recognize the contributions of diverse systems of knowledge, especially from the Global South. In particular, the ways in which individuals experience community, communal obligation, and faith must be highlighted. Engagement with the way local communities in developing or poor countries provide humanitarian support is necessary. It is crucial to recognize and write their contributions into the history of humanitarianism and highlight the processes through which other actors and modes of humanitarian action have been minimized.[40]

Recognizing and documenting the contributions of other "humanitarianisms" allow us to see local actors' agency and capacity for agency, which enriches interpretations of humanitarian action that have remained focused on the northern system.[41] We cannot ignore the process of globalization that shapes local experiences, but recognizing the contributions of the "local" is necessary to address northern biases in shaping humanitarianism.

Southern (and/or "Local") Faith-Based Humanitarian Actors and Local Faith-Based Initiatives

While the distinction between international and local humanitarian actors seems clear on paper, in practice, the interconnection among organizations problematizes the idea of local (South-South) assistance and highlights the blurred distinction between what constitutes "southern" and "northern" assistance. Networks of faith-based organizations are a clear example here. Elizabeth Ferris, a scholar of humanitarianism, explains that networks of FBOs "are unique players in the international humanitarian community in that they are rooted in their local communities and yet have global reach."[42] Regarding FBOs in Mexico, some shelters are part of larger religious networks like the Scalabrinian Network, Jesuit Refugee Service (JRS), and other international religious orders with work in Mexico. These interconnections must be considered when we analyze the distinction between northern-led humanitarianism and local or South-South humanitarian initiatives. In the analysis of different case studies, researchers sometimes find that the relationship between these actors appears in contraposition, but at other times it appears as a complementary partnership to deliver services to vulnerable populations.[43]

As has been noted, local communities are always first responders and those who stay in situations of crisis. NGO and civil society efforts at the local level have been offering humanitarian protection for displaced populations for a long time. These efforts have included both secular and faith-based initiatives.[44] At first, local and faith-based humanitarian actors may respond by providing basic humanitarian assistance, shelter, or first aid. However, faith-based institutions may also offer spiritual support as part of a holistic service to refugee communities and migrant populations. In this way, local faith communities (LFCs) and faith-based organizations are significant sources of social and spiritual capital for migrants and refugees. Though there is still resistance to using the "humanitarian" label to describe faith-based initiatives, it is more widely recognized that LFCs and FBOs are important in this area.[45]

The importance of faith communities relies not only on the provision of immediate basic humanitarian assistance, but also on the relationships that faith-based humanitarian groups may have with local communities and other actors. In one way or another, LFCs and FBOs emerge from within the community and have a more or less permanent presence in the local context that allows them to have closer connections and the capacity to develop medium- and long-term programs to serve displaced populations.[46] Furthermore, local faith communities and religious groups frequently represent a major proportion of the capacity of civil society to support displaced populations.[47] That is the case with *casas de migrantes* in Mexico. At the same time, the long-term presence of LFCs and FBOs serving displaced populations can face adverse reactions from local communities and local actors, especially when the populations receiving services are seen as a threat. In some contexts, FBOs may act in discriminatory ways toward vulnerable groups. This negative impact should be taken seriously.[48]

At this point, the issue is not to emphasize the value of local humanitarian initiatives as a form of humanitarian assistance. Rather, it is to highlight the lack of understanding and underappreciation of what faith and religion bring to the table. An approach to LFCs and FBOs that focuses only on commonalities misses the opportunity to see other ways that faith and religion can serve the needs of people in displacement contexts, even if, at first glance, they do not share some of the classical—northern—humanitarian principles like neutrality, impartiality, and independence. These groups mobilize significant human capital (volunteers), social capital (through pastoral and other religious networks), physical capital (buildings used to provide services), and financial capital or donations (secured from benefactors). Furthermore, the potential value of the "spiritual capital" mobilized through pastoral care and religious practices must be considered, as it is a resource for people in displacement to cope with the experience. Thus, international humanitarian agencies that work only with "secularized" faith groups may miss the opportunity to understand deeper dynamics that come from the continuous presence of LFCs and FBOs.[49]

What Faith Puts on the Table

Though contemporary notions of humanitarianism are considered secular and separate from faith or religion, it is impossible to study humanitarianism without recognizing the roles religion and faith have had in delivering aid to the poor and vulnerable.[50] A recent trend in world history is that people have been joining in large numbers on expressly secular grounds to alleviate the suffering of others and to coordinate relief by establishing local, state, and transnational institutions. However, just because there has been a more secularized conceptualization of humanitarianism does not mean that religion or faith has gone away.[51] In the analysis of humanitarianism, a rigorous distinction between secular and religious organizations often breaks down empirically.[52]

While acknowledging that the Catholic Church and other denominations have fostered the emergence of many *casas de migrantes* along migration paths in Mexico, some accounts of the roles of humanitarian actors in Mexico move quickly to talk about the actors in secular terms, referring to them as "civil society" without analyzing whether or not their faith-based ethos has anything to do with their work.[53]

Ferris highlighted the difficulties that exist in the field to offer a definition of faith-based organizations that could be accurate and could cut across multiple faith traditions.[54] To add further complication, there are different levels of analysis that can guide the understanding of FBOs. These can be classified or understood "according to their implicit or explicit connections to faith based on their organizational, administrative, environmental, financial funding, and programmatic characteristics."[55] Here, I follow the definition of Gerard Clarke and Michael Jennings because it is broad enough to apply to different settings and geographic contexts: a faith-based organization is "any organization that derives inspiration and guidance for its activities from the teachings and principles of the faith or from a particular interpretation or school of thought within that faith."[56] In addition, I also consider what Jason Scott has written regarding FBOs:

> At a minimum, FBOs must be connected with an organized faith community. These connections occur when an FBO is based on a particular religious ideology and draws staff, volunteers, or leadership from a particular religious group. Other characteristics that qualify an organization as "faith-based" are religiously oriented mission statements, the receipt

of substantial support from a religious organization, or the initiation by a religious institution.[57]

FBOs represent a wide range of organizations, from relatively large national organizations to small groups of individuals and individual religious leaders with different levels of power, structures, and religious affiliations across local and national levels.[58] Attempts to explain and understand the nature of FBOs have led to the emergence of classifications or typologies.[59] Available typologies emphasize three categories: organizational control, expression of religion, and program implementation. Organizational control relates to funding resources, power structures in the organization, and decision-making processes. Expression of religion refers to the self-identity of the organization, the religiosity of participants, and how faith is expressed in outcome measures. Program implementation deals with the selection of services provided, the integration of religious elements in service delivery, and the voluntary or mandatory participation in specific religious activities.[60] An additional framework or analysis refers to the size of the organizations. FBOs range in size from small-scale, local-level religious congregations to national interdenominational coalitions and networks, to international humanitarian agencies associated with a particular religion; equally, they have highly diverse histories, underlying motivations, fundraising mechanisms, and modes of operation.[61]

Ferris also indicates that there could be "major differences between organizations in terms of their relationship with established religious structures, the degree to which considerations of faith are reflected in their work, the scale of their operations, their ways of working, and their understandings of the political and social context in which they operate."[62] My research confirmed this idea since, even within Mexico, the ways these faith-based humanitarian actors operate could vary significantly. While some figures and organizations, like Father Alejandro Solalinde, Las Patronas, Father Pedro Pantoja, Bishop Raúl Vera, OP, or Fray Tomás González, OFM, have been significant in defending migrants' human rights and have dominated the spotlight in the Mexican media regarding migration, I emphasize the role that local faith communities have in the origins, operation, and development of shelters and soup kitchens serving migrants across Mexico. While living in shelters in Mexico, I identified some factors or characteristics that allowed faith-based humanitarian organizations in Mexico to emerge and operate somewhat effectively. In a way, the things faith brings to the table in the humanitarian architecture in Mexico are resources, power of convocation, trust, and the ability to mediate with other organizations.[63] The ways these traits operate in practice show a significant combination of institutional and communal dimensions in faith-based organizations.

Resources

Faith-based communities may have some material assets available to support or mitigate precarious situations for people in general or emergency situations. Often, meeting rooms, bathrooms, buildings, and other facilities exist in churches, mosques, and other places of worship. Narratives about the beginning of humanitarian spaces in Mexico repeatedly echo this idea:

> Back in 1996, migrants did not come to the church or the town center. They would remain next to the train tracks. Slowly, they started to make their way downtown and the parish began offering services. They used multipurpose rooms as dormitories, they built some bathrooms on the ground floor, and the community organized itself to offer food. In the cases when a woman with children may appear, a member of the parish will offer her and the children hospitality.[64]

This comment illustrates how infrastructure (resources) becomes available and is transformed and adapted to cover the needs of migrants. The role of local communities in sustaining the work of shelters is explained in this way by a shelter director in a state in central Mexico:

> The local bishop [an ecclesiastical authority] offered us a small house to run the shelter. In 2009 they tried to open the shelter but had no success, even when the need was there. When we arrived, we did not have expertise or money, only the desire to help migrants and this little house. We started working, selling things, and taking on donations. We tried to keep

the shelter clean and with a sense of home. People from the local parishes [communities] helped a lot, and slowly we put together the shelter.

Shelters often start in multipurpose rooms or the small and seldom-used facilities churches may have. The above narratives suggest that while the faith community quickly responds to immediate needs like food or clothes, as other needs arise—like shelter or bathroom facilities—people occasionally offer their own living spaces. However, it is the more institutional church that makes resources available for shelters to operate on a more consistent basis.

Power of Convocation

Faith communities can gather resources from larger pools of people and occasionally from external donors, especially since feeding hundreds of people regularly presents a challenge. During my time in Mexico, I documented why reaching out to the community was critical for gathering the basic means of food, clothes, and even volunteers for different projects. At a shelter in southern Mexico, I accompanied volunteers as they collected remnants of food donated by grocery stores. At the shelter in northern Mexico, various Catholic community groups came every night to offer dinner to migrants; a similar operation was in place in another shelter in the state of Veracruz.

Yet gathering goods that fulfill basic human needs is only one side of the power of convocation. Occasionally, shelters use the church's structure to extend their reach and help people in distress. In a state in southern Mexico, the main church is in the center of the town; however, several other small churches—called *capillas*—in the surrounding communities are attached to or have a relationship with the main church. While the shelter Casa Rojche now has its own facilities to receive migrants, it also offers training on human rights and issues surrounding migration to the communities that belong to these satellite churches (*capillas*). In this way, migrants who have to walk the fifty-eight kilometers from the border between Mexico and Guatemala to a town in southern Mexico have a network of people who look out for them and will be sensible enough about their needs. This is a way to educate people in the communities about issues surrounding migration, as well as a way to gather the community and extend the reach of care a shelter can provide.

Trust

Trust may be understood as the firm belief in the reliability of someone or something. Based on migrants' belief that those helping them belong to the church, migrants on the move or returning to the country regularly seek or accept support from faith-based humanitarian organizations. Thus, migrants feel that they can confide in those people. Often, migrants moving through Mexico find themselves vulnerable and seek help at churches because they feel they will receive support there. Uriel, a twenty-nine-year-old Honduran migrant, walked along the train tracks for several hours until nightfall, decided to look for shelter, and specifically looked for a church. He said, "We looked for a church because we knew they would be the only ones to give us food and shelter." Migrants often trust the shelters because they belonged to faith communities back home. Higinio, a twenty-two-year-old Mexican migrant traveling for the first time, said, "I came to this shelter because I trust the people here. I know several priests, nuns, and people who serve God, and I trust them. If the people helping in shelters are people of God, you can trust them." These testimonies confirm what other studies have shown: religious organizations are often perceived as more trustworthy because they are embedded in the local community and their faith component.[65] Additionally, faith-based organizations are often present in areas that are hard to access and therefore create links to small enclaves of priests and nuns whose legitimacy is based on decades of community service.[66]

Mediation

Since many shelters in Mexico are locally run, their presence and work allow them to serve as interlocutors—with good and bad results—with other local groups. Sometimes shelters serve as mediators between migrants and the government to gain access to some resources—especially medical ones—or as legal representatives and advocates. At other times, they mediate with the community itself. Just as the community gathers to provide support and help for migrants, the other side of that experience is the community that abuses and takes advantage of the migrants because it perceives migrants as a threat and blames them for social problems or shows resentment because migrants may receive help while the poor in the community are unable to access some services. We need to keep in mind that in local communities not everybody belongs to or participates in a church, whatever its denomination, or is sympathetic of the support that migrant shelters provide. Furthermore, since shelters in Mexico have been working for a long time, INGOs like the Red Cross, MSF, UNHCR, IOM, UN, or Asylum Access look to partner with shelters to provide ad hoc services.

Similar to how shelters' services affect the migration process, the faith-based nature of many allows *casas de migrantes* to emerge, sustain their work, and function at a basic level. Aside from the fact that support and aid are free of charge, the power of convocation, trust, and mediation are vital traits that impact how migrants engage with shelters. Furthermore, the mediation role of these humanitarian organizations needs to be highlighted. Thanks to shelters' abilities to mediate, migrants can access resources that otherwise may be out of reach, like legal representation or maintaining conviviality with a community that may see migrants' presence as a threat. As Ferris (2011), Ager, Fiddian-Qasmiyeh, and Ager (2015), and Fiddian-Qasmiyeh and Ager (2013) have indicated, some of these traits are not recorded or considered humanitarian contributions. Nevertheless, these traits make *casas de migrantes* key actors in the humanitarian landscape in Mexico.

Double Identities

Nowadays, in many cases, migrant shelters that have a Catholic inspiration or are faith-based have double identities: one as a civil organization and another as a faith-based organization. These identities allow them to be more successful not only in their daily work of providing humanitarian aid, but also in lobbying the government for the rights of migrant populations and partnering with INGOs.[67]

After the Reformation period and the first decades of the nineteenth century, the relationships between the Catholic Church and the state were difficult. The Reformation laws established a separation between the state and the Church (mainly the Catholic Church). This separation was enshrined in the Mexican Constitution of 1917. During the second decade of the twentieth century, the Catholic Church in Mexico was seen as contrary to the revolutionary movement, and an anticlerical movement emerged. During these years, the government suspended religious cult and activities, which led to what was known as La Guerra Cristera, or La Guerra de los Cristeros (Cristera War, or Cristeros War), which lasted from 1926 to 1929.[68]

Some of the articles in the Constitution and subsequent changes in the law prohibited the Church from having juridical recognition, limited its ability to own real estate properties, and sought to limit the number of priests. Subsequently, as there was official separation between the Church, in practice religion and religious activities were tolerated until 1992, when the Mexican government reestablished official relationship with the Vatican and promulgated the Ley de Asociaciones Religiosas y Culto Público (Religious Associations and Public Worship Law), giving churches a defined legal status, the right to own property, and the right to conduct religious education. However, it was not until 2003 that the regulations to operate this law were published. These regulations not only restated the legal recognition of religious institutions but also specified rights and duties. The regulations facilitated the process for faith-based organizations to become registered NGOs with legal recognition, which provided the opportunity to access funds locally and internationally. After 2003, *casas de migrantes* started registering as *asociaciones civiles* (civil associations, or formal NGOs), assuming a double identity, one of which let them engage more freely with other NGOs to seek grants and partnerships to enhance their services. The other identity allowed them to continue engaging with their faith-based ethos, maintain their membership in religious networks, and continue to foster their relationship with the local bishops and other religious leaders.[69] Today, these double identities may not seem significant, but at that time, this dynamic was a breakthrough in how this humanitarianism from below operated.

The way these double identities work was exemplified by the changes proposed at the Dimensión Pastoral de la Movilidad Humana (DPMH) annual meeting in 2012. At that time, the Catholic network of *casas de migrantes* had thrived and achieved great synergy in various projects and regions. The network was at its peak in terms of providing services and advocating for the rights of migrants. I attended the network's national gathering during the summer of that year. At that time, the bishops in charge of the network had close ties to the government. A reorganization within the network was presented and moved forward, in spite of the fact that the new arrangement did not favor or create synergy among its members. The 2011 Ley de Migración (Migration Law) had just passed the year before, and network members were creating pressure for the law to be applied. The 2011 migration law in Mexico had a human rights framework that made Mexico appear as a moderator country. In 2012 the main argument was that the changes aligned better with the pastoral approach needed to serve migrants. Members of the network felt otherwise. In practice, the changes meant dismantling different achievements, especially around advocacy. Due to the faith-based nature of the network, *casas de migrantes* had to align with the proposed changes. However, thanks to the legal status of NGOs that many of them had at that moment, they continued their advocacy efforts with the structures that facilitated their work without the interference of ecclesiastical leadership.

The double identities revealed some of the independent nature that humanitarianism from below in Mexico has. They empowered LFBs and FBOs to provide services on their own terms, navigating complicated political and social landscapes. They showed that even when some shelters are faith-based, they are not necessarily bound to hierarchical structures. They also demonstrated certain levels of autonomy and creativity to provide services in the ways organizations considered best. As *casas de migrantes* work under these double identities, one of the biggest challenges they face is the extent to which their faith-based identity is diluted as they perform as secular NGOs .

Conclusion

Casas de migrantes emerged in a fertile ground rooted in two experiences: the work of civic associations in Mexico and the experience of being a country of emigration. Mexico had a history of civic commitment efforts that provided care for vulnerable populations. These efforts were executed from local platforms, faith-based groups, and other networks. These efforts from the past show how Mexican society was sensitive to the needs of those in vulnerable positions and capable of organizing themselves outside government institutions. Experiences of emigration also embed in certain sectors of society a sense of solidarity with migrants and refugees. In a way, the work of *casas de migrantes* could be seen as a social movement of solidarity with people in contexts of mobility that emerges from local experiences and commitment to social justice. Mexican society has a history of these kinds of social movements.

In the past, Mexican society was used to seeing commitment from religious associations—that is, social commitments from faith-based groups. Expressions of religious affiliation do not necessarily mean regular attendance at religious services. The religious identity of Mexican society is not based on active participation and attendance at church as it might be in American society. However, in Mexico, anticlerical movements washed out efforts from faith-based groups to the point that nowadays, they are looked at with suspicion and undervalued. This perception remains today when we consider the work of *casas de migrantes*.

The lack of recognition of faith and faith-based affiliations in humanitarian work is not exclusive to the Mexican context. While humanitarian sentiments and concerns for the other echo religious sentiments and images, humanitarianism in the North has evolved to emphasize a secular framework guided by the belief that this approach will ensure respect for humanitarian principles. This dynamic not only fosters the undervaluing of the work of other people working on the ground to alleviate the suffering of vulnerable populations, but also leads to missing opportunities to create synergies or collaborations that could benefit the people humanitarians aim to serve, although international organizations do routinely partner with shelters.

In the Mexican case, federal requirements lead humanitarian organizations on the ground to have legal recognition. One of the unintended consequences of this requirement is the rise of dual identities in some migrant shelters in Mexico. While they keep the faith-based ethos and affiliations, migrant shelters use this other identity to network in ways that will allow them to serve migrant populations better. Hence, *casas de migrantes* have one foot in the secular world and another in the religious world. The challenge for them is navigating different relationships and scenarios while maintaining the foundational ethos that led to serving migrants.

4

An Informal Welfare System along Migration Routes

I was sitting down with Victor on a warm day at the shelter in Saltillo, Coahuila. I was on my second trip along the migrant routes, three hundred kilometers from the border between Mexico and the United States. We were watching other migrants play football. As we continued the conversation, he told me that he was twenty-seven years old and had been born in Guatemala. He had traveled for sixty days before reaching the shelter in Saltillo. While describing his journey, he exclaimed,

> Thanks be to God and the people of goodwill who have fed us along the way. For the most part, nobody denies food to you. However, people do not want to give you money anymore. Many Central Americans are panhandling, supposedly to eat, but they are drunk. So people do not give to you anymore. . . . I panhandled in Arriaga [Chiapas], in Corazones [Oaxaca]. I mounted the train, but migration authorities chased us again before arriving at Union Hidalgo [Oaxaca]. I had to walk thirty kilometers to Juchitan [Oaxaca]. It was dark when I arrived, and I had to sleep on the street. A lady gave me twenty pesos [one US dollar], and I traveled to Ixtepec, where I looked for *la casa del migrante*. . . . After a couple of days, I mounted the train in the direction of Medias Aguas [Veracruz], but migration authorities made us get off the train, and we had to walk to Matias Romero [Oaxaca], where I stayed for a couple of days at another shelter. . . . Unable to ride the train, I then walked another two days before reaching Medias Aguas [Veracruz]. . . . It took me another eight days by foot to reach the next town, which is Tierra Blanca in Veracruz. . . . If there was a shelter where we passed, we stayed at the shelter. If there was no shelter, one had to sleep on the street.

Victor's journey illustrates the complexities of migration journeys for poor migrants. He walked, rode on top of freight trains, and used public transportation to cover the 2,221 kilometers (1,380 miles) between his hometown in Escuintla, Guatemala, and the shelter in Saltillo where I met him. During his journey, he slept in churches, at shelters, next to the train tracks in deserted regions, and in parks when he passed through some towns. Occasionally, he waited for several days in different towns, and other times he tried to move as quickly as possible to cover more ground on his journey. On a few occasions, migration authorities chased Victor. He was deported from Mexico twice but resumed his journey again and again. He began his migration journey with less than thirty US dollars. Along the road, he panhandled to gather some money and often relied on people of goodwill to give him food. He has no relatives or contacts in the United States. It is not the first time he has traveled along the arduous migration route in Mexico. He crossed Mexico before, successfully entering the United States before being deported in 2013. When I met him, he was trying to reach Atlanta, Georgia. Victor's story, like the stories of many other migrants, poses an intriguing question: How did he make it to this point?

In migration literature, two general conventions are related to the intersection of poverty and migration. First, it is not the poorest who move, but those with the resources and the drive to do so.[1] Second, it is suggested that much of the experience of poverty connects to the idea or feeling of being poor when comparing personal situations to others' success or circumstances.[2] While these two ideas may remain valid on a large scale, the focus of migration research on the types of resources available for migrants has precluded deeper exploration of the role poverty plays in migration journeys. Furthermore, if migrants are poor, how do they cope with their migration project?

Migration literature does not explicitly sustain the notion that migrants are not poor. Geographer Ronald Skeldon states that the poor move, and my research in shelters along migrant trails in Mexico confirms that migrants who lack resources to finance their journeys use an array of strategies to cope with hardship and attempt their journeys.[3] Victor's story illustrates this: He begs for food, panhandles enough money to make it to the next town, looks for help at shelters and churches, and often uses his body (walks) to reach the next point of his journey. These types of experiences are not uncommon among migrants in different regions.[4] This chapter discusses two arguments that are critical to understanding how poor migrants cope with their journeys through Mexico: the notion of "an economy of makeshifts," understood as the strategies that migrants use to cope with the journey, and the emergence of the *casas de migrantes* as an informal welfare system that sustains the mobility of migrants in Mexico. The purpose of these discussions is to show that the mobile poor, like migrants today, were able to cope with hardship and that even before the rise of humanitarianism as understood today, there were ways in which aid was provided to these mobile populations by people tied to religious groups.

An Economy of Makeshifts

Poor migrants may move more than we expect or than researchers have been able to document.[5] While traveling along the migration routes in Mexico, I found that the incidence of poverty among migrants is double the incidence of poverty in each country of origin. The analysis in this chapter comes from using the Multidimensional Poverty Index (MPI) to measure the levels of poverty that migrants experience at the moment of their departure.[6] While the trend of higher prevalence of MPI poverty among migrant populations is seen elsewhere—like Vietnam and China—these trends refer to internal migration, particularly from rural to urban settings.[7] In contrast, the evidence here provides a snapshot of the poverty levels among migrants moving internationally. While the analysis cannot answer whether the *poorest* also move, future studies can use this same methodology with a larger and more robust sample to provide more information regarding the movement of poor migrants.

What is at stake here is neither establishing causality between poverty levels and migration nor making an in-depth analysis of poverty among migrants. The concern here is challenging some of the previous assumptions regarding the movement of the poor by making explicit and showing that poor migrants do move, and despite their poverty find ways to embark on migration journeys and cope with hardship. At the same time, while some migrants may feel that they are poor by comparing themselves to other standards, these feelings of being poor may be based on actual and specific deprivations (lack of nutrition, sanitation, water, and education), and not just on perception.

The poor do choose to migrate, but some resources, no matter how meager these might appear, are needed to initiate the move.[8] Skeldon writes that "migration always involves some costs of transportation and the abandonment of many of the few possessions the poor might have. The poorest of the poor cannot afford either risk or movement, and the majority starve in situ."[9] I consider this latter assertion too strong because it reinforces a sedentary bias and questions the agency that migrants may exercise in survival situations. However, one question remains: If the poor indeed move, what types of resources do they possess when they embark on their different migration trajectories? Conversations with migrants revealed that poor migrants use an array of strategies. Some of them launch their journeys with what I call "spark money," which is often enough to *start* the journey. Resources to *sustain* that journey, though, are a different matter, and may not come in the way of great financial resources but rather from unlikely places and in unlikely forms. As history has shown, the poor can develop their resources and find new strategies to cope with their deprivations and the lack of initial resources as they move.

"Spark Money"

Migrants must at least have meager resources to embark on a journey, but what do "meager resources" consist of? How much does "meager" translate to in terms of capital and social capital? Scholars have overemphasized the need for resources and the role of networks in the process of migration, but have rarely explored, addressed, or attempted to quantify the resources needed to embark on a migration journey. While in the field, I asked migrants how much money, contacts, and other resources they needed to start their journeys. While unable to afford smugglers, poor migrants knew that they still needed resources to sustain their continuous movement. They often started their migration projects with whatever amount of money they could gather, hoping that they could somehow cope or find resources along the way. Some of this spark money was borrowed, some came from gifts, some was from savings, and some represented what a migrant had available at that moment. In some cases, the cash that a migrant had was all that was available for their family.[10] Migrants took that money and relied on family networks to help those left behind cope with the departure. At times, it was clear that migrants felt pressure to reach their intended destinations because they had no more money available. This spark money was just enough to start the journey, but it was often gone by the moment migrants reached the border with Mexico or even earlier if they were robbed or had to bribe officials; in some cases, migrants were left with nothing very early on along their journeys. But, as has been documented in Mexico and other parts of the world, many migrants—like other poor people—are able to exercise creativity and agency to cope with hardship along the journey.

Interestingly, I found that women left with higher amounts of money than men.[11] Some women may have more access to cash either through income or because they could have acquired spark money from borrowing or selling assets. Although to be clear, the above factors do not mean that women are not poor. Also, migrants older than thirty-five embarked on migration journeys with more money than other age groups. It is plausible that an older person has more control and access to savings, loans, or cash that could be made available for the journey, as in the case of women.

There is an economic stratification in the migration process in Mexico. Those migrants who can hire a smuggler or have more contacts may have different strategies to reach their intended destinations than poor migrants who have fewer resources or contacts.[12] During my visits to detention centers in Mexico, migrants from India, Bangladesh, Pakistan, and Nigeria shared that they had paid large amounts of money to travel—between USD 20,000 and 25,000. Occasionally, migrants from African countries and other nationalities could be found at *casas de migrantes*. In these cases, they had usually lost all their resources or had made elongated journeys with meager resources. Regardless of their native country, Victor's story resembles the journeys of many poor migrants moving through or returning to Mexico.

The Mobile Poor and Their "Economy of Makeshifts"

Many poor people are not passive recipients of their fates and actively exercise their agency to overcome obstacles. Historian Olwen Hufton used the term "economy of makeshifts" to describe the different strategies that poor people in the preindustrial era used to deal with poverty and hardship: an extra job, seasonal migration, begging, burglary, or

TABLE 4.1. Strategies of an "Economy of Makeshifts" and Strategies Used by Poor Migrants to Cope with Hardship during Their Journeys

Strategies of an "Economy of Makeshifts"	Strategies of the Poor and Vulnerable Migrant
Begging	Begging
Neighborly and/or kin support	"Delayed activation of networks"
Loans	"Sustaining" cash transfers
Charitable doles	Humanitarian assistance (shelters)
Day labor (by employment and casual jobs)	Casual work
	The body

even getting involved in criminal activities.[13] Here, I draw a parallel between the poor during preindustrial times and poor migrants moving through Mexico. Similar to the past, when the poor and the vagrants were considered threats and thus needed to be controlled, nowadays, the migrant is seen as a threat that needs to be controlled.[14] And similar to the poor in the past, migrants rely on different strategies to cope with their journeys. Table 4.1 compares the strategies of the poor in the preindustrial era, as described by King and Tomkins, and some of the strategies migrants use along migrant routes in Mexico.[15]

I leave out the discussion of day labor because the migrants I found had always been on the move, even though begging could be seen as a form of work.[16] However, by 2023, many migrants trying to reach the US-Mexico border needed to work along the way. They often worked for a while until they gathered some money to continue their journeys. I also leave out the role of humanitarian assistance, which is at the core of this book and thus discussed throughout the rest of the volume. The discussion here offers insight into how, even though they actively employ these other strategies, the humanitarian assistance that this book describes is so essential for so many migrants.

The Strategies of the Poor

Begging

At the simplest level, to beg is "to ask someone earnestly or humbly for something" (per the *Oxford English Dictionary*). Without a doubt, begging entails dynamics of inclusion, exclusion, and power. Historically, begging has been associated with escaping labor—as the opposite of work—and has been treated by authorities as acceptable only for those who cannot earn their living in other ways. However, some argue that begging can become a career or a job. While begging, economic activity, and deservingness may all be interrelated, beggars often belong to vulnerable and excluded groups of society that may be perceived differently depending on the context and circumstances.[17]

Begging, or *charolear* (panhandling), is a common strategy used by poor migrants and deportees to cope with hardship during their journeys. While the prevalence of this practice is difficult to capture, it is common to find migrants begging for food or money in transit towns along migration routes in Mexico. But the practice takes different forms depending on the place and circumstances of the journey. Seeking aid at shelters along the routes, begging for food and shelter at houses in remote areas, and begging for money in different towns are some of the most common methods used by poor migrants moving through Mexico.

Knocking on the Door for Help

Rogelio, a twenty-three-year-old migrant from El Salvador, ran out of money when he and his friend reached the town of Tuxtla, in the state of Chiapas. They had to walk from the city's edge, where the bus dropped them off, to avoid a migration checkpoint. After several hours of walking, they reached a neighborhood, knocked on the door of a house, and asked for sustenance: "We asked a woman for water and food. We told her we were migrants and how we had been traveling [by bus and on foot]. She offered soup, and we ate. We asked her about the next migration checkpoint. She said that it was five kilometers ahead. We hurried to finish the soup and resumed our walking."

He continued his explanation by emphasizing that they had to walk around the checkpoint and stop and ask for water several times, mainly because they were walking in the sun. Rogelio said, "I think we walked more than five kilometers. But at some point, we moved and walked far away from the road to avoid the migration checkpoint. Thus, there were less and less houses, but from time to time, when we saw a little house, we stopped, knocked on the door, and asked for water. We asked for water four times before reaching the next point." Migrants who ask for food or water may concern local residents, especially those who have become suspicious of everyone since there is an exacerbated climate of violence in Mexico. Rogelio acknowledges this, saying, "People give you something, water or food, but they are suspicious of you. One time a man came out of his house with a machete in his hand. We asked him for water, and he gave it to us. But you could feel the tension. He was suspicious of us, and we were afraid of the machete. We kept walking, and thanks be to God, we avoided the migration checkpoint." The presence of strangers in local communities, especially isolated ones, may create anxieties because locals are unaware of the strangers' intentions. Hence, begging in remote places inevitably raises tensions with community residents. Mutual suspicion becomes the norm.

Standing at a Crossroad and Extending a Hand

Blanca, a twenty-six-year-old migrant from Honduras, *charoleó* (panhandled) during her journey, first in Coatzacoalcos (southern Mexico) and then in the town of Apaxco de Ocampo (central Mexico). Without money, she attempted to get on the freight train in Coatzacoalcos. A gang controlling access to the train asked for a *cuota* (fee) to let her jump onto the train. Unable to pay, she went to beg for money: "We went to a crossroad to beg, hoping to gather money for the *cuota*. It took us about an hour to gather the three hundred pesos (fifteen US dollars) that they were asking for. We returned to give them the money. We picked up our bags and waited for the train."

Blanca was able to reach Mexico City, but not having any money left, she asked for help at a nearby church: "I told the priest I needed to get to Huehuetoca [a town in the outskirts of Mexico City], but I did not have any money. He saw me with suspicion but gave me fifty pesos (three US dollars). So I made my way to Huehuetoca, where I sought the *casa del migrante*. We walked to the next town, where we stayed at another church. We went out to beg for money for three days. In three days, we gathered forty-five US dollars. At first, we thought about looking for a job, but then we saw that we were making like fifteen US dollars a day. Thus, we decided to continue *charoleando*. We just wanted to get enough to take the bus to the next town."

Often, I heard tidbits like these along migrant trails. I heard them from migrants who were both early on or deep into their journeys.

They could be in urban places or isolated areas with only small communities. I constantly saw migrants begging in different transit towns. They often validated their status by showing a banknote (bill) from Honduras, Guatemala, or El Salvador to prove that they were migrants. In some instances, begging is a coping or survival strategy. But this common practice along migratory routes has some significant implications relating to dynamics of power and (un)deservingness. This practice also challenges local authorities who want to contain migrants and dislike the idea of their spreading out in town. Begging is a fairly old practice; European states dealt with the poor and how local communities responded to the changing composition of a broader "economy of makeshifts" that the poor relied on to survive.[18] Beggars, the mobile poor, and migrants were seen with suspicion, and laws emerged to deal with them. Often the issues dealt with settlement, (un)deservingness, and criminalization of the migrants' activity. We see these dynamics in contemporary migration patterns, political discourses, and migration policies.

Delayed Activation of Networks

Migrant networks are sets of interpersonal ties that connect migrants, former migrants, and non-migrants in origin and destination areas through the bonds of kinship, friendship, and shared community origin. They can also be conceived as a form of location-specific capital that people draw upon to access resources elsewhere. Networks tend to decrease migration's economic, social, and psychological costs.[19] A network is useful only if it is active and can mobilize resources. At one of the shelters in southern Mexico, I assisted the staff with registering migrants passing through. During my time there, I registered 417 migrants. As part of those intake discussions, I asked about the ways they organized their journeys and the contacts they may have at their destinations. Migrants repeatedly said in one way or another that their social networks would help them once they reached the US-Mexico border. In other words, migrants must move through Mexico with their own resources, and hope that help—economic support to pay smugglers or to find ways to cross the border—will come when they arrive at the border. This is what I call the "delayed activation of networks."

There are also migrants who have no contacts or networks at their intended destinations, like Omar, a Honduran who is twenty-eight years old. He explained, "I want to get to Houston, but I have no one to help me. There is nothing I can do but to try by myself." Another example is David, an unaccompanied sixteen-year-old migrant from Guatemala, who said, "I am going to California, which is where the vast majority of people from my town go, but I do not know anyone over there. Furthermore, I did not tell my family I was leaving because they would not let me go. But someone has to help my family." These types of migrants become extremely vulnerable during their journeys, and hence rely heavily on support from shelters. Occasionally, they may be able to create ties with other migrants and use other networks that may offer support. In the meantime, they are on their own.

The delayed activation of networks may have two different modalities: First, there are migrants who have not talked to anyone in their networks at the point of destination but hope that those networks will help them to cross into the United States once they have reached the US-Mexico border. Second, there are migrants who have talked to their contacts at the destination and have been asked to aim at reaching the border, where aid would be made available. Thus, in many of these cases, the network does not become active or mobilize resources until a certain geographical threshold is reached. The reason for this dynamic is often cost saving, since it is cheaper to pay a smuggler to help someone to cross into the United States while at the Mexico-US border than to pay from a different departure point further south in Mexico, Latin America, or abroad.

"They do not know I am coming," said Emilio, a twenty-two-year-old migrant from Honduras. He has two cousins living and working in the United States, but has not contacted them. He said, "I am planning to call them, but when I am closer to the border. That way, it will be easy for them to help me [often this support comes in the form of money to pay a smuggler]." Ariel, a thirty-four-year-old migrant from Honduras, clearly expressed the nuances and complexities of the delayed activation of networks when he said, "God has the last word. I do not feel pressure or enamored by the idea of getting to the United States. I have family there, but I have not talked to them. They could potentially help me, but I believe more in friendship than in family. I will contact my family once

I am at the border between Mexico and the United States. We will see then. For now, I have no illusions of getting there." Some migrants thus generally embark on their migration projects with their own resources and at their own risk, hoping to activate their networks at some point. They also operate under the assumption of reciprocity, but assess that support could be easier to obtain at the border.

The fact that migrants do not want to contact members of their networks may signal that help may not be available at that stage of the journey, while proximity to the final destination may entice members of the networks to offer support. "Put yourself at the border, and we will see then"—that was the response that Filemón, a forty-four-year-old migrant from Honduras, got from his brother before departing for the United States. Similarly, Vinicio, a twenty-seven-year-old migrant from Honduras, described the agreement with his brother in this way: "He told me I need to get to the border of Nuevo Laredo. My brother said getting myself there is the only way in which he can help me." In these instances, migrants have made contact with their networks, and there is a willingness to help, but other resources could not be mobilized at that time, or there were not enough resources to cover the costs of supporting someone coming from the Mexican southern border.

I also encountered cases in which migrants moved through Mexico with the promise that they would receive help at the border, but at some point along the route, the promise was broken or other needs emerged for the contacts at their destination. Other times, a migrant may have received some help from his or her contacts, and the network was later deactivated. In other words, resources could not be mobilized anymore. Maria, a twenty-eight-year-old migrant from Honduras, left after her sister agreed to help her at some point in her journey. However, when Maria reached the town of Coatzacoalcos, her sister told her that she could no longer help. When I talked to Maria, she was in Coatzacoalcos, struggling with the decision to return and having trouble making a living. Similarly, José, a forty-four-year-old Honduran migrant, was on his way home when I registered him at the shelter. He had been on the road for several months because his nephews offered help. At some point along the journey, his nephews had an emergency in the United States and told him that they could not help anymore. It was then that José decided to make the journey back to Honduras.

Migrants often say that they have contacts at their intended destinations or in Mexico, but it is clear that not all family members are willing or able to help. Thus, having contacts or family members in a destination country is not necessarily a network or guarantee that aid will be provided. Historical accounts of the "economy of makeshifts" have indicated that support from kinship for poor people was common in the late sixteenth century. Still, evidence also shows that by the early seventeenth century, support from kinship was less available.[20] Today, as in the past, the availability of support from kinship may vary depending on the circumstances of the supporters, and reliance on networks may lead to social inequality among migrant groups.[21]

Sustaining Cash Transfers

Many *casas de migrantes* provide secure access to migrants' networks by offering means of communication, including free calls, texts, access to the Internet, or the reception of money orders on behalf of migrants. Some migrants may receive these small amounts of money once or twice during their migration trajectory. I call these cash transfers "sustaining cash transfers" because that is their function, as they help migrants to sustain their migration journeys. Moreover, the cash transfers do not necessarily come from the destination country; during the time I spent along migrant trails, I found that money they received came from Central American countries, the United States, Mexico, and even Europe.

It is difficult to accurately measure the percentage of migrants who receive cash transfers during their journeys. However, what I found volunteering at *casas de migrantes* was that 20 to 25 percent of the migrants who stayed at the shelters received cash transfers. For example, 727 migrants passed through one shelter in central Mexico during August and September 2015; 83 and 97 people received money orders during those months, respectively. Those migrants who were sent cash transfers received a median of forty-five US dollars in each transfer. *Casas de migrantes* have a rule against the reception of large amounts of money for security reasons and because transfer companies cap the amount of money a recipient can receive. Generally, a volunteer or staff member at the shelter receives the cash transfer on a migrant's behalf since migrants cannot cash a money order or receive a cash transfer unless they present official identification, such as a passport.

As mentioned earlier, migrants' narratives often refer to small amounts of transferred money that barely sustain their journeys. "They only sent me fifty US dollars. They are poor like me and are barely making it. Those fifty dollars were barely enough to move to the next town," said Blanca, a twenty-six-year-old migrant from Honduras, who left her country with forty-three US dollars and received a cash transfer in Coatzacoalcos. Similarly, Eduardo, a thirty-nine-year-old from El Salvador, shared, "One of my aunts is going to help me when I reach the border with the US. For now, I do not have anyone to help me. But one of my friends was kind enough to send me fifty US dollars. She said that she could not send more because she has other expenses." These narratives illustrate that people supporting migrants may also have limited resources, often having to borrow money themselves to send to family or friends along migration routes.

Some migrants may plan to have money sent to them by their family members at different points along the journey. Each time, migrants factor in different costs, which may include bribes to officials or *derechos de piso* (fees for criminal gangs). While this strategy seems like an efficient response to violence because it saves migrants from carrying all of their money at once and avoiding being robbed of large amounts of money, in practice, this is not as easy as it may first appear.[22] An intermediary who is a Mexican national, or someone who holds an official identification, is always necessary. This is also critical for Mexican deportees who return to the country without official identification. Sometimes in border towns, the post office is the only place that will accept a repatriation letter (the letter that a Mexican deportee receives upon return to Mexico, which supposedly serves as a form of identification). By the end of 2023, the practice of receiving sustaining cash transfers was much more common as migrants moving through Mexico came from South American countries as far as Chile. Anel, a twenty-six-year-old Venezuelan migrant traveling with five children, narrated the need, challenges, and risks associated with receiving cash transfers during her journey:

> I lived in Brazil for two years and a half before starting the journey. . . . [I] crossed the Darién Gap [a tropical forest in Panama] with my children . . .

but Mexico was very difficult to cross. In Tapachula [a border town in southern Mexico], my partner [who was already in the United States] sent me three hundred US dollars to pay for transportation from Tapachula to Mexico City. I asked someone [a Mexican national] to receive the money for me, but he robbed me. He went to withdraw the money from a different Western Union and when I looked for him, he was already gone. My partner had to send me another three hundred US dollars. This time he had to borrow money.

Anel also mentioned that she sold candy and begged for money during her journey through Mexico, but her comments made evident the need for financial resources to move quickly from one place to another, as well as the risk of relying on strangers or quick acquaintances to receive a cash transfer.

In January and February 2023, I spent a couple of weeks in Ciudad Juárez volunteering at the cathedral (the main Catholic church in town), which opened a soup kitchen to give food, information, and basic services to a large number of migrants arriving in town. Every day, an array of volunteers led by the pastoral team at the cathedral fed between four hundred and five hundred migrants—many of them from Venezuela— arriving in the city with the hope of crossing into the United States to apply for asylum using the CBP One app. While serving food, I had many conversations with migrants during those days. Invariably, migrants mentioned over and over having received one or two small cash transfers along the way to cope with the journey. Similarly, during another two-week visit to interview migrants at a migrant camp in Matamoros, Tamaulipas, a Mexican border town across from Brownsville, Texas, reception of cash transfers was mentioned in interviews not only as part of the journey but as an essential need for navigating the rough conditions of the camp for several months. The camp could hold between 800 and 1,500 migrants at any given time. Migrants waited here an average of three to four months to get an appointment through the CBP One app.

The strategies of an economy of makeshifts allow poor people to cope, not to move out of poverty. Thus, one must not assume that the strategies a poor person could rely on offer consistent and adequate income for poor people. In the case of migrants depending on shelters or in the absence of them, cash transfers have more of a sustaining role than ultimately supporting a migrant during her or his journey. Sustaining cash transfers are not a source of income. If that were the case, migrants might not rely on or seek shelters for support, especially when they have to abide by the shelters' rules and regulations.

The Body

Without minimizing the significance of understanding irregular migration from a socioeconomic-political perspective, I maintain that there is still a lack of understanding of the migrants' embodied experiences of being on the road. Blisters, scratches, dehydration, tired bodies, broken arms, and—in extreme cases—missing limbs are traces that the journey through Mexico leaves on migrants' bodies. In a way, migrants use their bodies as a resource not only to cope with the journey, but to defy the systems that try to contain them.

Walking long distances or for significant periods of time appeared as a constant feature as migrants described their journeys. When faced with a lack of economic resources, migration controls, and/or irregular options for transportation, migrants walk. As the freight train's schedule has become more erratic, migrants staying at *casas de migrantes* become restless and have to decide their next steps. "We decided to walk to Zapata" (the next town after one main city in southern Mexico), explained one migrant from Honduras, traveling with another three friends. He added, "We cannot keep waiting; with or without the train, we will continue our journeys. We do not have many options, so we will walk."

Filemón, a twenty-five-year-old migrant from Honduras, walked for two weeks and covered 420 kilometers (260 miles) before jumping onto the train. He said, "We walked through the mountains and along the train tracks. We moved to the mountains when we saw migration checkpoints, returning to the train tracks once we were sure we were far away from migration authorities. We spent two weeks just walking. We kept walking to the town of Juan Rodríguez Clara in the state of Veracruz. We jumped onto the train around one in the morning. My feet were full of thorns and raw blisters. We were exhausted, and our stomachs were hurting because we ate a lot of green fruit that we found along the road." Migrants often walk at different stages of the journey;

sometimes those journeys last a couple of hours until they can catch a freight train, but other times their journeys can last days or weeks. The physical demand is high. These experiences reveal how migrants use their bodies to cover long distances and how the journey takes a toll on their bodies, resulting in injuries and exhaustion.

The body is a human being's first instrument and the most natural object they can use in their interactions. Activity and movement such as climbing, jumping, walking, or trampling are among the most basic techniques of the body.[23] Migrants rely on walking, perhaps the most basic technique of the body, not only to avoid migration controls, but also as a tool to cover the distance toward their destination. Migrants "use" their bodies to overcome the constraints of their journeys.[24]

Occasionally, migrants pay a high price for daring to journey irregularly through Mexico. The price may come in the form of a limb, another part of the body, a life-threatening infection from exposure to different elements of the weather and landscape, or attacks by criminals. Valentín, a seventeen-year-old from Honduras, lost a leg while trying to jump onto the freight train. When I interviewed him, he was recovering at a shelter in Puebla. Like many other migrants who have suffered his fate, he will likely return to his country of origin. "Without a fully functioning body, how am I going to be able to continue the journey?" he asked.

Political geographer Alison Mountz argues that "the body is a crucial element to understand the operation of power in relations between states and migrants. . . . Embodiment locates power relations and contextualizes decision-making within workplace settings and life histories."[25] Furthermore, Thomas Blom Hansen and Finn Stepputat observe that mobile bodies defy disciplinary power and challenge manifestations of sovereignty.[26] Migrant protests against migration policies or injustices at detention centers, aimed at legal changes or better treatment in those contexts, take place occasionally and may involve different bodily acts, such as lip sewing or hunger strikes, which have political significance only if they are mediated by public media or mobilizations on migrants' behalf. To some extent, migrants' protests require the intervention of local citizens because they may witness, broadcast, or highlight the protest itself.[27] In the case of migrants in Mexico, using the body as a mobility tool to cover distances amid migration controls and limited resources emerges as an expression that defies the state. Walking is not often observed as or considered a public act of defiance. Nevertheless, migrants leave pieces of their bodies along the road when walking long distances to reach their destinations or to avoid system controls. This "use" of the body is an act of defiance to the system that attempts to manage migrants.

The caravans of late 2018 and early 2019 perfectly illustrate the use of the body as an act of defiance against a system that limits migrants' mobility. As noted earlier, the caravans were large groups of migrants moving through Mexico with the intention of reaching the US-Mexico border. They gained significant media and political attention, as the migrants were traveling primarily by foot. Walking in this context was an act of defiance and an embodied practice of resistance. It was a way to occupy physical space and political space. People put their bodies on the line because nobody can walk the journey for others. In doing so, they found that there was a price to pay. The body will be taxed with the physical demands of the journey.[28] Local humanitarian groups and migrant shelters aided the caravans' journey through Mexico. Churches and local communities scrambled to offer as much support as possible, especially to children and women. But migrant shelters are not designed to house thousands of migrants, and the services they offer have limits. Thus, local and state governments had to step in to guarantee safety, shelter, and food for migrants as the physical demands of covering the journey mostly on foot took a toll on them. Their worn-down bodies were a sign of the protest embodied in the caravan. Walking and moving in caravans triggered a political response. Still, even with all the media attention and the government's response, the risk of violence against migrants has always remained.

An Informal Welfare System

The opening quote in this book comes from the work of historian Lynn Hollen Lees on the English Poor Laws, a system of poor relief in England and Wales that developed out of late medieval and Tudor era laws and was codified at the beginning of the seventeenth century.[29] She argues that there is no simple solution to drawing the boundaries of individual needs and public and private resources, just as there is no simple answer about the motivations for people and groups to seek help and to offer aid. Sociologist and historian Marco H. D. van Leeuwen notes that during preindustrial times, diverse charitable bodies assisted the poor or gave relief in the form of an allowance.[30] The relief consisted of money, bread and other nourishment, peat, clothes, medical help, education, and Bible classes. These historical precedents show that providing welfare to vulnerable populations is not a new phenomenon, and groups have found ways to provide for the poor and vulnerable for centuries.[31]

With regard to the "economy of makeshifts" discussed above to explain how the poor and vulnerable populations made ends meet, it is useful to remember that the history of welfare is as much local as international, a history of clients and patrons, a story of hopes, fears, and assumptions.[32] Though there has been a rise in academic literature linking social solidarity, local efforts, humanitarianism, and migration, it tends to present the issue as a new phenomenon, though this is far from the case.[33] I offer here a brief historical framework in order to contextualize the analysis of solidarity with migrants. In engaging with this history, we must bear some considerations in mind: First, the distribution of welfare to the poor and vulnerable people varies across countries and regions, and even when support is available, the poor are not passive recipients. They frequently use other strategies to navigate hardship.[34] Second, delivery of welfare to the poor and vulnerable generally evolves from local and informal settings to more regulated delivery forms.[35] Third, a dynamic of (un)deservingness always remains present.[36] Hence, *casas de migrantes* in Mexico emerged as an informal welfare system along migrant routes, similar to how welfare was offered to the poor in Europe and England during preindustrial times and before the emergence of the welfare state.

Relief for the Poor

While discussing local relief as part of the "economy of makeshifts," professor of economic and social history Steven King and historian Alannah Tomkins state that relief needs to be seen more as a process than a single event or events.[37] The same is true for understanding the experience of poverty, which evolves and changes according to age, employment, and other factors. This understanding of relief and poverty (or precariousness) is important in migration processes, where policies and migrants' experiences constantly shape and reshape one another and any responses of aid that may emerge.

The statutory relief system and the welfare state are modern creations traced to preindustrial times in Europe, the Elizabethan Poor Laws in the seventeenth century, and later the emergence of state social provision after World War II. However, even before the Poor Laws, there were other regulations, such as vagrancy laws that aimed to control the movement of people, and the Ordinance of Laborers in 1349, which criminalized giving alms to beggars who refused to work. Forbidding giving alms to a group of people was a great challenge for a society with deep-seated beliefs and practices about poverty, charity, and Christianity. Furthermore, the vagrancy laws were used to encourage people to sell their work locally. Thus, these regulations were more than a simple prohibition on giving relief to the poor.[38] But before the Elizabethan Poor Laws, there was an understanding that relief must come not only from mandatory benefices, abbeys, and monasteries, but also from private donors. Modern research has shown that aid for the poor and vulnerable was also supplied through family or neighborly networks:

> Such support networks were sometimes formalized: "help ales" might raise funds to bail out people in difficulties; religious guilds supported needy members. Alms were sometimes bestowed on individual supplicants; sometimes selectively distributed among the poor of the neighborhood; sometimes more widely broadcast, at funerals, or on fixed days by monastic houses. Relief was sometimes institutionalized in the form of housing for travelers, the sick, or the aged.[39]

Delivering relief to the poor occurred locally with various levels of success and collaboration.[40] Religious activities were often the product of an association between laity and clergy, between political and religious power. This makes it challenging to distinguish between the secular and the religious. Furthermore, within the historical revision of relief to the poor, there are conflicting positions, and the evolution of the welfare system has many other layers that make it a much more sophisticated process.[41] This historical framing aims to highlight how the practicalities of relief distribution to the poor remained at the local levels even after different types of legislation and regulation were enacted. Similarly, the work of *casas de migrantes* remains primarily at the local level. Still, it plays a vital role in facilitating the delivery of resources to migrants in distress.

Casas de Migrantes *as an Incipient Welfare System*

Scholars have used the notion of welfare in different ways to describe material aspects of well-being, such as contentment, happiness, an absence of threat, and confidence in the future. At the same time, welfare can be defined as a statutory procedure or social effort that promotes the basic physical and material well-being of people in need. Welfare can also be thought of in terms of individuals, while "social welfare" can refer to more collective forms of well-being, such as the well-being of a community or a nation.[42] Thus, welfare can be seen from a person's everyday life perspective or in society at a macro-level and can be related to both the individual and the collective, involving material and immaterial needs.[43]

In academic literature, the word "welfare" is rarely used by itself; the field of social policy deals with the complexities of how social welfare is produced, sustained, and distributed.[44] Furthermore, there is increasing interest in how welfare has been provided, not only by the state but also by a mixed economy of welfare, which describes the variety of organizational and economic arrangements for the delivery, funding, and regulation of welfare. These organizational and economic arrangements may include the state, the market, and voluntary or informal forms of welfare, including NGOs, church groups, and individual personal networks.[45] In the case of the migration process in Mexico, the discussion of the meaning, production, and distribution of welfare relies on analyzing the practical function of humanitarian actors supporting migrants, deportees, IDPs, asylum seekers, and refugees.

There is also a growing interest in and an emerging body of literature that studies the link between migration and the provision and access to welfare or social protection.[46] Some features of these studies are the exploration of social protection within transnational space, the informal ways these social protections emerge among migrants, and the inequalities that access to social protection may create in migrant populations. This strand of literature uses the term "social provision" or "social protection" rather than "welfare" because of the negative connotation that "welfare" may have. Policy analyst Ian MacAuslan and development economist Rachel Sabates-Wheeler state that "social provisioning or what is (often pejoratively) referred to as welfare, relates to the provision of goods, services to protect people from, and prevent, the negative livelihood impacts of risk, and to reduce structural inequalities in opportunity."[47] They also emphasize that welfare or social protection can be understood from multiple perspectives, but often these perspectives are not mutually exclusive. Further, MacAuslan and Sabates-Wheeler consider that "social provisioning can be provided through a spectrum of market and non-market distribution systems or, in other words, through formal and informal channels, public and private sources."[48]

While other definitions of social protection have been provided, definitions to aid in understanding social protection or welfare across borders or within the transnational space are in the early stages of formation.[49] However, one of the most comprehensive definitions—and one that fits this analysis—is provided by Sabates-Wheeler and Stephen Devereux, who define social protection as "all public and private initiatives that provide income or consumption transfers to the poor, protect the vulnerable against livelihood risks, and enhance the social status and rights of marginalized; with the overall objective of reducing the economic and social vulnerability of the poor, vulnerable and marginalized groups."[50] This definition of social protection includes dimensions like human rights and social justice, providing a framework for understanding the role of the humanitarianism from below that has emerged in Mexico, which provides a type of welfare that goes beyond the coverage of migrants' basic needs.

The emerging literature on transnational welfare still emphasizes the interplay between citizens and the state, taking a top-down approach while paying attention to the possibility of a "global social policy."[51] However, there are examples of transnational social welfare, such as the services that the Mexican consulate offers to Mexican migrants living in the United States with irregular status.[52] Other examples and instances illustrating the welfare-migration nexus appear in an edited volume by migration and welfare scholars Oleksandr Ryndyk, Brigitte Suter, and Gunhild Odden.[53] Developing the notion of "transnational social protection" requires asking "when and how are people on the move protected and provided for outside of the traditional framework of the nation-state."[54] This inquiry necessarily takes us to explore what Peggy Levitt and colleagues call the "resource environment" available to migrants, which may include a combination of sources coming from the state, the market, and a third sector of social protection, alongside migrants' social networks, all of which may cross borders.[55]

The migration system in Mexico offers a unique response to the above line of inquiry from and for the migration-welfare nexus through the work of *casas de migrantes*. While the literature on transnational social protection highlights how social protection crosses borders through different actors or follows migrants through their networks, for *casas de migrantes* the transnational experience crosses them as international migrants and, more recently, forcibly displaced people are the primary beneficiaries of their work. Through the years, these local initiatives have developed and sustained the safety net that has supported migrants moving through Mexico.

While it has been pointed out that NGOs can support migrants in the country they move to, the number of local organizations providing support to migrants in Mexico leads us to see *casas de migrantes* as a welfare system spread out throughout the country. Furthermore, while we often use the general term "migrants" to talk about migrants, asylum seekers, refugees, deportees, and IDPs, in practice, each of these groups requires differentiated services and support. The welfare offered by *casas de migrantes* attempts to meet the diverse needs of people on the move.

The other element that guides the analysis of humanitarian assistance in Mexico as an informal welfare system is the informal delivery of assistance and access to welfare or social protection. Social protection assemblages include formal and informal, state and non-state dimensions.[56] Formal provision of welfare often involves publicly funded formal state regulations supported by policy, legislation, and regulations, including eligibility criteria. By contrast, the most significant source of non-statutory welfare seems to be provided by relatives, friends, and neighbors. This type of help is often called "informal" as it does not come from formal organizations, but rather from different kinds of relationships among individuals (kinship or mutual obligations developed between neighbors, friends, and communities). The support can also come from people in similar situations through self-help or other networks. Key features in the delivery of informal welfare are collective norms such as community solidarity, reciprocity, altruism, and obligations.[57] These collective norms explicitly or implicitly assume that help is offered in return for the support received in the past or that the support will be reciprocated in the future.[58] These networks or groups are an essential complement to formal social protections but are even more critical for irregular immigrants. In times of crisis, these networks offer perhaps the only support that irregular migrants can access.[59]

The work of *casas de migrantes* expands the notion of informal welfare because it is a kind of welfare offered by non-state actors that is not linked to migrants' social networks, and has temporal limitations. *Casas de migrantes* are local initiatives, many of them with faith-based affiliations, and with different kinds of organizational structures, but they are not formally sponsored by the state, even while some of them may have strong relationships with the government. The welfare offered by migrant shelters covers only basic necessities, even as services have evolved and become more specialized. Because *casas de migrantes* are not part of a migrant's network but external local sources that offer welfare to foreign citizens or people in displacement, while this type of welfare is generally free, migrants have no control or decision over the resources available. The expected reciprocity to the support provided comes in the form of compliance with norms and regulations, raising issues of deservingness. Finally, social protections offered by migrant shelters have a temporal limitation (the amount of time migrants can receive services), even as changes in migration patterns have required adjustments to the temporal limitations.

Conclusion

History reminds us that the mobile poor during the preindustrial era were not passive agents during times of hardship. Similarly, poor or less well-off migrants today are not passive subjects in their journeys. Despite the challenges that traversing Mexico presents, migrants use different strategies to achieve their goals. While some, such as begging, cash transfers, use of networks, and the use of their bodies, may be temporary to cope with hardship along the way, they create an economy of makeshifts that changes depending on the circumstances. *Casas de*

migrantes are not the only resources migrants use during the migra
tion project. However, the shelters have become a crucial element in
the migration dynamics in Mexico. Even if migrant shelters were not
in the equation, migrants still would find ways to resource their migration projects. However, the absence of migrant shelters certainly would
increase the precarity of their movement.

As humanitarian assistance in Mexico has developed, *casas de migrantes*, tending to the needs of migrants in distress, function as an
incipient and informal welfare system. Exchanges between migrants
and humanitarian spaces occur in a context characterized by violence,
heavy migration, and heavy enforcement. Without a doubt, *casas de
migrantes* reduce migrants' vulnerability by not only providing basic
humanitarian assistance but also advocating for structural changes to
ease their suffering. While *casas de migrantes* have formalized their
existence as more of them become official NGOs, their existence along
migrant routes still maintains a certain informality. Many migrant
shelters still function independently, rely on the community, and only
keep a local reach. The role of *casas de migrantes* remains crucial in
the provision of welfare. Only a few shelters have reached a level of
prominence in the humanitarian architecture of Mexico. Nevertheless, vulnerable/poor migrants use these humanitarian spaces as resources. This reveals the agency that migrants keep as they navigate
their migration journeys.

By looking at humanitarianism from below as an informal welfare
system, one finds a perspective that has an element of solidarity, and that
is not defined merely by a political economy approach, where there are
financial gains. Furthermore, the study of interactions between humanitarian groups and migrants provides insight into the role of groups and
institutions in facilitating, controlling, and aiding human mobility and
the internal dynamics of migrants' networks.

Work studying the link between migration and social welfare (social protection) is still emerging. Some studies may situate the migrant
as settled in a country and advocate for the portability of social protection.[60] Sociologist Thomas Faist and colleagues also look at social
protection in the transnational space, focusing on how these protections create inequalities among migrants.[61] However, they recognize
that in some instances, access to certain forms of social protection or

welfare may equalize the status of the migrant rather than contribute to inequality.[62]

Framing the role of *casas de migrantes* as an informal welfare system contributes to this emerging literature and adds novelty in three areas: First, the context, rather than being transnational—in the strict sense—is one of multiple directions (transit, return, and strandedness). Second, welfare is offered to migrants with multiple profiles: transit, deported, return, (im)mobile migrants. And finally, while there could be a discussion of shelters' formal or informal delivery of aid, migrants access welfare from a third party outside migrants' networks, making it possible to distinguish networks from resources. The migration process in Mexico cannot be limited to understanding migrants' journeys from the perspective of migrants; we must also consider how humanitarian actors perceive themselves and their roles while providing services for their targeted populations.

5

Brokers of Aid

Jorge was born in Honduras but grew up in the United States, where he fathered two children. He was initially deported from the United States in 2004, journeyed back to the United States in 2006, and was deported a second time in 2008. He tried another journey in 2009, but only reached the city of Puebla in central Mexico, where he decided to remain for a while. He voluntarily left Mexico in 2010 to go back to Honduras. Now at age thirty-two, he was attempting another journey back to Minnesota, where one of his children lives. He had left Honduras with USD 175.

At a migrant shelter located in the southern state of Chiapas in Mexico, eighty kilometers from the border of Guatemala, a tin roof on the patio provided us some protection from the blazing sun. Jorge had been on the road for eight days. Unable to shower upon arriving at the shelter, he was sweaty and dusty from the road. He also looked exhausted, but still was kind enough to have a conversation with me. While familiar with the journey up north, he was also aware of how dangers and migration controls had changed dramatically since the last time he had traveled. "El camino es mucho más peligroso" (The road is much more dangerous this time), he shared. "I was robbed in Ciudad Hidalgo [at the border] by police and other people. I lost almost all I had with me." With very little money that his mother had sent him from the United States, he relied on other strategies to cope with hardship along his journey.

> I reached the town of Tapachula, and I slept in the park. There, my
> mother, who lives in the United States, sent me thirty US dollars, and I
> was able to rent a dump [a small room] for a couple of days. I reached
> this town riding a *combi* [public transportation]. . . . The shelters are a
> tremendous help to the migrants. Remember that migrants do not bring
> money. Some do not even have bread to eat along the road; others only
> have water. Furthermore, some may eat mangos that you can find on the

trees because they do not have money to buy food. I have slept in the park, but with these places [referring to the shelters], at least we have a place where we can sleep.

Jorge recognized that no two journeys are alike. Even with previous knowledge of the migration routes, he still encountered challenges and precariousness. Since he had no money to pay for anything, staying at migrant shelters was only one of the strategies he said he would rely on for the rest of the journey. Reynosa, his intended crossing point into the United States, was 3,840 kilometers away. It was almost one o'clock in the afternoon when we finished our conversation. He got up, looked around, found another shaded corner at the shelter, threw his backpack to the floor, and got ready to rest a bit more before lunch. He knew that there was a long road ahead.

Migrants recognize the support and importance of shelters along the road. However, if migrant shelters are seen as "pockets of safety" or "oases" along migrant trails, questions emerge about them. How can they sustain their initiatives? How can they expand services? What kind of relationships do they forge with different actors? What are the implications of their brokering role for the migration process in Mexico? This chapter discusses the intermediary role migrant shelters play while providing services to migrants. It explains how dynamics of facilitation, control, and care emerge in migrant shelters, and discusses the understudied notion of brokerage. Moreover, it explores how *casas de migrantes* engage with different local, federal, and international actors, and considers the implications and consequences of this brokering role.

The Convergence of Facilitation, Control, and Care

In migration, many actors play intermediary roles. Travel agents, labor recruiters, money lenders, brokers, interpreters, housing agents, immigration lawyers, smugglers, counterfeiters who falsify official documents and passports, courier services, migration officers, and even banking institutions have become critical actors in mediating the migrations projects of many.[1] To describe and analyze the role of these migration intermediaries, the term "migration industry" emerged.

Rubén Hernández-León, a sociologist, offers one of the most compre-hensive articulations of the concept. He explains the migration industry not strictly as an industry but as

> a matrix of private and specialized services that facilitate and sustain international human mobility and its related behaviors, including set-tlement, mobility, communication, and resource transfers. Migration entrepreneurs render these services for a fee, and the main objective is turning a profit. Still, because migration industries services are often embedded in immigrant networks and ethnic economies, the behavior of these entrepreneurs is also mediated by relations of kinship, bounded trust, patron-client relationships, and coethnicity.[2]

His take on the migration industry includes many actors at different stages of the migration process and in different types of migratory movements (permanent, circular, undocumented). For him, these actors "grease" the migration system, characterized by restriction and border control.[3] Later on, he acknowledged the inclusion of the "control" and "rescue" industries as part of the more general concept of the "migration industry."[4] Still, his approach is limited to profitable aspects of migration intermediaries and to those actors that "facili-tate" the migration process. While there have been efforts to argue that the migration industry is not really an industry but rather a figure of speech,[5] empirical studies continue to emphasize its financial connota-tion, along with a multiplication of "industries" that only diminish the heuristic value of the term.

Some scholars argue that "facilitation, control, and rescue [industries] should be treated as different subcategories within the migration indus-try."[6] This approach certainly broadens the scope of the migration in-dustry, and helps to avoid seeing "facilitation," "control," and "rescue" in opposition to one another. Nevertheless, in practice, there are no clear-cut distinctions between "facilitation," "control," and "rescue/care," since these dynamics—or a combination of them—could be exercised by the same actor in the migration process, just at different moments and with different intensities.[7] Hence, facilitation, control, and rescue are seen now as subdivisions of the migration industry.

The interest in humanitarian actors as part of the migration industry is recent and has emerged alongside interest in the other subdivisions of the migration industry.[8] To make room for the multiple actors—in multiple contexts and with multiple agendas—that have intermediary roles in migration processes, scholars have started using the term "migration industries."

Migration law scholar Thomas Gammeltoft-Hansen and cultural sociologist and ethnographer Ninna Nyberg Sørensen acknowledge the increasing role of humanitarian actors in migration processes and briefly mention religious groups' roles.[9] The role of humanitarian organizations and faith-based organizations (FBOs) is occasionally discussed in connection with the "migration industry," often mentioned at the intersection between facilitation and migration management.[10] However, humanitarian actors justify their role based on other kinds of capital—for example, social or humanitarian.[11] Thus, while humanitarian actors may be driven by motives other than commercial gain, sometimes substantial funds may still be involved, both from migrants and through government contracts.

Despite its popularity in migration literature, the migration industry concept has yet to be fully accepted as an analytical category, even though it is "a useful shorthand term to guide inquiries" or theoretical analysis.[12] Scholars have argued that it is more helpful to focus on the essential functions of migration intermediaries than to focus on the term "migration industry": "We might do better to focus less on enterprises and entrepreneurs as our objects of study and more on the types of service provided to migrants, their families, and their employers, . . . along with the types of relationships that exist among the actors involved. . . . We would do well to focus less on what the migration industry is and more on what it does."[13] Hence, I move away from framing the work of *casas de migrantes* and their intermediary role under the umbrella of the migration industry. Focusing on facilitation, control, and care as essential functions of *casas de migrantes*—and not subsuming them under the rubric of the migration industry—is more useful for an understanding of the complexities and nuances of their humanitarian work in Mexico. However, we cannot fully understand these functions and their consequences without carefully considering

the many ways these local humanitarian actors interact with other actors to link migrants and other actors in the humanitarian landscape
in Mexico.

What Is Brokerage?

Brokerage is an essential yet understudied function in social life that
is rarely systematized in migration studies. Faist argues that brokerage
involves issues of connectivity between persons and groups as well as
trust.[14] Brokerage is defined as "the process of connecting actors in systems of social, economic, or political relations in order to facilitate access
to valued resources."[15] At the core of brokerage is the role of mediator
and facilitator; financial gain is not a central feature.[16] This idea is essential for understanding humanitarianism from below, where rather than
a financial gain, there is a moral gain in the process of intermediation.

Brokerage, as a social mechanism, makes sense only in a specific
context.[17] Here, "social mechanism" refers to the recurring actions and
events linking identifiable initial conditions with a specific result or outcome.[18] The recurring actions or events in the migration process are the
passage of migrants through migrant shelters. The initial condition is
their precarious and vulnerable situation as they move, and the expected
outcome is to ease their suffering. However, legal anthropologist Maybritt Jill Alpes emphasizes that the study of brokerage needs to be seen in
relation to "stateness"—by which she means the "ensemble of state actors
and institutions, as well as regulatory instruments (such as papers) and
normative frameworks (such as legality)"—and also within the boundaries of legality.[19] She pushes this notion to understand forms of power
and representation better. This is a critical idea because migrant shelters
inevitably broker with the government in different situations, and do so
within the boundaries of the law.

As migrants move through Mexico, they use different resources that
may come from different places and actors, such as local donations, volunteer time, medical services, or legal representation or advice; migrant
shelters mediate all of these. Shelters link these disconnected actors,
revealing that brokerage is "the linking of two or more previously un-
connected, social sites by a unit that mediates their relations with one
another and/or with yet other sites."[20] Understandings of brokerage have

generally been limited to mechanisms relating groups and individuals to one another in stable contexts. However, brokerage can also become a relational mechanism for mobilization during periods of contentious politics. As new groups and relations appear, their interactions allow them to discover common interests.[21] In migration processes, intermediaries or brokers help circumvent or overcome barriers that migrants could encounter at any moment in the migration cycle, and they may or may not have a financial gain, which is the case in the kind of humanitarianism that has emerged in Mexico.[22]

Since the study of brokerage is situated within the field of sociology and closely related to social network analysis, it provides a larger canvas upon which the role of intermediaries in migration can be explored. Faist writes, "Brokerage helps to conceptualize the broader infrastructure that makes spatial mobility possible in the first place. . . . Brokerage helps to break down unhelpful dichotomies (legal/illegal; altruism/ profit; formal/informal)."[23] The focus in the migration industry literature has been on the industry (profit) side, as well as the construction of illegality and control, while the connections and the purposes intermediaries have in different relationships have been largely ignored. However, understanding the types of connections and relationships helps us understand how a social mechanism works. Furthermore, analyzing brokerage helps to illuminate the creation of inequalities or the process of resource equalization in local and transnational spaces. The interactions that *casas de migrantes* have are not limited to those with migrants. Understanding brokerage permits a better analysis of the different links that shelters must have to provide services for vulnerable migrants.

Sociologists have identified three types of brokerage processes: First, transfer brokerage allows resources to move from one party to another. Second, matchmaking brokerage facilitates the formation of ties between third parties. And third, coordination brokerage allows third parties to interact without the formation of a tie.[24] Aside from the categories of brokerage mentioned above, there are other types of roles that a broker or intermediary may have, including liaison, itinerant, coordinator, gatekeeper, or representative.[25] In practice, these roles or structural positions represent concrete social roles in social interactions. While these roles have been identified for analytical purposes, individual actors can perform any combination of them simultaneously.[26]

Considering different types of brokerage provides a blueprint for inquiring about how shelters interact with other actors and migrants. The focus remains on the relationships and the roles played, not necessarily on the effects of these relationships and roles, which is the emphasis in the migration industry literature. While performing their intermediary role, *casas de migrantes* have become brokers of aid along migrants' routes. They perform critical intermediation roles, linking people on the move with local communities, local governments, and international organizations in order to alleviate the taxing experiences that migrants face while moving through Mexico.[27]

Local Communities

Up to this point, we have focused on the importance of understanding the bottom-up process from which humanitarianism from below emerges in Mexico, even though these humanitarian actors operate within a paradox. While there is a response from local communities to aid and support migrants, there is a different part of the community that preys on and abuses migrants. Shelters always have to mediate between migrants and the communities where these shelters are located.

The presence of migrants changes the landscape and the communities where they arrive or pass through.[28] Migrants' presence allows "migration economies" to arise. A town may benefit from irregular migration or deportees by offering various services such as telephone services, food, rooms for rent, showers, and so on, and may profit from migrants by overcharging them. Along the tracks of Medias Aguas in the state of Veracruz, many people sold goods ranging from toilet paper to soda to backpacks. The people selling goods often told migrants not to get close to the mobile soup kitchen, run by Catholic dioceses, because they could be handed over to migration authorities. In the town of Coatzacoalcos, a convenience store and an office supply store—offering Internet service and reception of cash transfers—overcharged migrants staying at the shelter. These migration economies were booming in certain towns when the presence of migrants was more visible. As migration policies have changed and violence has increased, migration patterns have changed as well. Thus, as in any economy that operates by supply and demand, some of these economies in transit places have disappeared.

For example, in the town of Palenque in southern Mexico, more than two hundred migrants could congregate at any time, waiting to jump onto the freight trains. Their presence allowed services like public bathrooms, convenience stores, and places offering telephone services to emerge. Even more noticeable was the construction of sleeping facilities where migrants could spend the night without being too far from the train tracks. As authorities started conducting raids along the train tracks, the migration patterns changed, and the number of migrants decreased, taking with them business opportunities for these places. Signs outside a few houses offering services and abandoned facilities were the only evidence of this "migration economy" left in the town.

Occasionally, communities do not allow shelters to operate for different reasons, such as in towns like Huixtla in southern Mexico. Father Angel Rodríguez, sharing his frustration, explained, "We were about to open the new shelter. It was a good space, with showers, dormitories for men and women, a good kitchen, a dining room, and common areas. However, a group of people came and put chains on the door. We tried to mediate with the government but could not agree. The government sent me a letter saying that the area was risky and creating tensions with the community was not a good idea." The shelter in Saltillo has suffered different threats; an unknown group has actually shot at the facilities. Their members also have received verbal threats through phone calls and anonymous messages. In this case, there was a need to activate a security mechanism with the National Human Rights Commission.

Other shelters, like Casa Portillo and Casa Cuc, were closed because of community pressure or increased dangers. However, they later resumed operations at another site at the local government's request. Casa Cuc, initially a soup kitchen, was forced to close due to security concerns. The shelter offered services in a neighborhood with social issues of homelessness, substance abuse, and drug dealing. At the beginning of 2015, despite safety protocols, drug dealers and drug addicts verbally and physically threatened some staff members. The shelter staff asked for more support from the authorities without success and consequently decided to cease operations until the local government could guarantee better safety conditions. The shelter's director explained, "So we felt there were no conditions to keep providing services, and at some point, we decided to close. We alerted the government about our decision.

A few weeks later, the local government contacted us to reopen services at another location." The shelter used the opportunity to grow and expand services.

It is evident that tensions and dangers exist, and shelters emerge or operate within the paradox of those who seek to alleviate migrants' suffering and those who prey on them. Shelters have to exercise brokerage roles as liaisons with those members of the community who want to support migrants. Still, at the same time, shelters must mediate with local communities that may see migrants as a threat. These roles must be played if a shelter wishes to succeed in supporting migrants or deportees. For example, Casa Rojche had to mediate a conflict between the community and several migrants who had been roaming around town. At a neighborhood community meeting, neighbors shared their concerns about the migrants' presence.

> These migrants are the ones that had been assaulting people and harassing young girls. Since the shelter opened, there has been an increase in the number of robberies and sexual assaults. Why are you defending these people and not us? Why are you not helping us to solve all the social problems that exist here? But we are sure it is the migrants who cause all the trouble.

In such moments, humanitarian actors must play a role that requires mediation and representative brokerage to continue operations. In this case, as in the previous anecdote about the soup kitchen in Guadalajara, humanitarian actors' brokerage role as representatives not only reaches out to the community, but also branches out to reach the government, seeking aid and support. This type of brokerage becomes crucial for shelters to continue their services; without it, they would most likely end up closing because of mounting pressures or dangers.

Local Government

The relationship between humanitarian organizations aiding migrants and the Mexican government has several layers and is not limited to migration regulations. Without a doubt, shelters mediate the relationship between migrants and authorities. *Casas de migrantes* are "spaces of exception" that migrants seek and use as sanctuaries to protect themselves from deportation or, in the cases of deportees, as immediate support after deportation. Additionally, shelters become "pockets of safety" for migrants and go beyond immediate assistance to develop diverse programs or initiatives related to the protection of migrants. However, other migrant shelters require different kinds of interaction and mobilization of resources to assist migrants, deportees, and refugees. There are three main areas of intermediation between *casas de migrantes* and local government actors: health, safety, and legal representation. Without the brokerage of migrant shelters, migrants representing themselves could not easily access such resources.

Health

While visiting shelters from 2014 through 2016, I observed that the largest shelters could have somewhere between 120 to 250 migrants spending the night. By the end of 2022, these numbers had changed dramatically as some shelters were hosting up to 1,200 migrants or even more on certain occasions. In southern Mexico the turnaround is rapid, since migrants move on rapidly. Even with that pattern, in 2023 some shelters could receive more than 700 migrants daily.

In central Mexico, numbers reached between 70 and 90 migrants a night, but the stays are more extended, as some migrants may stay for a few months. As shelters have become more specialized, some *casas de migrantes* can host up to 150 or 200 migrants. In northern Mexico, group variation and diversity of profiles are high, as well as shelters' capacity to serve people. Stranded migrants, deportees, IDPs, asylum seekers, migrants, and refugees are all mixed in shelters across the border. One shelter could have ten deportees one night and 30 or 40 at other times, along with 200 or 300 stranded migrants. Turnaround for deportees is pretty fast, as they try to rearrange their lives quickly. Usually, deportees do not stay at shelters longer than three days—although this may be extended depending on the circumstances. The length of stays for stranded migrants will depend on their circumstances and vulnerability. The largest shelter I visited at the northern border was hosting around 1,200 migrants. In any case, it is not easy managing the day-to-day activities in the shelters, which are comparable to the difficulties of managing those who stay in refugee camps.[29]

Humanitarian actors must link and establish rapport with health and sanitary governmental agencies to fumigate, prevent outbreaks of infections, and provide immediate medical assistance (or, in some cases, assistance in emergencies). At least two shelters I had visited were fumigated two times each during my visit. On a few occasions, it was necessary to request that municipal authorities supply additional potable water because of a drought in the region. Occasionally, it was also required to empty septic tanks because of the number of people at the shelter. Psychological support is also sometimes needed; I witnessed a couple of mental health crises—one person was actively suicidal, and another had a psychotic episode. My counselor and social worker background allowed me to assess those situations, but the shelter had to work with psychiatric hospitals to deal with these situations proactively. The vignette at the opening of this book also illustrates the link to other authorities when fatalities occur. What is at stake here is understanding that shelters do not own many of the resources that are made available through them to migrants. Thus, the need to broker with other constituents is essential to run humanitarian spaces safely. Although migrants may not link directly with those constituents that provide specific resources or support operations, they are still beneficiaries of those links.

Security

There are high levels of violence in Mexico, and sometimes this violence is directed or aimed at the shelters where migrants congregate. Thus, one of the priorities of any of the *casas de migrantes* is safety. Occasionally, humanitarian organizations need to establish links with local police, national human rights organizations, or federal police. Some shelters have received threats or even attacks on their facilities. Through legal means, the Mexican Human Rights Commission has established safety mechanisms consisting of bodyguards and direct access to federal police. There are at least three shelters that have these protection mechanisms activated. Other shelters, like the ones in San Luis Potosí and Guadalajara, have made arrangements with the local government to be protected by the police and to have additional security measures in place in the areas surrounding the shelters. Sometimes there are security cameras outside the shelters that local police can monitor.

While safety and security mechanisms are established to protect humanitarian staff, in practice, what matters for the shelter is also the safety of the migrants using the services. As the director of Casa Rojche attested, "We want everybody to be safe here. Thus, we have to pressure the government to provide the security that was supposed to exist in the first place." Thus, humanitarian organizations serve as representatives and liaisons for migrants and humanitarian staff when working with governmental bodies. The resources these NGOs mobilize ensure an intangible benefit: safety. Despite its intangibility, the effects of securing safety are felt since migrants repeatedly stated that they were willing to trade freedom for safety.

However, concerns for safety at migrant shelters are not only from significant external threats. There is always the risk of smugglers or criminals posing as migrants infiltrating the shelter. Prevention of violence or smuggling is an everyday dynamic that raises several issues. Intakes and backpack inspections at migrant shelters become a significant filter. On the one hand, migrants can prevent the coming of smugglers who could lure or convince migrants to go with them or prevent the introduction of arms and substances; on the other, staff and volunteers may foster dynamics of inclusion or exclusion based on perceptions or misperceptions. Shelters that network with other shelters may be able to flag people previously identified as smugglers and take precautions. Other times, the recurrent visit or passing of a migrant may raise suspicions. There are no easy solutions as to whether to provide services or deny them based on security concerns. This dynamic echoes what scholars have described as logics of care, where humanitarian workers discern and decide whether to provide care or not based on previous experiences and their encounters with migrants in their everyday work.[30]

Legal Assistance and Representation

Legal assistance is the more contentious area in terms of brokering to access resources. Migrants who have been victims of grave crimes by criminal gangs, federal police, local police, or migration authorities are entitled to a regularization of legal status in Mexico for humanitarian reasons. Humanitarian NGOs often have to represent migrants with judicial authorities to gain access to justice and due process. Along the northern border, deported Mexicans return without identification or money and are often disoriented within the cities they return to. As we have seen, upon return, Mexican migration authorities provide a simple letter of repatriation that is supposed to serve as identification. Deportees are often harassed by local authorities who detain and extort them, hoping to make some profit. In these cases, shelters serve as representatives and advocates for deportees who are detained or seek employment in border towns. Getting a new identification card—which in Mexico is essential for any administrative task—takes more than three months and requires a permanent residence or address. Furthermore, this identification, known as *credencial de elector* (electoral card), often needs to be processed in the district where the migrant is supposed to reside. Casa Leal offers its address to deportees as a reference for the ID card. Its staff also drive them back and forth to the town hall because walking around the city may be dangerous. Furthermore, criminal gangs may target migrants.

Casas de migrantes at the US-Mexico border may have to collaborate and advocate with US Customs and Border Protection (CBP). In January 2023, migration dynamics at the southern US border changed dramatically with the implementation of the CBP One mobile app, which, as noted, mandated that any request for an exception to Title 42 to enter the United States and file for asylum had to be done through the app. In March 2023, there was a sudden surge in rejections by CBP officials of families who showed up at ports of entry with appointments. These families were sent back to Mexico. A migrant shelter in Nogales, Sonora, documented over forty individuals who were rejected despite having an appointment confirmed through CBP One. The legal team at the shelter began communicating with local authorities, organized a protest at the border wall, and held a press conference to share information about the rejections. Members of the press at the shelter's event also attended a gathering with Alejandro N. Mayorkas, the US secretary of homeland security, who happened to be visiting Nogales the same day and was asked by reporters why asylum seekers with appointments were being turned away. These advocacy efforts worked, since CBP contacted staff at the shelter to tell them that it was prepared to receive the cases of people who had been rejected. The migrant shelter was able to contact some of the migrants who were initially rejected and accompany them as they presented themselves at the port in Nogales and were processed into the United States.

Without the efforts of *casas de migrantes* and other humanitarian NGOs to advocate for and represent migrants in front of Mexican authorities or lobby with CBP, migrants could face even more significant challenges when trying to access the judicial system or entering the United States to apply for asylum. While there is no guarantee that justice will be served for migrants, shelters persist in documenting human rights violations, crimes, abuses, or irregularities to push advocacy efforts. On the ground, shelters represent migrants to access justice; on a macro-level, shelters liaise with other organizations to advocate for the rights and well-being of migrants.

International and Other Actors

Casas de migrantes are also hubs for information. They offer general information about the shelter, education on human rights, emergency contact information, access to refugee status, and much more. Migrants who can reach the Mexican border with the United States have received a good amount of information along the way. That information comes partly from the shelters, but because shelters often have small staffs, humanitarian organizations liaise with multiple international actors to provide additional services. The Red Cross, the United Nations High Commissioner for Refugees (UNHCR), Doctors Without Borders (MSF), Asylum Access, the United Nations Development Program, the Inter-American Commission on Human Rights, and the International Organization for Migration are just some international actors that partner with *casas de migrantes* to provide special services.

The Red Cross provides medical relief and telephone services at different points during a migrant's journey, often operating outside *casas de migrantes*. MSF runs a program addressing mental health issues along migrant routes. It also provides counseling and social work services in cases of violence (particularly rape), and occasionally provides ad hoc medical services. UNHCR and the UNDP provide training on humanitarian practice standards and sponsor publications for migrants, often including information about the shelters along migrant routes.

Although the partnerships tend to work, there are tensions that exist. While shelters have been operating for a long time, international organizations often arrive with professional knowledge or "know-how" to run operations in humanitarian contexts, and frequently minimize the labor that people have done before. This attitude perpetuates dynamics in which local organizations are not treated as equals. Occasionally, this dynamic causes partnerships to end, or agreements to be terminated because of a clash in values. While in some cases it is appropriate to offer staff at each shelter some training and professionalization programs to improve the service levels—some may have very low standards of service—there are times when the experience of the place is not considered and organizations with significant histories and on-the-ground experience are treated by their international partners like children who must be taught the alphabet. In these cases, shelters may choose not to work with INGOs because the partnerships are not on equal grounds.

The shifting nature of the context and the required ability to adjust according to the needs of migrants requires *casas de migrantes* to serve as liaisons with INGOs to provide information, education, and other services. Occasionally, personalities, shelters' goals, needs, or actions may cause conflict and clash with the agendas of INGOs. However, these partnerships have also proven fruitful, challenging, and above all, beneficial for migrants, deportees, IDPs, asylum seekers, and refugees as *casas de migrantes* broker aid and information toward migrants and also liaise with external actors to make visible the realities of migration, deportation, and asylum in Mexico. By participating in different advocacy networks, shelters share information about what occurs on the ground. Furthermore, shelters also link to the academic world, as many researchers—like myself—have collected data at these places.

In January 2023, digital literacy, information, and collaboration with the US Customs and Border Protection became crucial with the rollout of the CBP One app. I was collecting data for another project at Casa Ixpertay during the initial rollout of CBP One. The shelter quickly set up workshops on how to use the mobile app and complete all the information in the application; it contracted additional internet lines so migrants could use them without cost. There were some changes in the physical facilities as a need for more electrical outlets—to charge phones—emerged. As the initial days of the rollout passed, there was a need to develop procedures and mechanisms to offer migrants updated information about the app's functionality.

By March 2023, the app was in its 2.43 version, while at the beginning of the year, when it became available to migrants, it was in its 2.26 version. During a visit to an informal camp in the town of Matamoros, migrants expressed their frustrations with the app over and over. "Lo intento una y otra vez, pero me saca cuando llego al calendario" (I try over and over, but the app crashes once I reach the calendar). "Me levanto a las tres de la mañana para ver si tengo suerte. Le pico y le pico pero nada" (I get up at three in the morning to see if I get lucky. I click and click on my phone and nothing happens). "He estado aquí dos meses. Intento sacar una cita todos los días pero es casi imposible. Todo mundo se quiere conectar a la misma hora" (I have been here two months. I have tried to get an appointment every day since my arrival but it is almost impossible. Everybody wants to get connected to the app at the same time). Migrant shelters and other humanitarian actors formed networks and established dialogues with US Customs and Border Protection to gain clarification on the use of the mobile app and share some of the difficulties people face while using it.

By the end of December 2023, the CBP One app had improved its functionality from the day of its initial rollout in January 2023. Still, the app was on its 2.56 version, meaning that the app had had thirty updates since it became a required step for those aiming to request asylum through the US southern border. These changes put a burden on migrants and organizations that support them. Migrants are required to have smartphones with the capability to handle higher wireless cellular technology and the app's functionality and Internet. *Casas de migrantes* must now offer mobile cell phone charging stations as well as strong and stable Wi-Fi networks. Legal teams and international organizations need to be on top of any changes in the app or new requirements to advise migrants about as they fill out the application. Collaborations between *casas de migrantes* and other organizations are crucial as changes in migration patterns and policies yield new needs and challenges.

Amalia, director of Casa Umaña, a shelter at the US-Mexico border, summarized how collaborations with different actors local, federal, and international translate into benefits for migrant populations:

> [At the shelter] we don't fill out the CBP One application, because once we fill it out, we will become an organization that has to offer that service. For that kind of service there are other organizations like HIAS [originally the Hebrew Immigrant Aid Society]. They come here, give them workshops, tend to the women [at the shelter], and they teach them how to fill out the CBP One application. . . . [These collaborations] are a benefit for the migrants; it is not so much a benefit for the shelter [staff and volunteers], but it translates into benefits for the migrants. . . . The shelter is not only a bed, it is [an array of services] offered for the integral attention of migrants. . . . The services at the shelter are offered because we have collaborations. We look for these collaborations. We didn't have a full-time doctor, but the IMSS Bienestar [a federal health agency] provided a team of doctor, nurse, and a psychologist to work at the shelter. I offered them the spaces that UNHCR occupied in the past [currently UNHCR does not offer services in the city].

During the interview, Amalia emphasized repeatedly that services at the shelter are free of charge. At the same time, she said that shelters do not own the resources to support migrants and that staff at the shelters do not get a direct benefit. Nevertheless, migrant shelters need to actively seek collaborations with different organizations to provide more complete services. Furthermore, she acknowledged that partnerships with different organizations end or change due to different circumstances like budget cuts or changes in the agendas of INGOs or local agencies. Nevertheless, shelters must keep seeking collaborations in order to continue offering services. Implicitly, Amalia's words describe how *casas de migrantes* function as brokers of aid.

Whose Agenda?

The moral and ethical basis for humanitarian intervention is the protection of vulnerable lives. However, in the moral economy of humanitarianism, there is always a political price to pay or loyalties to be remembered.[31] Humanitarianism from below is no exception to the dynamics and alliances that unfold in the humanitarian ecosystem in Mexico. The brokerage role that *casas de migrantes* play in Mexico has an inherent tension. As shelters start to gather, receive, channel, and administer resources, to what extent do donors' agendas and other external agendas shape or influence the ethos and work of shelters?[32] Fray Rubén cautioned that "we must be very careful about which hand we take the support from, because you will be in debt to them."

Donors, INGOs, and even the federal and local governments—occasionally supporting *casas de migrantes*—may feel entitled to shape shelters' agendas or condition their support. Collaborations between shelters and external organizations often emerge around specific projects and needs. Earmarking assistance is an example of how donors exercise power over beneficiaries, leading to dynamics in which the provision of services implies giving to a deserving or worthy recipient and occasionally not allowing shelters to decide the best use of those resources.[33]

An incident between Casa Rojche and UNHCR offers a glimpse into the issues that may arise in benefactor-beneficiary partnerships. The shelter serves women with children and family units, which means hosting many children at any time. While food was provided at the shelter, there was a shortage in the amount of food the shelter could serve at the time of the incident. The shelter had received a grant for an educational project; Fray Rubén decided to call UNHCR to ask whether funding could be diverted to buy food for children. After the conversation, he said, "They told me that I could buy as many notebooks and pens for the children, but I could not use money that had been tagged for any other purpose." This incident shows how sometimes the agendas and rules of donors can influence or limit the operation on the ground.

Migrant shelters often partner with INGOs to expand or fill gaps in services. Going around any shelter, one often sees signs from Save the Children, UNHCR, UNICEF, IOM, MSF, UNDP, International Red Cross, and others. International humanitarian organizations regularly offer different kinds of support to migrant shelters. Legal information, educational projects, medical support, mental health and social work services, and provision of supplies and food are some of the services and support offered by INGOs. Recognizing that migrants gravitate to shelters, INGOs often approach shelters to discuss projects, support, and collaborations. At the same time, shelters perform different roles and highlight various aspects of their work while interacting with INGOs in the hope of obtaining or forging a partnership.[34] Shelters may emphasize the surge of unaccompanied minors and their needs in order to attract the interest of organizations like UNICEF or Save the Children. With the support of these INGOs, shelters can run projects like the educational initiative at Casa Rojche referred to above.

Casa Requena worked with UNHCR to become more LGBTQI+ friendly after emphasizing to the INGO the vulnerabilities of transgender migrants arriving in the city. Shelters in Ciudad Juárez at the northern border of Mexico have adapted to the mobile services provided by Jesuit Refugee Service (JRS), emphasizing the needs of women traveling alone and their commonalities as faith-based organizations.

While emphasizing different aspects of their work is part of how *casas de migrantes* bring about collaborations, sometimes these alliances also carry the burden of accommodating and adapting to the needs of particular projects and the aftermath when those projects and collaborations end. For example, office space is required to provide services, such as MSF needing private offices to provide mental health services or Save the Children needing dedicated areas for children's activities. These needs require an investment or adaptation in infrastructure on the part of the *casas de migrantes*. Amalia's quote from earlier illustrates that occasionally, as agendas and needs shift and budgets are cut, INGOs terminate or finish collaborations they started. Spaces that once thrived at migrant shelters look empty or unused once projects end. Sometimes spaces are repurposed with other goals or to meet other needs. Local humanitarian work relies on negotiation, interest-seeking, and compromise. However, the issue of sustainability follows collaborations. When INGOs or other organizations leave, migrant shelters remain to provide services; they often then need to broker again with other actors to continue offering particular types of aid. Shelters serve as the "middle institution," linking services to the populations they serve. However, INGOs come from a position of power because they set agendas and rules for providing these services. In the collaboration, the donor-recipient dynamic is often evident. The agenda of INGOs remains at the forefront of the relationship, sometimes with organizational and infrastructural costs to migrant shelters. Collaborations of this kind are rarely between equals.

The COVID-19 pandemic provided another good example of how collaborations between *casas de migrantes* and INGOs work. Sister Angélica from Casa Caal shared that "every week, three laywomen and us [two religious sisters] gathered to decide whether we needed to stop providing services. But migrants never stopped coming. UNHCR and IOM were supportive to the extent that they always provided supplies, but in the end, we were alone in the field." Thus, while some INGOs continued to provide services remotely and supported migrant shelters with supplies at critical times, they retrieved their personnel from the field, leaving shelters' staff to tend to the needs of migrants who, regardless of the pandemic, continued coming. This experience at Casa Caal confirms that INGOs collaborate on their own terms and agendas, leaving or staying in the field at will, even if they remain sympathetic or supportive. In contrast, local humanitarian organizations, as first responders, may see contexts of mobility from different perspectives. In their everyday lives, the needs of migrants remain in the forefront.

Conclusion

We have seen how facilitation, control, and rescue/care are vital functions of intermediate structures in migration processes and how these functions inevitably overlap. Furthermore, analysis of shelters' brokerage roles and the different relationships they develop deepens our understanding of the spatial dimension, which refers to the place where the social facilitation, control, and/or care occurs, and the role of "network externalities," which refers to the relationships of migrants with other actors.[35] In the migration process in Mexico, *casas de migrantes* become brokers of aid to support migrants effectively. An analysis of their partnerships reveals and illuminates the role of humanitarian organizations as intermediary actors in migration processes and how they broker to gain access to resources for migrants. Nevertheless, local humanitarian organizations need to be attentive to the partnerships they enter into and consider how they broker in benefit of migrants. Migrant shelters, as brokers of aid, must navigate an array of bureaucratic hurdles and contextual predatory forces (enforcement authorities, police, and even criminal groups).[36] At the same time, they have to deal with demanding beneficiaries of aid who may not be aware of all the intricacies involved in the reception and administration of resources, as well as the arrangement and delivery of services.

Brokerage in migration processes may mean collaboration, but also could also mean complicity. To broker aid is also to take the risk of others shaping the agenda to support migrants or benefiting from the support provided. This has been especially true in the relationship between migrant shelters and the Mexican government at the local and federal levels. *Casas de migrantes* have been lauded and recognized for their work at many levels. However, they also have been changing and performing to relate to the government in other contexts. The government has used that recognition to reinforce its image as a country of emigration, transit, destination, and return committed to protecting the human rights of migrants. The results of brokering with the state indicate that with varying degrees of awareness and willingness, *casas de migrantes* have become tools of the state agenda, which is the management of migrant populations.

6

Between Welfare and Containment

After a year and a half of living and volunteering in shelters and conversing with migrants and humanitarian workers, I recognized how savvy migrants are in engaging with *casas de migrantes*. In short, migrants seek what they need. As much as they are grateful for the services they receive, they are also aware of the rules, benefits, limitations, and dynamics that emerge when they seek assistance. In conversations, they often highlighted the tension between receiving welfare and being contained in migrant shelters. They also often expressed a willingness to exchange freedom for safety. Benjamín, a thirty-year-old migrant from Honduras, had been on the road for a month when we met at a shelter in San Luis Potosí in central Mexico. He was on his fourth attempt to reach the United States. He sold his motorcycle to jumpstart his journey. His wife, who lives in the United States, sent him some money three times. "It was not much money, but enough to keep moving forward," he said. We talked about his journey, his life in Honduras, his desire to join his family in the United States, and his perceptions about the *casas de migrantes*. He said,

> I am not happy about the fact that you cannot go out of the shelter, but when one makes the journey riding the train and coming to these places, you accept whatever they offer you and obey the rules. . . . Here, you are confined and not being able to go out affects you; it kills you. That is why people sometimes come and stay for a short period of time and then move on. . . . I understand that the rules are a question of internal security. The presence of the federal police means that you are safe, and I feel safe. . . . In a way, there is internal and external security. Here I am safe, even if I cannot go out.

Through the narratives of migrants and humanitarian workers, this chapter explores and discusses the inherent tension between welfare and containment present in humanitarian work, which appears clearly in the work of *casas de migrantes*, pointing out the rise of the humanitarian governance of migration. It highlights that, in practice, the line between a migrant shelter and a detention center can be blurred, while questions of citizenship and the creation of a containment regime emerge.

To Care Is to Control

There is growing recognition of the importance of everyday practices in managing borders and human mobility. Didier Fassin argues that humanitarianism needs to be analyzed broadly; the theoretical and political ideas used to explain and justify it, and practices employed in humanitarianism to manage human beings and their lives require deeper consideration. Focusing on everyday life reveals how power and discourse operate in specific times and places.[1] Hence, to care for migrants is also, in some sense, to control them, and controlling them requires a degree of care.[2]

Looking at the shelters' everyday practices and the context in which they operate, one can see that migrants cannot fully reciprocate the support they receive. This asymmetrical relationship gives control to the shelters over the populations they aim to serve. Issues around the distribution of resources are common at migrant shelters. Who gets the best clothes, who gets additional food, or who gets some other preferential treatments are often issues that migrants point out. In the structures of aid distribution, there is a transference of responsibility from the donor, to the recipient, to the administrators of aid at the shelter.[3] If staff are not careful, these asymmetrical relationships may resemble the power dynamics at detention centers and foster bordering practices emerging far from the border.

I have recognized this issue at different moments in migrant shelters. At Casa Portillo, a group of migrants defiantly told the staff, "Why don't you give us those clothes? Those donations are for us." At Casa Chox, the director shared, "At the beginning, I let them [migrants] distribute the donations, but there were many cases of abuse. Now, I spend entire nights bagging beans to distribute them. Like it or not, I have a responsibility to administer the resources we have." Sometimes migrants, in their search for resources, may feel entitled to all of the aid and resources offered at the shelter at a particular moment. Still, there is also the responsibility that shelters may feel to sustain care for migrants yet to come. Hence, migrant shelters develop rules and systems for rationing clothes, phone calls, reception of cash transfers, charging phones, and facilitating access to other services. Sanctions and consequences often accompany rules, regulations, and organizational systems. These dynamics are sometimes not-so-subtle forms of control and deservingness. Still, unaware of the challenges of administering aid, migrants occasionally do not ask but demand that their needs be fully met.

Migrant shelters are often understaffed, underfunded, and overworked, thus the need to rely on migrants' participation and collaboration as a solution. This could be seen as a form of reciprocity, but it is part of the contractual dynamic of receiving services. At many migrant shelters, it is expected that migrants will collaborate at least to support basic cleanup and daily chores. There are further complications when migrants have to contribute economically to the running of the shelter. This often happens in shelters at the US-Mexico border that have no support from faith-based communities or where migrants must wait lengthy periods either to decide to cross to the United States irregularly or for their asylum claims to move forward.

However, beneficiary participation is not a panacea and can occasionally lead to problems in humanitarian settings, especially around needs assessment, performance, relationships, and impact.[4] While some *casas de migrantes* try to foster participation and enable migrants to embrace their process and advocate for themselves, some forms of participation, especially those related to rules' enforcement and distribution of resources, may reflect socioeconomic differentiation, ethnic, national, religious, or regional differences, and increase status differentiation among migrant populations.[5]

Services at *casas de migrantes* are designed to ease the precarious situations that migrants experience, and providing food is one of the most basic needs addressed in these humanitarian spaces. However, sometimes food waste emerges as a point of contention. "Do not waste food. Only take what you are going to eat." These are words that migrants repeatedly hear at different points of their migration journey. Being local initiatives, migrant shelters offer food from whatever donations they receive or prepare the ordinary diet of the region. Sometimes it is not that migrants are not hungry or want to waste the food; it is more about the fact that some foods may be foreign to them.

Children refusing to eat or getting sick illustrate the challenges of food provision. In a shelter at the northern Mexican border, Graciela told me, "I am not sure what to do. My little boy is sick; he is not eating because he cannot handle the food. . . . I may have to return to my country." Another time, at a shelter in central Mexico, Joaquín, a Honduran migrant, told me that he had lost ten kilograms (twenty-two pounds) because he could not handle the food. "I eat a little from time to time, but Mexican food is not for me." Behind these instances is the assumption that through the act of receiving, migrants have accepted a contractual obligation to consume whatever gift has been given, regardless of the adequacy or appropriateness of the gift.[6]

Care and control appear intertwined in shelters' everyday life, along with issues of deservingness, expectations of having "well-behaved and grateful" migrants, and inclusiveness. In humanitarian ecosystems, there is no way around these tensions. How do you administer resources for seven hundred people who may stay at the shelter for two or three days? How do you ensure sustainable care when people are stranded at a migrant shelter for three months or more? How do you address the mental health needs arising from grueling mobility journeys or the uncertainty that the inability to move generates? How do you promote processes of inclusion, leadership, and ownership in contexts of mobility? These are questions that, in practice, may have different answers in different locations and in the face of different local challenges.

Like a Jail

The experiences of Mexican deportees at the northern border of Mexico exemplify how containment is experienced by migrants using *casas de migrantes*. The process of deportation is simple but taxing for deportees. US migration authorities—either Customs and Border Protection (CBP) or Immigration and Customs Enforcement (ICE)—drop deportees at the border. At some ports of entry, like Reynosa/Hidalgo, migrants arrive in chains and receive no information other than an indication to walk across the international bridge toward Mexico. Often, deportees arrive with no documents or identification other than an order of removal from the United States. On the Mexican side, authorities verify that the deportee is truly a Mexican national by asking a couple of questions; once verified, they proceed to register them in a database. As we have seen, once registered, the deportee receives a letter that is supposed to function as a form of identification but is rarely considered valid among local police. Some support information is provided, and those deportees with fewer resources or networks rely on the help offered by migrant shelters. The team working at the shelter in Reynosa used to wait for deportees at the international bridge. That is how I met Carmen, a forty-three-year-old deportee.

Carmen had been in jail for three years in the United States. After completing her sentence, she was deported to Mexico through the city of Reynosa, one of the most dangerous cities in the country because of gang and drug cartel presence. Even though there was an agreement between Mexico and the United States not to deport people in the evening, she was left at the international bridge around 7:30 p.m. She explained that when migrants come back, they often return in highly vulnerable positions: "You come back, and you do not know anything; you do not know anyone. Everybody is suspicious of everyone. You start looking around, and everybody is nervous. I was terrified. . . . I stood by the door with another woman because I did not know what to do. I think they saw us very confused and afraid, so the person at the counter came to tell us, . . . 'A religious sister or a priest will be here soon, and they will help.'"

Shelters offer services that help migrants to cope with distress, and migrants often are appreciative of that. However, as we have seen, shelters have rules, schedules, areas reserved for women or men, and policies that must be followed to check in and out. Thus, sometimes the boundaries between a shelter and a detention center are blurred.[7] Carmen clearly expressed this tension:

> Thank God for the *casas de migrantes*. . . . These places are extremely helpful. If the officer did not tell us about the shelter, we could have spent the night on the street. . . . I am extremely thankful for the help, the roof, the food . . . but, when they turned off the television at 8:30 p.m., told us to go to bed, closed the door, and turned off the lights, it reminded me of jail. But I also felt this during the day. The door to the street is locked, and

we cannot go out even to the convenience store. I know it is for security reasons; we do not know the place, and people do not know us. Still, for a moment, I feel like back in prison. . . . The more days you spend here, the more you feel like in prison. At the same time, I feel safe.

In the end, *casas de migrantes* are spaces where migrants can be controlled and contained and where migrants can be protected and supported. As Michael Barnett rightly asserts, "Any act of [humanitarian] intervention, no matter how well intended, is also an act of control. Humanitarian governance may have its heart in the right place, but it is still a form of governance, and governance always includes power."[8]

Carmen described the often chaotic and dangerous circumstances to which deported Mexicans return. Some may have assistance and find their way quickly, while others, like Carmen, return to the country with minimal to no support. Regardless of their location—southern, central, or northern Mexico—shelters become a significant social safety net that aids vulnerable migrants and deportees, giving them some relief as they consider their options moving forward. However, Carmen's observations about the rules, the impossibility of going out, and the feelings of being in jail reveal the tension in providing humanitarian aid, and its function of containment.

Shelters operate in a liminal state where welfare and containment become a double-edged sword. Humanitarian actors seek migrants' and deportees' emancipation through their services and advocacy efforts. However, they also confine a captive audience who seek their services and are willing to trade their freedom for safety, food, and shelter. In all, it seems that the government, shelters, and migrants themselves are all willing to be part of this dynamic.

Migration patterns in Mexico move through a south/north axis. Migrants often go north (which they refer to as *pal' norte* or *pa'rriba*, which means "going up"), while deported Mexicans travel south and are pushed far from the border by assistance programs for deportees. While Mexican authorities frame migration policies as humane and respectful of human rights, with their main goal the safety of migrants, in practice, the country is heavily patrolled and surveilled by migration authorities and by local and federal police. The gap between migration policies and enforcement practices affects the migration dynamics in three ways:

First, an internal border that fosters deportation and containment is created. Second, questions of citizenship for deportees returning to the country are raised. And third, the emergence of spaces of confinement is fostered.

A Deportation and Containment Regime

The internalization of borders in Mexico promotes the identification, detention, interdiction, and deportation of irregular migrants, asylum seekers, and occasionally refugees as they move north or as deported Mexicans return to the country. This policing of internal borders across Mexico has two effects. On the one hand, there is a benevolent government that uses humanitarian language and places migrants in a "victim-savior" relationship, and on the other hand, there are poor migrants who see the "threat of deportability" at all times and hide, run, and seek to evade controls, thereby putting themselves in precarious situations.[9]

Since November 2014, as part of its use of humanitarian language, the Mexican government consistently began using the term *rescate* (rescue) rather than *detención* (detention) to refer to its practices of migration control. Bulletins from the Instituto Nacional de Migración (INM) reveal trends about INM. Headlines like "INM rescues 12 Hondurans kidnapped by a criminal gang in Tabasco" and "INM rescues 61 migrants in Chiapas and Coahuila" appeared, and in April 2015, INM reported rescuing 804 migrants from risky situations.[10] Similar headlines abound in communications from INM. Consistent with the way language is used in migration law, Mexico has preferred the term "assisted return" when referring to the removal of irregular migrants rather than the term "deportation." This preference in language seeks to position Mexico as a country with humanitarian practices of removal. In practice, the difference between deportation and assisted return is only semantic.[11]

The official discourse and media coverage present any operation from migration authorities as a rescue operation. However, how these "rescue" operations occur is never discussed, and the outcome often leads to migrants' injuries or distress. From my time along migrant trails, I perceived a clear gap between the way control is enacted and the "rescue" discourse. Migrants often describe running away or hiding from the threat of deportation. Migration authorities chased Gerardo, a twenty-two-year-old migrant from Honduras, in the town of Bojay in central Mexico. Ivan, a twenty-nine-year-old migrant from Honduras, described how migration authorities chased him and his friend just outside the town of Palenque in southern Mexico. Migration journeys are filled with episodes like this. Migrants' escapes from migration authorities or police often lead to scratches, injuries, twisted ankles, and broken bones. Evidence shows that, more often than not, rather than rescuing and respecting migrants, Mexican authorities attempt to forcibly control and contain migrants' mobility. The presence of the National Guard has only aggravated this situation.

In practice, no matter how migrants move, efforts to control and contain their movement appear everywhere; yet despite these efforts, migrants continue to venture on with their migration projects. Bernardo, a twenty-nine-year-old migrant from Honduras, explains the constant threat of deportation and his desire not to be caught, because being caught often means removal from the country: "You do not want to be caught. You must stay at the detention center for weeks, only to be returned to your country. Then, one has to start again, hoping that one will not be caught this time, but the risk is always there. The road is hard, but it is harder to let life slip through your hands if you get caught by migration authorities." These words illustrate how migrants live under the threat of deportation. Sometimes this threat becomes real, and migrants must run from police and migration authorities. But most of the time, migrants must deal with the anxiety and fear of getting caught.

Questions regarding Citizenship and Context

At the northern border of Mexico, deportees return after experiencing the power of another deportation regime. In addition to arriving without identification, they occasionally have only limited belongings, often having just experienced days, weeks, or months in detention. In addition, some deportees return to the country after serving years in prison for illegally reentering the United States. In many ways, they end up becoming "de facto aliens in the country of citizenship."[12] Over the past decade, a growing body of literature has emerged that covers different aspects of the consequences after deportation.[13] I emphasize the immediate aftermath of the actual moment of deportation (the moment when deportees are left with or handed to Mexican authorities at international bridges) because without resources and with limited social networks and little information, deportees return to highly vulnerable conditions.

The return to the country of origin always involves a process of waiting and questioning. It is difficult to generalize about deportees because their circumstances range from separation from families, to years in prison, to recent crossings. Thus, their needs are always different. Of concern here is the questioning that deportees endure to prove Mexican citizenship. The reception process involves several questions regarding their place of origin, the entry of deportees' names into a database, and the presentation of a repatriation letter to deportees as proof of return to the country. Larger reception centers like Tijuana offer more on-site immediate support, but there is little to no assessment of the deportee's particular situation. Smaller reception centers like the ones in Nogales or Matamoros offer minimal assistance.

There is always confusion at the moment of return, mainly because groups arriving at the reception centers can vary in size from 10 to 70 to 135. As has been noted, official transactions at banks or some commercial activities in Mexico require a form of official identification. Only two banks accept the letter as official identification, making it difficult for deportees to make any financial transactions. Furthermore, police in border towns harass deportees or extort them, telling them, "That piece of paper is worth nothing." While the Mexican government has tried to speed up the process of providing official documentation for deportees, obtaining a national identity card can take up to fifteen working days and requires a proof of residence.

Thus, deported Mexicans return to Mexico only to be regarded as aliens in their own country for a while. Support for deportees often comes from NGOs and other outsourced programs that the Mexican government has implemented, but at most immediate moments after deportation, there is limited support for deportees.[14]

In contrast, the reception for Mexican migrants legally residing in the United States has become a successful program that has expanded through the years. Thus, the context or circumstances for the return matter deeply.

Zones of Confinement

Roads and train tracks, detention centers, and *casas de migrantes*, in one way or another, have all become zones of confinement and spaces of exception. Mexico's geography limits mobility opportunities for migrants; as much as there is a discussion of new migrant routes, the mobility patterns followed by poor migrants often consist of deviations around checkpoints, eventually returning to train tracks or main roads further ahead.[15] The routes get activated or deactivated according to the presence of migration or police authorities. In practice, the train tracks and the main roads that migrants use have become zones of confinement. As irregular migrants move from south to north, they avoid "belts of control" that appear along the road.[16] These belts of control refer to the checkpoints that have become fixtures along migration routes. Migrants who can use the train at different parts of the journey are often aware of where to get off so that migration authorities will not catch them. Some migrants walking along the train tracks hide in the mountains when migration authorities conduct raids but still use the train tracks as a compass to keep moving north. Similar to deterrence, the control and policing strategies used in Mexico confine migrants to isolated and dangerous routes.[17]

Detention centers are premier examples of the confinement of migrant populations, and are often perceived as static entities. In the case of Mexico, it is not only the number of detention centers that have appeared everywhere in the country but also the possibility of setting up mobile detention centers—sanctioned by the law—that complicates an understanding of confinement as a static form of control. Mexico's migration policies and enforcement foster the emergence of itinerant forms of control or mobile spaces of confinement.[18] Even when mobile detention centers can hold migrants for limited periods of time, the centers can also appear and disappear according to the way migration routes are activated or deactivated. Furthermore, their emergence functions as a way to channel and contain mobility, since migrants' mobility responds to the presence of migration controls.

Mexican migration laws appear on the face of it to be concerned with respecting human rights and caring for migrants. Yet in practice, the emphasis is on managing migration patterns, as shown by the implementation gap between migration laws and enforcement. Whether intended or unintended, the result fosters migrants' containment along migration routes and transfers or outsources responsibility to humanitarian actors for the care of migrants and deportees. Mexican migration law protects migrant shelters from any intervention by police or migration authorities, reinforcing the fact that migrants need to seek support at migrant shelters, and also highlighting the funneling of migrants into places that are well known along migration routes.

Blurred Lines

Mexican migration laws protect *casas de migrantes* or any humanitarian space from acts of control or surveillance by Mexican authorities. Such policies create de facto sanctuaries and safe havens. Nevertheless, it is essential to highlight that the boundaries between humanitarianism and control are often blurred. Anthropologist Michel Agier argues that inherent to humanitarian interventions are forms of control and confinement: "There is no care without control."[19] The protection migrants receive from the law in Mexico creates a significant ambivalence for the shelters' role in the migration process.

On the one hand, shelters support migrants out of genuine humanitarian concerns. On the other hand, migrant shelters end up being part of a functional solidarity system sanctioned by the state. In this system, *casas de migrantes* end up being spaces of exception and confinement, which exemplifies the blurred line Agier described when discussing refugee camps. Regarding the effects of humanitarian aid on the migration process, it is critical to note that power is exercised at the institutional and ground levels, where humanitarian agencies use different techniques to regulate behaviors in emergencies.[20] In the case of *casas de migrantes* in Mexico, location and delivery of services also function as forms of containment embedded in humanitarian aid provided to migrants in Mexico. Many shelters are located along migratory paths or border towns; the shelters' presence makes these routes more visible, while at the same time encouraging migrants to remain around those geographical locations and promoting a captive audience that regularly occupies humanitarian spaces.

Migrants using the shelters are, for the most part, those unable to afford paying smugglers and who use other strategies and means of transportation. Furthermore, migrants recognize that shelters are protected spaces and seek their services precisely for that reason. What matters to migrants is safety. Thus, there is a trade-off in the relationship between migrants and shelters, which is migrants' willingness to exchange freedom for security, even if they sometimes do so reluctantly. While this is not surprising due to the high levels of violence, the dangers, and the threat of deportation that migrants may experience outside migrant shelters, it still seems that in some shelters, the lines between a detention center and a migrant shelter blur.

Casa Ceballos, a migrant shelter at the border between Mexico and the United States, is one of the few shelters in that town that provides services free of charge. However, people need permission to go out. The National Guard, migration authorities, local police, and criminal groups prey on migrants wandering throughout this border town. Even more, taxi drivers deny services to migrants who need them. Some migrants have waited at the shelter for over six months. Thus, it is not surprising that migrants feel that their mental health is affected by the inability to go out. I heard variations of this concern at Casa Lucas, Casa Maldonado, and Casa Varela, all shelters along the US-Mexico border. Isabel, an asylum seeker from Venezuela staying at Casa Leal in the border town of Reynosa, reflected, "I am grateful for the support we receive here. However, I never gave an account of my whereabouts before. Here I have to ask for permission if I want to go out. I cannot remain here. I need to go to a place where I can be free." This comment and Carmen's observations about the rules, the impossibility of going out, and the feelings of being in jail reveal the tension between providing welfare and containing migrant populations.

In the end, *casas de migrantes* can be seen as spaces of exception that confine and control migrant populations. "*Casas de migrantes* are the solution for those of us who do not have money. Those who travel with coyotes [smugglers] have no need for places like this. . . . Aside from the attention that we received here, one feels safe here. Here migration authorities cannot detain you," attested Rubén, a twenty-seven-year-old migrant from Honduras. While discussing the different rules shelters have, Gustavo, a twenty-eight-year-old migrant, opined that

> the rule of not going out is a good rule. It is also OK if they check that you are not carrying guns or drugs. . . . One is safe here. Here nothing is going to happen to you. I trust the people that help here. Here nobody is coming for you to kidnap you or hurt you. . . . Outside, people ask many questions. Where are you from? How are you traveling? Do you have money? Who is waiting for you in the US? Those are strange questions that make you not feel safe. . . . I am fine following the rules if that will provide safety.

As we have seen, alliances between humanitarian actors and the government prevent migrants from spreading throughout the cities or towns where shelters are located. They also contain migrants in one space, making control easier if needed. It is thus inevitable that the politics of humanitarianism reveal the complex relationship between humanitarianism and power that is understood as "those effects that shape the capacities of actors to determine their own circumstances and fate."[21] In all the ways described above, humanitarian aid offered by *casas de migrantes* is a double-edged sword. As much as shelters function as an informal welfare system for migrants, the shelters' internal rules, policies, and relationships also foster different forms of containment.

Between Welfare and Containment

Using *casas de migrantes* is one strategy that poor migrants frequently rely on to cope with hardship. Soup kitchens, shelters, and community or neighborly support fall into the category of informal social resources. As we have seen, migrants, asylum seekers, refugees, and deportees use *casas de migrantes* because they do not have many options, mainly due to a lack of money and for security reasons. Hence, shelters exist as resources along migrant paths instead of being integrated into a migrant's social network. The distinction between networks and resources allows migration scholars to recognize how resources may be available outside migrants' networks. Migrants' narratives illustrate these points clearly.

Angel, a forty-two-year-old migrant from Honduras, noted, "I am traveling with my own means. I am on this road because we are poor, and I need to. I left only two thousand lempiras [eighty US dollars] for my family, and I need to cross to the US as soon as I can to start working before they run out of money and have nothing to eat. I have no money, so I have slept on the street, in the mountains, and in some shelters. That is why I came here." Angel had been on the road for twenty-four days before reaching a shelter in central Mexico. In the absence of money or other means to move through Mexico, migrants use shelters as one type of resource, among others, for their journeys.

Shelters are also social hubs that provide access to other types of resources (information, healthcare, legal opportunities, and so on). While most of my conversations with migrants occurred while they were staying at shelters, I also conversed with migrants who did not use shelters. I met a family from El Salvador outside a shelter in San Luis Potosí who said that they did not want to miss the train, which was why they did not enter the shelter. Another migrant I met by the train tracks in the town of Tenosique indicated that he did not like rules and, therefore, he preferred not to use shelters. Following international development expert Michael Titterton's argument that vulnerable and poor populations may rely on social support as an informal resource to cope with hardship, I argue that migrants use shelters (social support) as resources according to their circumstances and their perceptions of these places.[22] Indeed, the geographical distribution of these places along migration routes in Mexico fosters their use. But migrants may choose whether or not to use them, and migrants who have attempted the journey before and are familiar with the shelters may decide to skip a particular shelter if they did not have a good experience there the last time they visited. They may even sleep on the street if that is more conducive to their needs or seek another shelter with more relaxed rules.

Casas de migrantes aim to care and provide basic welfare for migrants in distress. In this case, welfare or social protection should be understood as public and private initiatives that provide consumption transfers to the poor, protect the vulnerable against livelihood risks, and enhance the social status and rights of the marginalized.[23] Thus, while humanitarian actors aiding migrants in Mexico have become a social safety net distributed throughout the country to alleviate their suffering, migrants engage with them on their own terms or in emergencies. Migrants repeatedly agreed that shelters provided basic needs; for instance, Arturo, a seventeen-year-old migrant from El Salvador traveling with a friend, said, "I think shelters are a great help. They treat you well; you have food and a place to sleep. Here you can get clothes; the doctor checks you if you arrive dehydrated, you eat well, I can take a shower and rest for a couple of days, and then get on the road again up north. . . . I will use other shelters. Now, I have the map that they gave me here."

Migrants using a particular shelter for a second or third time express their continued appreciation of the basic welfare they receive but are also aware of how the delivery of services changes over time. Gonzalo, an eighteen-year-old migrant from Guatemala traveling for a second time with two other migrants, said, "I am surprised how everything has changed in this shelter. The shelter has grown and there are more people to help. This is how a 'migrant shelter' is supposed to be. It is not only because of the facilities but also because of the staff and rules that one can be completely convinced that one is safe here. At the same time, staff encourages us to continue with our journeys and provide everything you may need." These words show not only how shelters may change over time but also how they can improve their services and how they interact with migrants.

In humanitarian assistance and the care for vulnerable populations, the tension between welfare and containment is anything but new. In the history of welfare, rulers have been concerned with controlling the mobility of people. Vagrants and the wandering poor were threats that rulers believed needed to be controlled.[24] At the same time, in the delivery of welfare, another concern deals with the issue of who is entitled to aid and support.[25] In the past, some regulations attempted to address this. For example, the Law of Settlement regulated the immigration of the poor; "letters of surety" (letters ensuring payment for the sustenance of the carrier) were required to allow settlement; and "wardens" at the doors of several cities identified "valuable migrants" from liabilities.[26] Thus, requirements and regulations to settle, suitability inspections, and proof or assurance of support are forms of control exercised by those providing aid. Similarly, many shelters utilize different forms of control, requesting proof of identity to document who comes to the shelter to receive aid.

Casas de migrantes are not spaces designed for long-term stays. As we have seen, some shelters may have rules aimed at leading migrants to decide to resume their journeys, others to allow shorter stays, and others do not allow migrants to go out until they are ready to resume their journeys. Shelters reassess and adjust their rules on a need basis. By 2023, some *casas de migrantes* served as spaces of transit (migrants staying less than twenty-four hours) while larger shelters located in cities with greater access to resources and services offered more comprehensive care models. Stays at these shelters can last for months. Still, the expectation is that migrants will continue their journeys at some point. Even in those shelters that allow indefinite stays, rules that regulate migrants' coming and going make them want to move quickly rather than remain in an environment that may resemble a detention center.

Furthermore, as time has passed and migration policies have become more restrictive, shelters have recognized that some migrants decide to settle in particular towns. Recognizing this reality has led *casas de migrantes* to develop support programs for migrants remaining in the area. Casa Melara and Casa Ixpertay have developed programs to help stranded migrants, deportees, or asylum seekers integrate into the local community.

Within the dynamics of migrant shelters, mobility restrictions, security measures, and other forms of control point to a form of migration governance. While describing the role of walls and other border infrastructures, political geographer Polly Pallister-Wilkins indicates that these structures produce and reproduce border logic of territorialization, separation, and exclusion. But they also reinforce a governance role where filtering, bridging, disciplining, and regulating population control circulation.[27] Similarly, *casas de migrantes* are porous humanitarian spaces of control and welfare. They are porous in the sense that they contain and control people within a space where they can receive welfare, but migrants can always move on with their migration projects. Without a doubt, migrants are beneficiaries of these spaces, but the Mexican government benefits from deflecting its responsibility to care for migrants. In cases where migration journeys are elongated for months, questions arise about the role of shelters and their ability to support people in deciding how to face the roadblocks in their projects.

By March 2023, Mexico had seen more migrants, asylum seekers, refugees, and IDPs along the migration routes and at its northern border than in previous years. It is difficult to capture how many people were stranded at this border. CBP enforcement statistics reported nearly 258,000 migrants apprehended or expelled under Title 8 and Title 42 during January and February 2023.[28] These statistics do not include people who had newly arrived at the border but had yet to attempt to cross and ask for asylum because of the likelihood of expulsion. Furthermore, it was unclear how many people were currently along migrant trails or in border towns in southern Mexico waiting for an opportunity to reach the northern border.

Casas de migrantes and other humanitarian organizations continue to provide services for migrants, but as their capacity is tested because many shelters are overcrowded, informal camps have emerged.[29] The phenomenon of informal camps is not new at the northern border of Mexico; cities like Tijuana, Ciudad Juárez, Reynosa, and Matamoros have seen informal camps appear, disappear, and reappear in recent years.[30] In the context of humanitarian governance, informal camps develop as a form of resistance and contestation to the system that tries to control and contain migrants. They all seem driven by a mix of self-organization, care, control, and concrete and explicit forms of violence.[31]

Still, informal camps remain monitored and surveilled by local authorities and under the watch of some international organizations that occasionally provide services. While visiting informal camps in Matamoros, Ciudad Juárez, and Reynosa, I encountered international humanitarian organizations including Doctors without Borders, IOM, and UNHCR providing different kinds of support. Volunteers and small NGOs always tend to the precarity of those who inhabit the camps. While informal camps may appear as an outlier in the dynamic of welfare and containment, in practice, states may tolerate them because it is convenient for them.[32] Informal camps in Tijuana, Ciudad Juárez, and Matamoros have emerged, been cleared out by the Mexican government, and reappeared at other moments.[33] This shows how, despite its neglect, the Mexican government remains in control, and even in informal ways, migrants remain contained in specific areas.

Waiting, Idleness, and Uncertainty

Esperanza, an Indigenous woman from Guerrero and mother of four, had been waiting at an informal camp in Matamoros for five months. Juliette, a woman from Haiti and a mother of two, sighed and smiled nervously when I asked about all the free time she has since she cannot leave the shelter unless she leaves for good. Mario, a man from Venezuela, said he has been coming for four months to have a meal at the cathedral in Ciudad Juárez while he awaited an opportunity to enter the United States. Waiting, idleness, and uncertainty have become unintended consequences of the tension between welfare and containment and of increasingly restrictive policies and lack of access to asylum in the United States.[34]

Moving through Mexico could take weeks to months, depending on the resources and networks available to a particular migrant. As migration journeys elongate, journeys and migrant populations become stranded, especially at Mexico's northern border. The humanitarian ecosystem in Mexico now includes shelters for medium- and long-term stays, usually located in larger urban cities.[35] As movement through Mexico has become more complicated and costlier, waiting has put migrants' lives in a state of limbo or suspension. Waiting here is part of the temporal dimension of migration and the politics of mobility.[36] It involves more than physical immobility; it also involves a sense of existential immobility.[37] Christian, a migrant at a shelter in Reynosa, shared, "I have been here for more than three months, and I do not know what to do. I can only hope and continue waiting, I guess." His words express awareness of the concrete act of waiting and the existential uncertainty it generates, even if this uncertainty comes with a hint of hope. However, waiting appears as "the temporal process in and through which political subordination is reproduced."[38] Hence, waiting burdens marginalized populations and functions as a deterrence and containment strategy that eventually leads migrants to change, alter, or desist from their migration projects.[39] For migrant shelters, waiting brings a new set of challenges as they have to help migrants cope with uncertainty and imagine opportunities or foster collaborations that will allow people to move out of the shelter and attempt to integrate into the local community. That is easier said than done, as the location of the shelter will determine the opportunities available for migrants.

Waiting refers to those periods of time when migrants have to stay at shelters due to restrictive migration policies or because it is hard to continue the journey. Idleness, understood as a state of inaction and inactivity, comes hand in hand with waiting and uncertainty at migrant shelters. It expresses an imposition of immobility within the tension of welfare and containment.[40] Sometimes idleness is exacerbated because migrants cannot go out due to shelters' rules, unfamiliarity with the locality, or a lack of opportunities outside. Migrant shelters have rules and structures that help to organize the day, but shelter activities cannot fill all the migrants' time as they wait. Some shelters have psychosocial programs, but psychosocial interventions may not be designed for long-term stays. Abundant and unstructured time becomes problematic for the long-term mental health of migrants.[41]

As migrants face waiting, idleness, and uncertainty, they can also transform their temporal and spatial dimensions of waiting. Sociologist Gil Everaert, in her article "Inhabiting the Meanwhile," describes some of these practices of asylum seekers at a shelter in southern Mexico. She argues that placemaking and rebuilding a home are a way to cope with waiting. "Sleeping arrangements and bunk beds were not only spaces for sleeping and resting, but they have become, for many, the possibility of building a home. Of claiming a space as their own, at least during a few hours each night."[42] In shelters across Mexico, it is not uncommon to see migrants and asylum seekers claim spaces and develop routines as they wait. Bunk beds at a shelter in Tijuana resemble small households covered with blankets to offer some privacy. The tent's interior in an informal camp in Matamoros resembles a small room where everything has a place, from clothes to food, to an invaluable electric outlet to charge the cell phone. Arranging and tending to these improvised "home settings" allow people to cope, defy uncertainty, and wait.

Conclusion

Humanitarian actors have several not-so-subtle ways of controlling and exercising surveillance of migrants. Mandatory registration, photographs, and even digital fingerprinting are some requirements that migrants must accept to receive support. Paradoxically, shelters' forms of surveillance aim to make *casas de migrantes* safer. However, there is no doubt that while registration and pictures occasionally help identify potential smugglers or criminals, these practices echo preindustrial times that aimed to ensure that aid was being delivered to the right people. From a more contemporary perspective, scholars have indicated that humanitarian aid always has a component of control. Barnett states that at the core of humanitarianism, there is the paradox of emancipation and domination:

> Humanitarianism operates in the best tradition of emancipatory ethics. It aspires to keep people alive, to expand their opportunities, and to give them greater control over their fates. It does so through various interventions, all defended on the grounds that they improve the health and welfare of others who are too weak and powerless to help themselves. . . . Yet any act of intervention no matter how well intended, is also an act of control.[43]

Humanitarian actors in Mexico epitomize the tension described by Barnett between emancipation and domination by blurring the line between being an oasis—as some migrants call shelters—and functioning as de facto containment or semi-detention centers. *Casas de migrantes* serve people on the move with the best of intentions. Even when the success of particular shelters is questioned, one can see the efforts made to provide assistance or the reasons migrants perceive them as oases that offer respite and support. The same can be said about how shelters morph to meet the needs of migrants or the efforts of the main shelters in advocating for migrants. However, shelters' policies and regulations and the dynamics involved in the migration process (violence, control by migration authorities, and migrants' agency) lead shelters to foster settings that can be contentious. Restrictions placed on going out, predetermined schedules, idle time, bag searches before entering the shelter, the possibility of seizure of belongings, and uncertainty about the journey are some of the elements that make migrants feel that shelters' policies and practices can create detention-like environments. At the same time, migrants often express their willingness to exchange freedom for safety, which again indicates that, indeed, some of the shelters' settings resemble detention.

In Mexico, policies, alliances, location, and services converge to stimulate a type of humanitarianism that functions not only as welfare, but also as containment and control.[44] Migration policies in Mexico make humanitarian spaces a kind of sanctuary that migrants use to guard themselves against migration and police authorities. Intended or not, the migration policy funnels vulnerable migrants toward humanitarian spaces throughout Mexico. Furthermore, as the political landscape has changed, the length and timing of migration journeys have changed too. Waiting, idleness, and uncertainty emerge within the inherent tension of welfare and containment in humanitarian work.

At migrant shelters, control may happen in everyday practices resembling bordering practices that sometimes emerge far from political borders. Control also occurs through the different alliances migrant shelters enter into, no matter if these alliances are with local communities, INGOs, or state and federal government agencies. In various degrees, these alliances and collaborations shape and condition the agenda and the work of migrant shelters.

Contestation, Alliance, and Institutionalization

Moving along the migration routes in Mexico is an eye-opening experience. The differences in geography, climate, and culture show a diverse and divided country. The Indigenous faces in the south change as you move through the "sierras" and toward the center of the country. The striking size of Mexico City replaces the rural areas and the highlands. The city itself, with all its busyness, also shows many differences. You see rich and poor, White, Brown, and, more recently, Black people, but above all, you see a city divided by class. The landscape changes again as you leave Mexico City and move toward the north. The valley and its dry vegetation are home to a mix of urban and industrial sites. Small towns with rural flavor appear and disappear frequently. The language accent changes as you move north, and the warm temperature from central Mexico becomes abrasive heat at times as desertic areas emerge until you face the "wall" between Mexico and the United States. Along the way, *casas de migrantes* appear in small towns along the train tracks leading north. They also emerge in the bellies of the larger cities far away from the train tracks. Finally, there are those *casas de migrantes* that operate in border cities, near or close to the border wall, points of entry, or places near crossing points.

Just like the Mexican landscape of the country, the most striking things about migrant shelters are the particular personalities and rules of engagement they display. "Trump, you will be the fire that will ignite the fury of the people," reads a mural at Casa Rojche. "I was here," reads a mural in a shelter in central Mexico. The LGBTQI+ rainbow dominates the shelter in Saltillo, along with a poster that reads, "I know I can, I believe I can, I will achieve it." A large altar to Our Lady of Guadalupe dominates the shelter at the border town of Reynosa. Five large panels with religious motifs dominate the common area at the new facilities of the Casa Ixpertay. The style of each shelter reflects not only the personalities of founders and directors but also the roles they play in the migration process in Mexico.

This chapter discusses why geographical location matters in how migrant shelters interact with different actors. I highlight contestation, alliance, and institutionalization as three different ways of engagement in different geographical regions along migrant trails. Acknowledging geographical location is important to understand why migrant shelters are different. These ways of engagement are both strategies and consequences of the role that humanitarian organizations play in the migration system in Mexico.

Geography Matters

Migrant shelters take on different brokerage roles depending on the needs that they try to fill while aiding migrants in vulnerable situations. Shelters' particular styles and forms of operation are highly influenced by the contexts and regions in which they provide services and how they broker with different actors. In other words, geography matters.

Historically, southern Mexico has a history of social movements where people fought for justice and equality. Many Indigenous groups live in different parts of southern Mexico; these groups have always lived in tension with the government and fought for their rights to be recognized and respected. The Zapatista movement, a fight for Indigenous rights, emerged in this region in 1994 and created some independent areas. Border cities and towns like Tapachula, Tenosique, and Frontera Comalapa have been known not only for being points where migration journeys start but also for being places where migrant protests and movements have started. The Viacrucis Migrantes, the Caravan of Mothers of Missing Migrants, and even the Exodo Migrante all have started in southern Mexico and beyond.

The center of Mexico has tended to be more politically and religiously conservative. It is also more centralized, mainly because it includes larger urban areas and cities. Some of the more industrialized regions in the country are near Mexico City or central Mexico. Mexico's geography contributes to this centralization since most roads have to go through Mexico City, diversifying up north. In central Mexico, relationships between migrant shelters and state or religious authorities tend to be more visible. Shelters in central and western Mexico have strong relationships with the state governments and local authorities; a diocese of the Catholic Church sponsors a shelter on the outskirts of Mexico City and has had a strong relationship with the government.

Proximity to the United States has always shaped Mexico's northern border dynamics. Migrant workers with regional cards and visas cross every day to work in the United States. To ease living costs, some Americans have moved to live in Tijuana while still holding jobs in San Diego. American-born students cross the border daily to attend schools in the United States because their families have moved to border cities in Mexico due to deportation. After the ending of some restrictive US policies like Title 42, migrants have arrived in growing numbers hoping to file for asylum in the United States. Relationships with federal, state, and local governmental actors are crucial. In some states, governmental organizations called Institutos Estatales de Migration (State Migration Institutes), Institutos de Asistencia al Migrante (Institutes to Assist Migrants), or Institutos de Atención al Migrante (Institutes for Attention to the Migrants) engage migrant shelters to serve the needs of Mexican nationals and migrants.

The need to understand contestation, alliances, and other relational expressions is accompanied by the need to consider the roles of space and geography—localized, global, or networked—in the expressions of social groups.[1] Thus, by looking at how shelters present themselves, operate, and relate to other actors, we may see these humanitarian spaces as places of contestation, alliances, and institutionalization.[2]

Contestation

Casa Rojche is a well-known shelter in southern Mexico. The shelter has allowed several artists to paint different works with human rights and justice motifs. Many motifs include quotes from Che Guevara, Mario Benedetti, and Monseñor Oscar Romero and reference to migration and social justice. The shelter's profile has grown enormously in past years, mainly because Fray Rubén, the shelter director, has been a key figure in Mexico's migration advocacy landscape. In 2014 the shelter promoted the Viacrucis Migrante, which was a mix of a religious practice and pro-test movement. Fray Rubén described the experience:

> The first time we did [the Viacrucis Migrante], we just wanted to ride the freight train to Palenque. There were, like, two hundred people, including migrants and volunteers. Once we were on top of the freight train, the rail company decided not to depart. So we decided to walk to Palenque. It was a way to emulate Jesus's journey to the cross. The journey of these migrants is a calvary. So we arrived at Emiliano Zapata and walked to Palenque from there, but more people joined us. From there, you know, we went to Villahermosa, and then we got transportation to reach Mexico City. By the time we reached Mexico City, there were close to a thousand migrants taking part in the caravan. The support we had from shelters and civil organizations was unbelievable. But above all, migrants felt em-powered, and their movement was a way to assume their fight for justice. This journey is an act of civil disobedience.

Participants and organizers from the Viacrucis Migrante met with government officials in Mexico City. Their original intention was to meet with president Enrique Peña Nieto to request free transit through Mex-ico so they could avoid violence from organized crime and migration and police officers. While they could not meet the president, they met senators and members of Congress to discuss the experience of being an irregular migrant. They also requested changes to the migration laws and the enforcement code. The movement of over one thousand migrants who reached Mexico City forced the government to pro vide *pases de salida* (exit documents) to guarantee free transit to migrants throughout the country.[3] From Mexico City, the Viacrucis Migrante branched out to different destinations along the US-Mexico border. When the Viacrucis Migrante dissolved, it was unclear how many migrants had reached the Mexican northern border and how many had entered the United States. Shelter directors in Tijuana and Ciudad Juárez reported the arrival of different migrant groups. However, Sor Teresa, director of Casa Leal in Reynosa, recalled, "When the Viacrucis Migrante arrived, we started to receive threats from criminal groups in the city. They said, 'Sister, you need to send your people away. We do not want to bring attention here [to the city]. If you do not do that, things are not going to end well.'" The members of the Viacrucis Migrante who arrived in Reynosa returned to Saltillo, a city 188 miles from the border, so as to avoid any risks for the group and for the staff at the shelter.

When it began in 2014, the Viacrucis Migrante caught the Mexican government off guard. In 2015 the Viacrucis Migrante took a different approach, and each shelter organized particular activities. Casa Rojche organized a hunger strike and a rally outside the detention center. The strike concluded with the celebration of Mass during Easter. The shelter in Chahuites, Oaxaca, promoted a Viacrucis Migrante through the Pacific route. I met people from this shelter at the beginning of the event in Tapachula, Chiapas, where I was collecting data at another shelter.

At that time, the group was small, close to twenty or twenty-five people. As in the previous year, the group started to grow as word got out that it was marching north. The Mexican government reacted differently this time and tried to block the caravan in the town of Ixtepec. Police and federal authorities surrounded the shelter and threatened the migrants with deportation. Amid tensions and with the support of Father Alejandro Solalinde, the Viacrucis Migrante 2015 continued its trajectory. A smaller group reached Mexico City, where it decided to finish the caravan.

Due to previous experiences and the pressures from the Mexican government, shelters organized more local activities in 2016. Still, while these later efforts were on a smaller scale than the first Viacrucis Migrante, they reveal the ethos of these humanitarian organizations. "We want to empower migrants so they can participate in the change we want to create," said Fray Rubén.

Casa Rojche actively documents abuse and human rights violations perpetrated by migration authorities and federal, state, and local police. The shelter has become very active in accompanying asylum seekers through the legal process. As a result, it can be said that the shelter exercises representative and liaison types of brokerage. However, taking a representative role and pushing advocacy efforts create enormous tensions between local authorities and the shelter. Immigration officers have filed lawsuits against different staff members of the shelters, including Fray Rubén. The shelter has received threats from criminal groups as an organization, as well as threats to individual staff members.

Tensions reached a point where Fray Rubén had to participate in a safety procedure offered by the National Human Rights Commission. This procedure provided bodyguards for Fray Rubén and an alarm system to contact federal and local police in case of an incident. The security guards often remain outside the shelter 24/7, providing a minimum level of protection for Fray Rubén and another layer of security for the shelter and migrants.

The shelter known as Casa Santos also has a long history of providing support to migrants in a contested setting. Located in the state of Oaxaca, the shelter started operations in 2007. Father Alejandro Solalinde was the founder, and he quickly became a prominent figure in the advocacy landscape for the rights of migrants. As noted earlier, he won the Mexican National Human Rights Award in 2012 for the shelter's work and for confronting authorities about abuse against migrants.

Like many others, the shelter is next to the train tracks at a critical intersection along the migrant trail. The town where it is located is around five hundred kilometers from the border with Guatemala. Migrants arriving at the shelter have already passed dangerous points, including Arriaga in Chiapas and Chahuites in the state of Oaxaca. Casa Santos functions as a respite along the first leg of the migrant route on the Pacific Ocean. Throughout the years, these roads have been heavily patrolled by migration authorities and, more recently, by the Mexican National Guard. The freight train stopped operating a couple of times in 2014, again in 2017, and more recently in 2019. This has not stopped migrants from arriving at the shelters, though; they have continued to move either by walking or using public transportation along secondary roads. These alternative forms of transportation increase migrants' vulnerability.

The shelter played a critical role in 2015 during the Viacrucis Migrante. As the number of migrants joining the event increased, Mexican migration authorities established more controls to block migrants' attempts to journey north. That year, migrants remained stranded for some time at the shelter because a group of migration authorities and police officers threatened to enter the shelter to detain migrants. After some negotiations with migration authorities, the group of migrants left the shelter on their way to Mexico City. Father Solalinde filed a claim with the National Human Rights Commission to denounce abuses from authorities and stress the rights of migrants to free transit. Ultimately, the migrants were granted special permission to transit through the country. Upon arrival in Mexico City, they met with the local chapter of the Human Rights Commission.

These two shelters in southern Mexico may be seen as the most emblematic for their active and visible roles in advocating for migrants and confronting and denouncing Mexican authorities' abuse against migrants. But they are not the only ones that play contested roles in the humanitarian architecture of Mexico. As we have seen, the leader of Las Patronas, another emblematic group of women in southern Mexico, won the National Human Rights Award in 2013. Casa Requena, in northern Mexico, also has been a prominent agent in the fight for migrants' rights through the work of Father Pedro Pantoja. Until the caravans of late 2018 and early 2019, the Viacrucis Migrante was one of the most prominent and visible acts of protest and mobilization of migrants.

The Viacrucis Migrante is an act of contestation and part of the growing number of immigrant protests, such as migrant workers' rallies in the United States during 2006, a No Borders camp in Calais, protests in immigration detention centers in the United Kingdom, and protest marches by Tamil migrants in Toronto. It could also be framed within the sociological debates about the nature of camps, the role of camp-like institutions, and the agency of those who are part of them.[4] In this case, the Viacrucis Migrante is mediated and led by intermediate actors, *casas de migrantes*, and occurs in a country of transit, combining both the agency of irregular migrants and the advocacy efforts of citizens running humanitarian organizations in Mexico. At the same time, it turns a religious practice into an expression of migrant resistance.[5]

Without a doubt, this practice has emerged due to the intensification of border security, which is highly influenced by pressures from the United States on the Mexican government to manage migration at the southern Mexican border. The slogan during the Viacrucis Migrante in 2015 was *Tránsito Digno* (Transit with Dignity), which reflects the tension between irregular migration and a humanitarian government. Furthermore, the Viacrucis Migrante shows how humanitarian protection becomes mobile and portable since humanitarian actors promoted the activity and traveled with irregular migrants throughout the country. The long-term effects the practice has had on the migration process are unclear. Still, the caravans of 2018 and 2019 were a clear development that emerged from the Viacrucis Migrante, as migrants used the cara-vans as a form of contestation, mobilization, and protection. The cara-vans gathered a more significant number of migrants and allowed the emergence of different leadership figures who used social media to give voice to the migrants' cause. The caravans gained even more attention because of the constant attention the Trump administration gave them to promote an anti-immigrant sentiment.[6] The director of Casa Rojche, Fray Rubén, played an instrumental role in organizing the initial cara-vans, reflecting the influence that he has had in shaping the agenda of the shelter in the southern part of the country.

Casas de migrantes mirror their founders' and directors' personalities. Casa Rojche and Casa Santos, as well as the Las Patronas group and other migrant shelters, have gained prominence because of the roles their di-rectors have played in the political migration landscape in Mexico. The volunteer programs at both shelters have evolved and developed to in-clude international volunteers because of their orientation to social jus-tice. Las Patronas became a staple among speakers invited to share their experiences of humanitarian assistance, participating in events at places ranging from the University of Oxford to the Gregorian University in Rome. Humanitarian actors in Mexico keep pushing the boundaries of their advocacy for migrants and asylum seekers. Paradoxically, there has not been a similar effort to advocate for deportees returning to Mexico.

By 2023, the United States had implemented a process of border ex-ternalization that Mexico operates. Despite Mexico's efforts to present it-self as interested in human security and a protector of migrants' human rights, enforcement and militarization are the main approaches through which the Mexican government "manages" migration.[7] However, fol-lowing philosopher Thomas Nail, we see that the migrant is not only a figure whose movement results in a certain degree of social expulsion but also a figure whose movement, social motion, and other forms of resistance—riots, revolts, rebellions—contest and disrupt the systems and forces that aim to control them.[8] In this figure of the migrant, we can include asylum seekers, refugees, deportees, and IDPs, who to dif-ferent degrees experience social exclusion in the migration system in Mexico. Still, people in contexts of mobility in Mexico have found ways to create alternatives to social expulsion, subverting and contesting sys-tems aimed to control their movement.[9]

Migrant shelters in Mexico contest an oppressive migration regime that puts migrants in vulnerable and precarious situations. Initially, advocacy and contestation were performed mainly by migrant shelters, their directors, and staff. More and more, *casas de migrantes* encourage migrants to become protagonists of their migration projects. Thus, one can now see migrants participating in rallies and offering testimonies of their struggles at different advocacy events. This process was well explained by Miguel, director of operations at Casa Ixpertay: "*Amigos* [friends], we [migrant shelters] should not exist; we want you to be protagonists of your process and learn how to advocate for yourselves."

Alliance

You can feel the climate changing when traveling from southern Mexico to central Mexico. The hot and humid weather is replaced by cold and foggy air. Migrants riding La Bestia describe the train's ascent through the mountains and a series of tunnels, which make the air even chillier. Those venturing on public transport must endure winding roads and stops at different rural towns. Once the ascent is complete, small towns start to appear; upon arrival at the city of Puebla, the terrain is downhill to the valley, where Mexico City awaits. Next to the train tracks, a small shelter in the town of Apizaco, Puebla, offers another small respite. Migrants stopping there spend long hours on the patio under the sun, waiting to warm up. Other small shelters throughout the city offer different kinds of assistance. Staff and shelter directors know that migrants pass through the city quickly on their way north.

Without a doubt, central Mexico is a different story from southern Mexico. Located in larger cities and more populated areas, *casas de migrantes* in this region have to create different kinds of alliances, which means teaming with religious authorities, the state government, or local councils. The shelters in Huehuetoca, San Luis Potosí, and Guadalajara are good examples of humanitarian organizations that broker with other actors to provide services to migrants. Above all, these are shelters whose particular alliances make it possible to offer assistance with certain levels of quality and stability. The emphasis here is not so much on their brokerage role but on the need to establish alliances with specific actors to navigate the sociopolitical landscape of different regions, mainly central Mexico.

In a town on the outskirts of Mexico City, Casa Villamil has gone through different iterations. Starting in 2005, a small chapel began providing services to the growing number of migrants resting there on their way to the United States. Overcrowding, violence in the surrounding areas, organized crime, and lack of attention from civil authorities were some of the dynamics documented about the shelter during those years.[10] In 2009 the shelter officially became an NGO and connected with organizations like Doctors Without Borders to continue providing services. However, the relationship with the local community was always tense, and the lack of space and the continuous presence of migrants exacerbated those tensions. Furthermore, there were rumors that organized crime had infiltrated the shelter. In 2012 the shelter moved to its current location, avoiding permanent closure.

The local Catholic diocese sponsors the shelter. At the time of its opening, the local bishop had a strong relationship with former president Peña Nieto.[11] When the bishop visited the shelter on opening day, he fiercely defended the migration authorities and praised the government's efforts. The prelate repeatedly insisted on the need to collaborate with immigration authorities to try to help thousands of migrants. His message had a clear, supportive tone toward migration authorities and the government, which resulted in the constant presence nearby of migration officers and local police. Migrants avoided the shelter because of this, in spite of its good facilities and open spaces, as well as services offered by international humanitarian organizations. Migrants often referred to this shelter as one with the strictest rules, most abuses by staff, and shortest time of stay.

The sponsorship of the diocese and the close relationship with the local bishop guarantee stability for the shelter. That was noticeable as the shelter transitioned from its original location in a small church to the facilities it has now. The sponsorship has made a difference in what is offered at the shelter and the relationships that can help to sustain its work. Nevertheless, the shelter limits its work to humanitarian assistance, avoiding participation in advocacy efforts that may question the role of government authorities. For example, at all costs, the shelter avoids conflict or clashing with migration authorities and local police. This way of working reflects the leadership that sponsors it. In this case, the alliance is necessary for survival.

Further north, but still in what is considered central Mexico, there is a shelter in the city of San Luis Potosí that had operated out of a parish on the city's outskirts for several years. Citing a health hazard to the migrant population and the community, the city council ordered the shelter to cease operations, which it did. As a result, migrants who previously remained close to the shelter or in the neighborhood were dispersed throughout the city. The city council asked the local Catholic bishop to reopen the shelter and offered to provide facilities and other services. The shelter reopened a couple of weeks later. Since then, it has received support from the city council and state government to assist migrants. It is one of the few *casas de migrantes* operated by the local chapter of Caritas (one of the Catholic Church's largest assistance institutions). Hence, the local government supports the shelter, ensuring that there is no crime in the surrounding areas, and a police officer comes through the shelter twice a day to verify that there are no issues. Cameras also record foot traffic and serve as a form of security. Some of these cameras are visible to the police, and the shelter has a direct line to them in case of an emergency. Caritas's sponsorship allows the shelter to focus more on its services and cultivating relationships with other actors than struggling to determine where the next food stock will come from.

There is no question that Casa Sutuj in San Luis Potosí has strong ties to the government. The state governor has visited the shelter, along with high-ranking officials from the state security and police sectors. The director of this *casa del migrante* won the state human rights award for his work. Hence, the alliance with the government and the shelter's reputation allow access to good emergency services. For migrants, the journey through Mexico can be gruesome. Miguel and Blanca, a couple I met at the shelter, shared the horrors of a gang rape before reaching the shelter. Alicia, another woman from Honduras traveling alone, was also raped while she was going north. The State Institute for Women received and followed up with their cases, including physical and psychological assessments and legal assistance. A social worker was assigned, and the service was impeccable. As a result, and thanks to the collaboration between the migrant shelter and the local government,

Miguel and Blanca obtained visas for humanitarian reasons. When I left the shelter, Alicia was still receiving services. Since tracking migrants or staying in contact with them is not a common practice at *casas de migrantes*, neither the shelter nor I knew her whereabouts after she left Casa Sutuj.

As we have seen, life at migrant shelters can be tedious; while cleaning and some other activities keep people busy, migrants may not have much to do during the day except find ways to fill their time between meals. Thus, it is not surprising that depression and anxiety are common among migrants, as I witnessed during my field research. One rainy and dark night, I was summoned from my room in the volunteers' wing. The women's dormitory was buzzing; women staying at the shelter at that time gathered in different corners of the big room. Someone approached me and said, "Gabriela has been crying all night. She is seeing things and keeps saying she wants to kill herself. We are terrified and worried." After a short conversation with Gabriela, and another with the shelter director, I could see that Gabriela needed psychiatric services, either for depression, suicidal ideation, or a psychotic episode. The psychiatric hospital was forty minutes from the shelter. It was a long night, but the shelter was able to secure services of sufficient quality for her. Those services would have been complicated to obtain without the existing networks and relationships with government authorities.

Casa Cuc, a shelter in the western city of Guadalajara, is an interesting case. The shelter emerged in 2007 out of an initiative from a group of students who decided to start a comprehensive intervention project after volunteering in different migrant shelters. Initially, their project centered on running a small soup kitchen for four hours daily. There, they offered essential services, food, showers, phone calls, and general information about the route. The group became an official NGO in 2009. As mentioned in chapter 5, in early 2015, despite existing safety protocols, some staff members faced verbal threats from drug dealers and addicts. The shelter sought additional support from local authorities but was unsuccessful. The shelter director explained that the organization believed conditions were insufficient to continue offering services and, after consulting with team members, decided to suspend operations until the local government could ensure improved safety. He emphasized that their decision was communicated to the government.

Similar to the shelter in San Luis Potosí, a couple of weeks later, the city council, upon realizing that migrants had dispersed throughout the city, contacted the organization to reopen services at another location. A site was selected through negotiations between Casa Cuc and the city council. The organization sought funds and grants to reopen the shelter in a former warehouse. Thus, in 2015 it opened new facilities called the Migrant and Refugee Care Center, extending its service hours and humanitarian services to include medical, psychological, and legal services.

The professionalization of leadership in Casa Cuc has allowed the shelter to survive, thrive, and emerge as an important actor in Mexico's migration and refugee advocacy landscape. The shelter is located in one of the largest metropolitan areas in Mexico and has over 180 volunteers, the vast majority of whom are college students. They are capable of coordinating the provision of essential services, as well as promoting campaigns through social media when specific needs emerge.

Casa Cuc is one of the few shelters without a faith-based connection and no alliances with a church. Its staff and collaborators include professionals, activists, academics, and religious members, among others. They have been particularly savvy in mobilizing resources through social media and lobbying with different actors, but especially in making the local government accountable for tending to the needs of migrants, refugees, and asylum seekers.

The shelter director explained his mode of operations: "We do not have the safety nets of a religious congregation or a parish; I cannot call the superior and say we do not have food to give to the people. Thus, I need to make alliances with the government. In fact, part of our work is to push the government to do its job and provide what is needed for the migrants in vulnerable situations. We cannot confront the government like Fray Rubén from Casa Rojche or Father Carlos from Casa Santos. That confrontational model will not work in this region. Thus, we have to negotiate, to lobby."

Thanks to the alliances it has formed and its ability to constantly hold local authorities accountable, its services have grown. Now, the shelter serves as a place where asylum seekers can stay long-term. The evolution of the shelter has allowed it to enter into leadership roles with different networks of migrant organizations in Mexico, like Red de Organizaciones Defensoras de Migrantes (Network of Organizations for the Defense of Migrants, or REDODEM). Casa Cuc has also entered into partnerships with UNHCR and participated in international forums, including the consultation for the adoption of the Global Compact on Regular, Orderly, and Safe Migration. These alliances, necessary for the shelter's operation, are not confrontational.

But how do the state and local governments benefit from the alliances? As we have seen, at least in central Mexico, many shelters are "closed," with migrants unable to go freely in and out of the shelters unless they are ready to continue their journeys. In practice, this way of operating that many *casas de migrantes* follow in order to afford the migrants with safety has the unintended consequence of containing migrants, refugees, and asylum seekers in their facilities. Government authorities benefit by having migrants concentrated in one place, avoiding having them spread throughout the city or on the streets. Additionally, government authorities capitalize on the perception that they support humanitarian efforts.[12]

Institutionalization

"Aquí es donde rebotan los sueños" (This is the place where dreams bounce), reads a message at the border wall in Tijuana. That is the reality of many migrants once they reach the border with the United States. Facing the border wall in different regions of the northern Mexican border reminds people of the power of political systems. Surveillance systems, powerful tower lights, small monuments commemorating the passing of a migrant, ports of entry, traffic coming and going, and long lines to cross international bridges on foot are some of the city's main features. As we have seen, largely lost among that landscape everywhere along the border is a steady flow of Mexicans being deported back to Mexico, and, more recently, many asylum seekers stranded at the border, as well as a surge of IDPs from Mexican states like Guerrero, Michoacán, Morelos, and Chiapas among others.

As we have seen, at the northern border of Mexico, *casas de migrantes* have served Mexican migrants aiming to cross to the United States and have also tended to deported Mexicans as migration trends reversed. As conditions have changed, the increasing number of Central American migrants, the movement of certain groups like Haitians and Africans in 2016, and the caravans from late 2018 and early 2019 forced migrant shelters to adjust their services.[13] In 2023, after visiting different official ports of entry, I saw how *casas de migrantes* support stranded migrants waiting to enter the United States to file for asylum.[14] Shelters now serve a wide range of nationalities, including Venezuelans, Ecuadorians, Colombians, Haitians, Central Americans, and internally displaced Mexicans who have to wait for months at the US-Mexico border. In some parts of the US-Mexico border, there is a presence of people from African countries, the Middle East, and China.

NGOs, FBOs, and local organizations often fill the vacuum when governments fail to provide structures, mechanisms, and services to guarantee the welfare of vulnerable populations.[15] Migrant shelters have become institutions that provide some form of welfare, information, and safety. Institutionalization in this context means a process of state divestment of responsibilities for the welfare of migrants, refugees, and asylum seekers to NGOs and other non-state actors.[16] At the same time, migrant shelters willingly or unwillingly replace the government in caring for migrants and become the institutions where migrants and asylum seekers seek support. Inevitably, this means that shelters have become a significant part of Mexico's humanitarian architecture of migration management.

There are other circumstances in which NGOs and FBOs coexist with the government or in which the government has little participation. In the city of Ciudad Juárez, Chihuahua, which is just across from El Paso, Texas, migrants and asylum seekers find support in facilities or locations run by the local and federal government, in shelters run by faith-based and private NGOs, or in other community settings (camps and shared living arrangements). You can also find people who are seeking nonresidential assistance from NGOs and international organizations, like the many migrants who come to the cathedral in downtown Juárez for a free meal. In January 2023, out of the cathedral facilities, different faith-based groups served six hundred meals daily, primarily to Venezuelan migrants arriving in the city. People in these different contexts seek assistance from institutions to cope with their needs.

Following its rhetoric of protecting migrants' human rights, the Mexican government opened the Centro Integrador para el Migrante (CIM) "Leona Vicario" (Integration Center for Migrants "Leona Vicario") in

Ciudad Juárez in August 2019. This was the first of three governmental shelters that provided services and support for migrants during the implementation of the Migrant Protection Protocols (MPP) and Title 42. Some states and municipalities have opened shelters in different cities across the border like Mexicali, Ciudad Juárez, and Matamoros. Thus, while government-run shelters exist, the Mexican government cannot tend to the needs of all the migrant population along the Mexico-US border. Hence, FBOs and NGOs fill the vacuum left by the Mexican government.

A different case is the camps for asylum seekers and stranded migrants that have popped up in cities like Tijuana, Ciudad Juárez, Reynosa, and Matamoros. These cities are among the most dangerous in Mexico. Walking through the camp in Matamoros, Tamaulipas, one can see the pressing need for all kinds of services: sanitation, showers, water, and health. Even if there are common areas for meetings in the camp, there are usually no educational or structured activities for the many children.[17] The local government in Matamoros has not done much but team up with Doctors Without Borders to provide medical services in a small clinic at the camp. The federal and local governments have let many volunteers, especially those linked to FBOs, carry the weight of providing for some of the most pressing needs.

As noted earlier, in the Institutos Estatales de Migración, each institute has different goals depending on its location. In the case of the state of Tamaulipas, which borders the United States, the institute has an agreement with six other *casas de migrantes* to provide services for deported Mexicans, and Mexicans with legal status in the United States who are returning to visit family members in Mexico. One of the government's aims is to aid deported Mexicans as they return to their places of origin. At the reception centers located near different international bridges, migrants are rushed to make decisions about returning to their places of origin.[18] Those who cannot return immediately are offered the opportunity to stay at the shelter, although the shelter policies only allow them short stays. Migrants are not allowed to go out, and the rules pressure deported Mexicans to move quickly. Neither the government nor the shelter assesses whether or not there are particular needs or options for returning Mexicans. The shelter director in Reynosa reported that part of the reason for these rules is the high levels of violence in the region: "We want them to move quickly. Reynosa [the city where the shelter is located] is too dangerous, and they can be kidnapped or killed. The presence of drug cartels makes this place dangerous, and people can recognize if someone does not know where to go or if someone is an outsider."

During my stay at the shelter, I had to abide by a strict security code. At one point, there was a shooting, and the city was in lockdown for several hours. In this context, for some shelters, their ties and alliances with the government make them operate as part of a larger apparatus of institutionalization of services for deported migrants.

Sometimes the reach of institutions and the protection they can offer are limited, even through NGOs or humanitarian groups. Andrea was the last person I interviewed at the *casa del migrante* in Reynosa. She had been recently deported to the farthest part of the country, and she spoke about her years in the United States, her two little girls (who are US citizens), and her husband, who lived in California. She was planning to spend time with her parents in central Mexico as the family tried to figure out their next steps. Some days later, after leaving the shelter, I received a phone call from the shelter director, who asked whether I knew anything about Andrea's whereabouts. After some conversation, the director asked me to contact Andrea's husband to share any information I had about her stay at the shelter and departure.

That phone conversation was one of the saddest I have ever had; the sadness and frustration in the voice of Andrea's husband impacted me deeply. He said that Andrea was kidnapped and raped after leaving the shelter on her way to her parents' house. She was held hostage for a couple of days before being let go. There was silence between parts of my conversation with Andrea's husband, and even though I tried using a comforting tone of voice, it was difficult to know what to say at that moment.

I also learned that Andrea had returned to her family, while her husband was far away in the United States with their two children. Mexican authorities were not being held accountable because Andrea never reported the incident, since she did not trust that the government would do anything about it. Andrea's experience illustrates the institutional vacuum left by the government in the protection of migrant populations.

As much as humanitarian organizations want to fill that vacuum, some circumstances are entirely out of their reach.

Humanitarian Governance in Mexico

Casas de migrantes emerge locally but deal with transnational movements. While well-intentioned, they occasionally stretch themselves beyond what they can do well, raising questions of effectiveness and safety. Due to their critical intermediary role, they also influence the ways migration patterns are "managed" or "controlled" and enter into the politics of humanitarianism, understood as "those effects that shape the capacities of actors to determine their own circumstances and fate."[19] The politics of humanitarianism reveal the complex relationship between humanitarianism and power. Inevitably, as migrant shelters interact with the Mexican government and other international actors, *casas de migrantes* become part of the humanitarian governance of migrants. Furthermore, regardless of size, shelters exercise different forms of control and power while assisting migrants.

The interplay between migration policies, enforcement, and humanitarian work in Mexico reveals how humanitarianism is connected to governance.[20] Here, humanitarian governance refers to "the increasingly organized and internationalized attempt to save the lives, enhance the welfare, and reduce the suffering of the world's most vulnerable populations."[21] This notion does not consider particular forms of state or nonstate actors as the foundation or model for governance. It may include governmental institutions but may also encompass two political figures: one governmental and the other nongovernmental, which have concrete ways to exercise power in everyday life and become part of humanitarian ecosystems that manage migration.[22]

Even though "regimes of care" and humanitarian assistance do not intend to be about politics, but about emergencies, protection, care, and compassion, humanitarianism has come to play a more significant role in the management and governance of migrants and people in displacement.[23] For Barnett, humanitarian governance is less concerned with effectiveness and more interested in the effects of the effort to reduce human suffering. These effects might be intended and desirable, but others might be unintended and harmful. At the same time, humanitarian governance can be associated with either emancipation or domination; but without a doubt, it fosters distinct forms of power.[24] Ultimately, humanitarian governance is about the "politics of precarious lives."[25]

While the Mexican government presents itself as a humanitarian government, in practice it has left most of the work to ease migrants' precarity to *casas de migrantes* along migrant trails and borders in Mexico.[26] While the humanitarianism from below that exists in Mexico is utterly concerned with the reduction of suffering in multiple forms, the effects of its actions and efforts vary enormously. Humanitarian work in Mexico has intended and unintended consequences.[27] *Casas de migrantes* believe that they give voice to the voiceless and accompany them in search for justice and *un trato digno* (a dignified treatment). Yet undesired outcomes may emerge from a policy perspective, as shelters' work functions as an unofficially outsourced system that facilitates and sustains the mobility of migrants through Mexico. Since migration patterns in Mexico have become more complex, with multiple profiles and legal statuses, this movement could be perceived as a threat to national security in Mexico and the United States. This perception is confirmed by the heavy presence of the National Guard along migration routes and border cities in Mexico and the support given to the US Customs and Border Protection by the US National Guard at the American southern border.

Humanitarianism from below in Mexico lives within the tension of welfare and containment. On the one hand, *casas de migrantes* empower migrants to gather strength, to continue their journeys, and to rethink their trajectories. Furthermore, migrant shelters' advocacy efforts and accompaniment practices yield good results that are appreciated and valued by migrants with limited resources. Nevertheless, the different surveillance and registration practices at every shelter indicate that migrants are subject to varying levels of control.

The transient nature of migrants' presence at the shelters raises the question of how to protect the migrant population and humanitarian workers from external threatening forces that may infiltrate humanitarian spaces. The more fragile the infrastructure, rules, and internal control at shelters, the more vulnerable those occupying shelters are. The shelter in Coatzacoalcos exemplified this dilemma. Located in a very dangerous area in the town, the space had limited resources and staff. The only control was an old notebook where migrants wrote their names and identification numbers. A couple of gangs monitored the shelter, tracking people coming and going. The dilemma was apparent: while welfare was provided, migrants became easy targets for other groups, raising the question of whether the shelter was doing more harm than good.[28]

Casas de migrantes serve migrants from a position of power and control. They establish the rules, and in the humanitarian transaction, migrants, asylum seekers, refugees, and deportees have to abide by them, even when migrants may have agency and freedom to engage with those who provide services. Migrants know this power differential and engage with it on their own terms. It is important to highlight that as much good as *casas de migrantes* do, they always do it from the perspective of the provider, supporter, and advocate. They see migrants passing, coming, and going. Ultimately, *casas de migrantes* remain in their localities to provide for those migrants who will come.

The Mexican government has an ambivalent relationship with humanitarian organizations. The government has remained close to and interested in the labor of humanitarian organizations, praising their work but minimally supporting them. At the same time, federal and municipal police and the National Guard have harassed and threatened migrant shelters, like Casa Requena, which has a prominent role in defending migrants' human rights, or the soup kitchen for migrants at the cathedral in Ciudad Juárez, which has played a critical role in tending to migrants who do not stay in shelters. Through the years, humanitarian organizations in Mexico—with varying degrees of awareness and willingness—have also become tools of the state agenda. Thus, what is at stake is the issue of collaboration and complicity from humanitarian organizations and how humanitarian organizations may involuntarily serve the interests of powerful actors, particularly the state.

The Human Rights National Awards won by Father Alejandro Solalinde and Norma Romero in 2012 and 2013, as well as other human rights awards given to humanitarian organizations in different states in Mexico, have provided a platform to humanitarian organizations advocating for migrants, raised their profile, built trust with the general public, and brought migration forward in the Mexican political agenda. At the same time, they have increased the credibility of shelters as interlocutors in migration policy and provided some sense of security for *casas de migrantes* with larger public profiles. It is easier for criminal groups or the government to harass or threaten small shelters like some along the train tracks in central Mexico than bigger shelters in larger cities or with more prominent advocacy roles.

Through the years, the Mexican government has had a vested interest in presenting itself as a humanitarian government that deeply cares for the rights and welfare of people in contexts of mobility.[29] Recognizing advocates of migrants' human rights serves well the idea and the image that the government collaborates significantly with humanitarian actors and reinforces the Mexican government's human rights rhetoric. However, humanitarian organizations or shelter directors may feel pressured to back up the government or at least not openly criticize it at the risk of losing its support. Casa Villamil and Casa Portillo have strong relationships with the government and rarely criticize or challenge it. The shelter director of Casa Santos has been a strong supporter of the López Obrador administration and regularly justified the government's approach to managing migration.

While embracing euphemistic rhetoric, Mexico has become the migration enforcer of a process of US border externalization.[30] This has taken place not only through the deployment of surveillance and control but also through the deployment of the National Guard along migration routes and border towns.[31] The National Guard has been assuming policing functions and supporting migration enforcement authorities to conduct detentions along migrant routes. It has also been documented that the National Guard extorts and robs migrants regardless of their legal status.[32] In this context, the development of this humanitarianism from below in Mexico has led *casas de migrantes* to become part of Mexico's increasingly complex humanitarian architecture, which inadvertently manages, controls, and governs migration patterns.

Conclusion

Geography, leadership style, and relationships significantly shape the work of the growing humanitarian ecosystem in Mexico and the notion of humanitarianism from below. Migrant shelters are deeply humanitarian and political, and their work challenges the common notions of sheltering, aid provision, and advocacy. Due to their local nature, *casas de migrantes* across Mexico differ significantly in leadership style, size, services, and capacity. While shelters share some best practices, it is impossible to have a single model for a migrant shelter across the country. The geographical location and the changing profiles of migrant populations determine the emergence of *casas de migrantes* as places of contestation, alliance, or institutionalization in the migration process. These different ways of interacting with and engaging actors are critical in facilitating the provision of services across the country. A shelter's relationship to the federal and local governments, the local community's size, and the timing of migrants' journeys determine its ways of operation. Furthermore, *casas de migrantes* play different brokerage roles in obtaining resources or advocating for migrants' rights. How they exercise their brokerage role calls into question the possibility of living or operating under the humanitarian principles of neutrality and independence.

Seeking help in southern, central, or northern Mexico is not the same. In the south, migrants start their journey, criminal groups prey on them, and migration controls fiercely try to contain them. Responding to this context, migrant shelters contest the government, criminal groups, and even local communities to ease the violence migrants experience. Central Mexico, with its array of larger urban areas, requires alliances to provide services to populations that, at this stage, often become stranded, have been abused on many occasions, and need some respite to gather strength and continue the journey. Northern Mexico, where a fence, a wall, the river, or the desert separate migrants from the "promised land," is a violent region that can engulf any migrant, asylum seeker, refugee, deportee, or IDP. Thus, geography matters and determines the rules of engagement for the provision of welfare and safety.

The leadership style of each shelter fosters different ways of navigating diverse contexts that are constantly developing and presenting many challenges in terms of migration control and violence. Shelters are highly politicized, as are their sheltering practices. We must remember that these places are sanctioned by law and occasionally supported by the local and federal governments. Relationships with diverse actors, especially the government, may sometimes seem challenging, odd, or convenient. Still, these relationships and those with other actors and the local community are key to providing services.

By 2023, strandedness, deportation, fast turnarounds, and new arrivals at the northern border contrasted with the respite that migrants take in central Mexico on their way north. The situation at the northern border also contrasted with the contained populations in southern Mexico. These contexts always represent a challenge for the provision of welfare and advocacy for migrants' rights. Thus, migrant shelters need to engage with different actors in different ways depending on the regions where they are located. In the effort to provide support for migrants, different ways of engagement emerge in the form of practices of contestation, ambivalent alliances, and attempts to fill the institutional vacuum left by the Mexican government. Furthermore, as *casas de migrantes* navigate the politics of reducing the suffering of precarious lives, they become part of an evolving humanitarian infrastructure and ecosystem that governs migration patterns in Mexico.

Conclusion

There were folding chairs, an ambo, and a small electronic keyboard in a multipurpose room that looked extremely familiar. Over the ambo, a sign read, "Jesus the Savior." Outside, it was sunny but crisp, unsurprising since it was still January. It was 2022 and we were at a migrant shelter in Ciudad Juárez, a northern Mexico city across from El Paso, Texas. Jean Pierre and I were having a conversation about his migration journey. I leaned over to get closer and hear more clearly since we were still some distance apart because of concerns over Omicron, the latest variant in the COVID-19 pandemic. Jean Pierre told me about his journey and how he had fled Port-au-Prince and went to the Dominican Republic because of concerns for his family's safety since his father worked with one of the politicians in Haiti. He shared his pain when he received word that his father had been killed, leading to his decision to move from the Dominican Republic and go to Chile with his wife. Once there, he said, he worked several jobs to keep the family afloat; a couple of years after arriving in Chile, his family expanded to include a daughter. Trouble did not stop during those years in Chile, though; his mother was kidnapped by a gang back in Haiti. Despite the efforts from family and friends, he could only gather a third of the ransom, and just like his father, his mother was killed at the hands of criminal gangs.

In early 2021, still during the pandemic and without too much to hold onto in Chile, Jean Pierre made the difficult decision to journey north. Using public transportation, he and his family reached the now infamous Darién Gap. He could not articulate the things he saw there. "It was difficult. . . . We walked for days, and we were afraid," he said. Somehow, with the help of friends who would send money occasionally, they reached the city of Tapachula in southern Mexico. There his family was granted a visa for humanitarian reasons. During the six months the family stayed there, Jean Pierre's wife fell seriously ill, finally losing her battle with cancer. He decided to resume his journey north with their little girl. They reached Ciudad Juárez a month and a half before our conversation.

An evangelical church sponsored the migrant shelter where I met Jean Pierre. The pastor told me that they were hosting thirty-six migrants from Haiti, and eighteen of them were young children. He also shared that early in November 2021, the Mexican government sought help from an NGO in Ciudad Juárez to find shelter for the increasing number of Haitian migrants arriving in the city. The pastor responded to the call and offered the church as a shelter. He adapted and reconditioned the facilities, adding bathrooms and showers to the space. He also started to ask for donations of food and clothes to meet the needs of migrants, saying, "I have been doing this as part of my calling to serve God . . . and God has provided through the community. I spent long nights bagging rice and beans and assembling kits with supplies, but I have a family to sustain and I do not know how much longer I can sustain this work. I tell people we cannot host more people, but they continue coming. Often, because they hear from the people that are already here."

In 2020, at the beginning of the COVID-19 pandemic, El Colegio de la Frontera Norte mapped ninety shelters along the route that connected border towns between Mexico and the United States. Two trends remain significant among the surging number of humanitarian organizations serving migrants in Mexico since then: First, many of them continue having a faith-based identity, and while the Catholic Church continues running many of those, evangelical churches and other faith denominations, including Islamic ones, have emerged on the scene to fill critical needs. Second, there is a greater specialization in how *casas de migrantes* operate. There are shelters hosting women with children, shelters catering to the LGBTQI+ population, shelters receiving Haitians—who may require translation services—shelters receiving single men, shelters accepting only families, and shelters working with deportees and IDPs. With the diversity of profiles, a wide range of services and alliances have emerged. Different arrangements tend to the educational needs of children, with help ranging from international organizations like Save the Children, UNICEF, Nest Global, the Sidewalk School, and Border Youth Collective to national and local organizations like CONAFE (Comisión Nacional de Fomento Educativo) and local universities like Universidad Pedagógica Nacional (Tijuana), IBERO Tijuana, and Universidad

Autónoma de Ciudad Juárez. In addition, there is limited enrollment in local schools.

Other initiatives have addressed the need for legal services; this has been done in collaboration with many organizations on the American side that do advocacy work and provide legal services. Still, new conditions are constantly emerging, especially concerning public health (attention to infectious outbreaks, the need for clean water, bathroom facilities, safety, and lack of social spaces) and mental health. Mental health is one of the most critical needs as people remain in crowded facilities and wait for uncertain periods of time. Several of the migrants mentioned in this book had been waiting anywhere between two months and two years. In all of this, as this book has made clear, the Mexican government seemed to have left most of the responsibility to care for these migrants to all the NGOs (faith-based and non-faith-based) on the field. As of 2023, there were only three migrant shelters run by the federal government, and a few shelters run by state or municipal governments in the cities of Tijuana, Mexicali, and Ciudad Juárez, all in border towns with the United States.

While the pandemic and different migration policies brought the world to a halt, migration patterns in Mexico and the work of migrant shelters never stopped. The need for them to continue providing services became even more critical. As this book has shown, two of the main traits of "humanitarianism from below" are their ability to adapt and their local nature. These traits were critical in navigating the pandemic and all the changes that came with it. Some shelters capped their capacity and adapted procedures that allowed them to continue operating. At the same time that personnel from international organizations retreated, local staff remained to continue providing services at migrant shelters across Mexico. Migrant shelters were effectively the informal welfare system needed for migrants stranded along migration routes.

While the services provided by *casas de migrantes* remain essential, they could be better, and sometimes their role in the migration system may seem questionable; stories like those of Jean Pierre and the pastor at the migrant shelter in Ciudad Juárez illustrate the realities on the ground and the ways many organizations shape and structure humanitarianism from below in Mexico. They show how migrant shelters have become essential actors in the Mexican migration system as they provide for the needs of people in contexts of migration in increasingly complex and ever-changing ways.

By the end of 2023, the humanitarian complex in Mexico had evolved to include FBOs, NGOs, municipal and federal government agencies, and an array of INGOs working to provide diverse services to ameliorate the human costs of human mobility within and through Mexico. For decades now, the backbone of this humanitarian complex has been the many *casas de migrantes*, soup kitchens, and humanitarian pop-ups along the migration routes in Mexico. With the changes in migration patterns, the migration routes have extended to include paths through Central American countries and the Darién Gap in Panama. At the same time, the humanitarian support has also extended south of the Mexican border as local communities, FBOs, and other INGOs have responded to the needs of the increasing numbers of Venezuelans, Haitians, Colombians, Ecuadorians, and migrants from other nationalities that dare to embark on migration routes through the Darién Gap.

This book has analyzed the role of *casas de migrantes* in the migration process in Mexico, exploring their context, work, and ethos, as well as the tensions inherent to humanitarian work. The accounts shared throughout the book have illustrated the critical role of these shelters in humanitarian work in Mexico, emphasizing that their work is a kind of "humanitarianism from below" with a faith ethos and an uncanny ability to adapt to emerging patterns. However, humanitarian work in Mexico operates in a context of many levels of violence, and a political desire to manage and control human mobility. *Casas de migrantes* have become places where poverty, violence, and care converge. Through the years, inadvertently and unintendedly, migrant shelters have become part of the humanitarian architecture in Mexico.

The Convergence of Poverty, Violence, and Care

My time along migrant trails, my conversations with migrants and humanitarian workers, and my stays at different shelters showed me that poverty, violence, and care emerge as three interrelated and mutually reinforced dynamics in the migration process of Mexico. Migrants, without means to migrate in safer ways, embark on perilous journeys through Mexico. Their lack of resources makes them highly vulnerable along the road as they enter or return to a country that has increased levels of generalized violence that can be attributed to larger structural causes like endemic corruption, poverty, and the illicit drug and arms trades. Thus, a humanitarianism from below emerged as a response to migrants' vulnerability and violence. At the same time, *casas de migrantes* are also vulnerable to the increasing violence in the country.

Migrants' levels of poverty, lack of opportunities, and risk of violence in their hometowns reveal the inability of governments to foster conditions that allow people to flourish or choose to stay rather than to migrate. Migrants relying on *casas de migrantes* to sustain their migration journeys are not the poorest or destitute, but are still poor. They often start their journeys with meager resources and little certainty of what lies ahead. However, using *casas de migrantes* is only one of several strategies that they employ to cope with hardship. Some of the stories shared throughout this book illustrated that migrants using shelters are indeed poor and unable to migrate in other ways. Others showed how poor migrants rely on different strategies to cope with hardship. In this way, *casas de migrantes* appear as one of several strategies—but a critical one—in migrants' "economy of makeshifts." In the case of deportees, they return to the country in vulnerable positions. Deportees' profiles vary from those incarcerated for several years to those removed after some time in detention centers. In either case, deportees often lack immediate resources, identification documents, and the possibility of communicating with family members. Thus, many return to Mexico in precarious and highly vulnerable positions, especially during the initial moments of the aftermath of deportation. Migration patterns in Mexico are a "living matter," constantly changing, requiring diverse actors to adapt and adjust. This dynamic is illustrated by the increasing number of migrants stranded along the way or at both Mexican borders and the growing numbers of asylum seekers and refugees in Mexico.[1]

Violence appears as the larger canvas for migration and humanitarian responses in Mexico. It is a contextual dynamic for the migration process and the country. At the same time, it has attained a status of normalcy, an experience that is just part of the journey. Instances of violence occur often and at any moment. For many migrants, it could be the trigger for departure from their hometown, or they may experience violence at the hands of state and non-state actors at any point along the journey or upon return to Mexico. Migrants' comments often refer to the National Guard, migration authorities, municipal, state, and federal police, staff from bus companies, and unidentified criminal groups among the most common actors taking advantage of them along migration routes, often asking for bribes, harassing them while they are using public transportation, or chasing them when they have to walk from one town to another. Cristina recalled, "The bus left us in Nueva Rosita [a small town in the state of Coahuila, seventy miles from the border town of Piedras Negras] and we had to walk from there until Piedras Negras. Even when we paid the full price for the bus ticket. It was dark when we started walking. . . . We were coming from Monterrey. . . . Two times different groups got on the bus and asked us to get off, demanding money, taking pictures of us, and checking our documents if we wanted to continue our journey." By 2023, violence and abuses against migrants along migration routes are not only a dynamic of the route, but have become a barrier to access asylum in the United States or to find safe harbor in Mexico. Thus, it needs to be considered within the larger increase of violence in the region.[2]

Humanitarian groups in Mexico, fostered mostly by faith-based groups and local communities, have taken on the responsibility of caring for the needs of migrants, a responsibility that belongs to the Mexican government and the international community. Willingly or unwillingly, they exercise dynamics of facilitation, control, and assistance and play brokerage roles with local communities, government institutions, and other international humanitarian actors. In this way, they become migration intermediaries. And, as much as shelters work as an informal welfare system, they also serve as a form of containment for migrants along migratory paths, exercising new forms of domination and power.

Migration never happens in a vacuum. Analysis of human mobility must not be reduced simply to dichotomies like push-pull factors, sending and receiving communities, or regular versus irregular migration. On the contrary, a more comprehensive analysis of migration needs to consider other dynamics at play in the migration process, including aspirations, capabilities, agency, local development, the role of networks and cash transfers, and labor markets, among others. While the analysis of the role of casas de migrantes is positioned at the meso-level of analysis, their role in the migration process in Mexico cannot be properly understood without consideration of the role of poverty, violence, and government efforts to manage migration. Analysis of migrants' accounts of their journeys and experiences cannot be limited to heart-wrenching stories or quotes. They need to provide us with a larger picture of the different dynamics and actors at play, revealing the human costs of migration policies and containment and deterrence practices.

While the migration routes through Mexico have extended to include Central American countries and the Darién Gap, other regions and countries in the world are coping with becoming transit regions, part of smugglers' routes, or (un)desired destinations for migrants. Different migration routes, in one way or another, are gaining more visibility, such as routes in the Horn of Africa, routes in Asia that include countries like Bangladesh, Myanmar, and Malaysia, and more well-known routes through East Africa and the Mediterranean Sea.[3] For migration scholars, it is paramount that research studies contribute to understanding the interrelated dynamics and changes in migration routes and patterns at large.

In the Mexican case, the increasing violence remains one of the most significant dynamics affecting people on the move. Further studies need to explore how violence and abuses against migrants have become part of a lucrative business for different actors in Mexico and how violence interplays with human rights and restrictive migration policies or programs. Furthermore, as migration patterns continue to evolve and mobile phones have become a necessity, research on the role of information and communications technologies (ICTs), migrants' digital practices, the role of social media as a source of information, and the effects of surveillance is needed to enhance our understanding of human mobility through Mexico and the role of humanitarian actors.

Humanitarianisms, Intermediaries, and Migration Dynamics

An analysis of the role of *casas de migrantes* in the migration process of Mexico contributes to the emerging literature of humanitarian assistance in contexts of transit and return migration, which do not fit the label of "emergency."[4] What I have called "humanitarianism from below" distinguishes it from the kinds of humanitarianism provided in emergency settings, and reinforces the idea that we live in a world of humanitarianisms.[5] There are contextual and historical reasons why a "humanitarianism from below" has emerged and remained in Mexico. Comparing this type of work with other experiences of humanitarian assistance to migrants in distress, such as those in the Mediterranean, provides insight into how migration policies and context shape how humanitarian aid may emerge and unfold.[6] Nevertheless, even when problematized, humanitarian work has at its core the notion of giving a compassionate response to those suffering in precarious situations.[7] Invariably, *casas de migrantes* see themselves as resources that alleviate the suffering of migrants, refugees, or deportees.

While I was writing this book, one of my biggest concerns was to provide an in-depth analysis of how *casas de migrantes* emerge from the ground and local communities, and to highlight the faith ethos of many of many of them as well as their adaptive nature. The work, stories, and commitment of many humanitarian workers along migrant trails in Mexico have shown how this "humanitarianism from below" is deeply humane and local, with a wide range of organizational structures and strong faith-based affiliations. The notion of humanitarianism from below, as exercised in Mexico, recognizes the tireless work of many faith-based communities and other local organizations and their ability to offer resources to tend to migrants' needs. Their efforts and contributions should not be taken for granted or lightly, as they are the backbone of humanitarian work in Mexico. Removing their contributions could increase migrants' vulnerability significantly. Furthermore, *casas de migrantes* offer an interesting gendered perspective on humanitarian work, as evidenced by the many female religious congregations operating migrant shelters and female staff members and volunteers working with them.

The convergence of Mexican migration policies with their abundant humanitarian language and the shelters' process of institutionalization has led to a form of "humanitarian governance." Humanitarian governance means "the increasingly organized and internationalized attempt to save the lives, enhance the welfare, and reduce the suffering of the world's most vulnerable populations."[8] Thus, on the one hand, Mexican migration policy moves in that direction, linking humanitarian language to development and collaboration, though an implementation gap exists in the way these policies are enforced.[9] On the other hand, humanitarianism from below, as a particular form of humanitarianism that extends beyond emergency relief situations, aims to protect the welfare of others and gets involved in advocacy efforts. As shelters go through processes of professionalization and institutionalization, their operations and internal rules lead to new forms of control and domination and inevitably become part of humanitarian governance; as much as they seek to emancipate and care for the well-being of vulnerable populations, they also create new forms of power.[10]

Functions of Migration Intermediaries

The analysis of migration intermediaries has become more nuanced, so facilitation, control, and care are seen as subcategories of the so-called migration industry.[11] However, the dynamics of facilitation and control shift and blur when we analyze humanitarian work in Mexico.[12] This book has stressed an understanding of facilitation, control, and care as essential functions of migration intermediaries. These functional characteristics often overlap and may be exercised by the same actor at any time in the migration process. Thus, I have advocated for moving away from the notion of a "migration industry" in favor of the more neutral term "migration intermediaries."

Migration intermediaries may facilitate, control, and care for people in contexts of mobility. But, rather than seeing these as distinct industries or subsets of a general concept, viewing them as operations or functions of migration intermediaries provides a specific answer to the question, What do migration intermediaries do? Furthermore, it removes the emphasis on the financial gain prevalent in the migration industry literature. It also allows for including different actors in the migration process, including humanitarian actors. These functions may be singled out and highlighted as a way to analyze them. In practice, these functions are intertwined and may be exercised by migration intermediaries at different degrees and at different moments in the migration process.

There is no denying that some actors, operating as intermediaries, profit from human mobility. A clear example is the vibrant economy emerging in the Darién Gap region. My interviews with migrants along the US-Mexico border in 2022 and 2023 illuminated the challenges of crossing the Darién Gap. The migrants described paying for guide services to cross the region, recalled a system of color-coded bracelets to distinguish groups and different points of access, and mentioned that services may include boat rides, guides, and security.[13] Though the economy of mobility in the Darién Gap region remains highly visible, wire transfer companies (i.e., banks or another kind of financial institutions) have received less attention while still profiting enormously from people on the move. There is little research about the amount of money that wire service companies make from cash transfers to migrants; data are difficult to track because international wire transfers are usually compiled with the remittances that a particular country receives.

The Significance of Brokerage

This book has emphasized the need to focus on the types of relationships developed and maintained by migration intermediaries. It has demonstrated how humanitarian actors engage in different types of brokerage, each of which significantly affects the migration process. Analysis of brokerage advances meso-level theory, revealing how linking happens in the migration process. Brokerage is an understudied function of social life.[14] While sociology has a larger tradition of studying brokerage, in migration studies, brokerage has taken a back seat because the theoretical debates have been around developing the understanding of the migration industry. However, if the meso-level links micro- and macro-realities, the study of brokerage is essential to an understanding of how intermediate migration actors connect through different relationships. Hence, the analysis of the complex web of relations of diverse migration actors aids with understanding how the meso-level works.[15] Furthermore, a better sense of the context and different types of brokerage contributes to an understanding of how social mechanisms link and work.[16] An analysis of brokerage may include the types of relationships that migration intermediaries develop, how these are shaped and in which context, and what effects the linking has in the migration process. In the case of shelters in Mexico, *casas de migrantes* connect migrants (micro-level) to governmental entities, local communities, and international humanitarian actors (macro-level), revealing how meso-level actors serve as a link in the migration process.[17] Sometimes relationships and connections between migrant shelters and other actors may seem disjointed, but they still work. Casa Ceballos, in northern Mexico, received 100,832 migrants in 2023. The shelter, located in a former school, is sponsored by the local Catholic church, and the day-to-day operations are run by a female religious congregation. The shelter has collaborations with MSF (Doctors Without Borders) and has a team of lawyers and a social worker who are sponsored and supervised by another shelter in the city of Saltillo. The religious sisters at the shelter, the local community, and volunteers from the United States work together to find resources and donations to sustain the basic needs of migrants. In a way, the shelter functions as a hub where different actors come together to tend the needs of migrants. The arrangement works, but it would benefit from deeper dialogue and coordination among the actors who come to the shelter to develop a more sustainable model of attention. This example illustrates how even when shelters broker to get services, deeper collaboration is needed to foster better practices in contexts of mobility that change constantly. Hence, the insights that surface from an analysis of facilitation, control, and assistance/care in migration processes are limited if the types of relationships developed by migration intermediaries and their collaborations are not considered.

Adapt or Close

The COVID-19 pandemic brought the world to a halt. Borders closed, and human mobility seemed to slow down as nations around the globe scrambled to understand the virus and how to handle it. Along the migrant trails in Mexico, the effects of the pandemic were felt, but in different ways. While some of the movement of migrants continued, other migrants became stranded for months in different cities, and some started to return home. With increasing restrictions, changing guidelines, smaller staff, and scarce resources, *casas de migrantes* faced the dilemma of remaining open or adapting during the pandemic. The experiences of Casa Caal, a small shelter in Veracruz, run by a female religious congregation, exemplify the challenges that many *casas de migrantes* dealt with during the pandemic.

The shelter was receiving an average of four thousand migrants a month during the time before the first lockdown due to the pandemic in

March 2020. Those numbers started to decrease slowly, but seven hundred to a thousand people were still recorded as passing through the shelter in the summer months of 2020. A staff of usually around twelve people was reduced to five during the pandemic—three sisters and two volunteers, all women. The team constantly had to face the question, Do we close or do we continue? "Migrants did not believe the virus was real. Thus, that was a challenge since we needed to justify all protocols with them. We were fearful and were well aware that we could get sick. But, in the end, we could not let people on the street without services," said Sister Joanna, the shelter director.

In response, they adjusted services; while they did not let people stay at the shelter, they started providing three meals daily and streamlined the reception process. As migrants arrived, they showered, received a change of clothes, had some food, and then participated in a short interview. Sister Joanna recalled, "While social distancing was difficult among migrants, we tried to take as many protections as possible. . . . We adjusted our protocols over and over." However, the challenges were not limited to dealing with the pandemic, as migrants dealt with the same roadblocks along the journey. Sister Joanna explained some of the difficulties that the migrants faced:

> Because the train was not running regularly and public transportation was difficult, migrants walked. They arrived with their feet destroyed, covered in blisters. We had to tend to them. . . . One of the most dramatic cases we had was one of a young migrant woman who was sexually abused at home and along the road. There was a need to look for additional services for her, which was extremely difficult because everything was closed. This young woman fell from the train upon leaving, which severed her two legs. We needed to be there.

Brokering became critical in times when resources were scarce. The shelter partnered with UNHCR, Doctors Without Borders, the Red Cross, the local dioceses, and REDODEM to meet the needs of migrants. While limited, these crucial partnerships allowed the shelter to update protocols, access supplies, and connect with additional services like mental health support and hospitals. Furthermore, these partnerships were necessary to help the shelter search for solutions instead of shelter staff being faced with that responsibility on their own. "International organizations and members of the network were very supportive when the local community could not sustain us anymore. While we were the ones that remained on the ground, INGOs were attentive to our needs and requests," said Sister Joanna.

During the pandemic, migration patterns in Mexico continued to change. There was still movement toward the United States, but shelters also noticed that migrants became stranded in different cities along the migrant trails. Strandedness was much more evident at the border between Mexico and the United States because of the Migrant Protection Protocols and, later, Title 42. Nevertheless, shelters also documented a reverse movement, applying to migrants who became stranded and then decided to return to their countries of origin. Not wanting to wait anymore, they started to walk or move south. Sister Beatriz, director of Casa Sohom, in southern Mexico, explained,

> We started to notice that entire families were arriving at the shelter. We weren't sure what was happening. They were on their way to Central America. . . . Many said they did not want to wait at the border, and because they could not move, it was better to start the journey back home. . . . Thus, we needed to adapt. Longer stays were the rule, but we also adjusted the dormitories. . . . Some people were going north, but others were going south. Even more, the threat of the pandemic was always present.

Like the shelter in Veracruz, Casa Sohom regularly operated with a staff of twelve people. Having received seven thousand people a month before the pandemic, during the pandemic, the team was limited to six people: three religious sisters, the cook (who went only to prepare food), and two night guards. Revised protocols and the question about closing were ever-present issues. The challenges were even more significant when two migrants were diagnosed with COVID-19.

In February 2020, Casa Ixpertay closed its small soup kitchen next to an international bridge in northern Mexico to move to its spacious, brand-new shelter with offices, recreation areas, eighty beds, and a big dining hall. But as the pandemic hit, Casa Ixpertay staff could not use the new facilities. People enrolled in MPP and on other waiting lists were stranded there; meanwhile, deportation, removals, and expedited returns from the United States continued. People needed services despite the borders closing and the limitations during the pandemic. Thus, the shelter adapted and evolved. "We could not leave people without services. We needed to reimagine ourselves in these circumstances because we did not have volunteers. Initially, staff was limited to a handful of people," said Bernardette Fortitude, the shelter's executive director.

As a solution, Casa Ixpertay started to offer food to go. The shelter developed protocols to provide food in containers. Families or one family member would come to pick up the food. The shelter also found ways to continue providing legal services—initially over the phone and later with social distancing and adherence to safety protocols. In the later months of the pandemic, as the needs of asylum seekers became more pressing (especially for women with children), they adapted dormitories to allow some vulnerable people to remain there. The challenges and adjustments were similar to those taken by southern and central Mexico shelters. Still, the pandemic brought new opportunities for the migrant shelter as advocacy efforts moved entirely to social media and later to some in-person events in Mexico. Several campaigns were run to bring attention to the issue of people stranded at the border. The #SaveAsylum campaign and the "100 days later" initiative were two critical efforts that Casa Ixpertay was able to weave as part of its service to migrants, asylum seekers, and refugees during the pandemic.

We have seen that humanitarianism from below, at its core, is a type of humanitarianism that is deeply humane, local, and adaptable, and often has a faith-based affiliation. We have also seen that it plays a vital brokerage role in Mexico's migration process while pushing the boundaries of advocacy to promote migrants' human rights. While it seemed that the world paused, the pandemic highlighted these traits. As the world and INGOs retreated, the small staff and local communities remained on the ground. Shelters adjusted protocols and rules over and over to serve migrants and to protect staff. Since many shelters have a faith-based affiliation, those who remained on the ground were generally members of religious congregations. Many who risked their lives were religious sisters and women volunteers. Their connections and relationships with many actors allowed *casas de migrantes* to broker aid at a critical time.

Above all, the pandemic revealed how humane this humanitarianism from below in Mexico is. As shelters dealt with the pandemic and did so without a savior complex, the deeper question shelters dealt with was, Who will take care of these migrants if we stop providing services?

The ability to adapt is key in humanitarian work. As migrants' profiles change, immigration policies are implemented, and violence continues as a constant threat, new needs emerge and flexibility to provide services becomes paramount. Occasionally, INGOs have trouble keeping up with change, as their mandates, protocols, and institutional agendas sometimes do not allow them more flexibility to provide services or strengthen partnerships with migrant shelters, as in the case of UNHCR not allowing the diversion of funds tagged for school supplies to buy milk for children. "Adapt or close" is a way to say that not adapting would increase the vulnerability of people trying to make their way along migration routes in Mexico and at the border.

The Humanitarian Architecture in Mexico

Lack of recognition of a humanitarian crisis along migration routes in Mexico has prevented the development of more coordinated efforts to provide support for migrants. Larger structural dynamics like poverty, arms smuggling, the drug trade, smuggling networks, the US labor market, and generalized violence play important roles in the larger context of human mobility through Mexico. Mexico's response has been reactive and has lacked the implementation of effective migration policies and regional cooperation. The emphasis from governmental authorities and some INGOs has been on efforts to manage migration and to contain migration flows.

When we think about the architecture of migration governance, we must recognize that humanitarianism from below is part of this dynamic. As this book has argued, humanitarianism is not just a top-down process where governments and international agencies deliver aid; it is also a process where local actors emerge and, in many cases, are the first responders to distress and vulnerability. At the same time, while deeply rooted in humanitarian values of compassion for those suffering, humanitarianism from below has ambiguous effects, manifested in the tension between welfare and containment.

Undoubtedly, migration policies shape migration processes and determine who moves through territories and how they do so. Sometimes, as in the case of Mexico, policies shift from criminalizing migration to including abundant humanitarian language that guarantees safety and justice and values migration. However, if an implementation gap exists, those attributes held high in migration policy may become simply words without real impact. Occasionally, they can appear deeply contradictory due to how migration enforcement and detention actually operate.

The emergence of humanitarian actors as a response to migrants' vulnerability and contextual violence may lead to a deflection of responsibility by governments. In Mexico, NGOs and local actors have emerged to fill the gap in protection left by the government. In turn, the government has let humanitarian actors take the lead while offering minimal support other than the recognition of the work of humanitarian NGOs in migration law. Furthermore, humanitarian operations can be outsourced and stratified to tend to specific populations, such as the differentiation in care for deportees and visiting migrants with legal status in other countries.

Similarly, as humanitarian organizations become part of the humanitarian governance structure, they must be aware of how their work reshapes structures and dynamics of power and domination. In particular, *casas de migrantes* need to be mindful that their practices and regulations may risk resembling detention centers. In the case of Mexico, it may be challenging to find a general model or structure for delivering humanitarian assistance to migrants in distress. Their local nature and particular contexts preclude a unified model of service, and their differences enrich the humanitarian model and help them navigate the changing sociopolitical contexts. Nevertheless, solid organizational structures, professionalization, and implementation of best practices are essential components for the effective delivery of humanitarian assistance. Thus, NGOs must be aware of and acknowledge their limits by asking themselves when the desire to support vulnerable populations may cause harm or endanger the people they attempt to serve.

One of the biggest challenges for this humanitarianism from below is creating synergy to advance advocacy efforts. Humanitarian action requires work and resources, but efforts to aid are easily duplicated. As multiple humanitarian actors emerge, so do particular agendas and per-sonalities that dominate the landscape of humanitarian assistance. There is always the risk of losing sight of the focus of humanitarian efforts: empowering migrants and preserving their well-being.

In this book, *casas de migrantes'* role in the migration process has taken the spotlight, but this does not take away from how migrants cre-atively navigate a complicated sociopolitical arena with the hope of a better life. As I moved along migrant trails and among shelters, I was always impressed by the migrants' stories. At the same time, my appre-ciation for those who work at shelters grew more and more. I was deeply moved by the commitment of an array of volunteers from all over the world, as well as religious sisters, priests, and people in local communi-ties who generously support migrants. While writing this book, I con-stantly kept in mind people's motivations to engage with and remain in humanitarian work. Norma, the leader of Las Patronas, expressed this clearly: "These poor people are suffering, and we must do something. Let's start by cooking some food for them. . . . Migration patterns may change, but we also have to change if we want to keep aiding and sup-porting migrants in need. As long as there will be migrants in distress, there will be Patronas to tend to their suffering."

New challenges loom on the horizon as US migration policies have fostered a process of border externalization, with Mexico as the enforcer. This situation is causing increasing pressure in cities such as Tapachula, in southern Mexico, Monterrey, in northern Mexico, and even Mexico City, where many migrants are waiting or assessing their options before mov-ing forward. The capacity of migrant shelters and local communities is being tested, raising questions as to whether they can continue to provide effective support for many migrants and whether there is a limit to their capacity. The growing number of migrants from Venezuela, Haiti, Central America, and other countries who are forced to settle in Mexico as their final destination has also led to an increase in xenophobia. While organi-zations such as *casas de migrantes* are often the first point of support for migrants in the country, addressing prejudice against migrants and pro-viding opportunities for their integration cannot be solved by them alone.

Though *casas de migrantes* cannot do it all, this book has shown that they provide much-needed humanitarian support to a vast number of migrants, deportees, refugees, asylum seekers, and IDPs. Yet, due to their local emergence and their characterization as primarily faith-based organizations, they are often perceived as "charities" rather than professional humanitarian organizations, and not afforded the recognition and attention they deserve. We must reorient our understandings of what counts as humanitarian aid. In order to recognize the full ecology of migration, we need to understand not only how large institutions like UNHCR, Doctors Without Borders, or the Red Cross work, but how these smaller organizations with fewer resources do. Their local efforts play an outsized role in shaping migrants' experiences on their journeys and influencing their outcomes.

ACKNOWLEDGMENTS

Writing this book has been a long journey in which many have been great companions and supporters. As they say, "It takes a village to raise a child." Foremost, I am grateful to all the migrants, asylum seekers, and refugees who participated in interviews and conversations. I am indebted to all of you. I hope that this book gives voice to your concerns, experiences, stories, hopes, and aspirations. I wish the best for all of you. Also, I am deeply grateful to the many *casas de migrantes*, their staff, and volunteers who allowed me to explore their lives and challenges. During all these years visiting migrant shelters, I have always been impressed and inspired by the significant number of religious sisters and female staff and volunteers accompanying, serving, and advocating for migrants. They all provide a powerful gendered perspective to humanitarian work. Special thanks to las Hermanas de San José de Lyon, la Compañía de las Hijas de la Caridad de San Vicente de Paul, las Hermanas Escalabrinianas, las Hermanas de los Sagrados Corazones, las Hermanas Franciscanas Misioneras de María, las Hermanas Josefinas, las Hermanas Franciscanas de María Inmaculada, las Hermanas Misioneras de la Eucaristía, the Providence Sisters, the Sisters of Mercy, Norma Romero and Las Patronas, Gery Estrada, Lupita Serrano, Cristina Coronado, Joanna Williams, Ivonne López de Lara, Irazú Gómez, Anel Ortíz, Erika Clairgue, and many other women who work tirelessly along migration routes.

I have been privileged to have several mentors and colleagues who helped, provided feedback at different stages of this project, and sustained me all along the way. I am grateful to Hein de Haas, who patiently challenged, guided, and helped me hone my academic skills during my doctoral work, and to Agnieszka Kubal, who became a sounding board, a compass for direction, and a beacon of light in critical points during my time in Oxford. Thanks to Alexander Betts, who was always open to conversations and provided helpful insights. I am deeply grateful to

Maria Vidal de Haymes, who has been not only a mentor but also a great collaborator and friend in this journey. Also, thanks to Maryanne Loughry, who has accompanied me in different settings, providing advice, support, mentorship, and friendship.

Collaboration and conversation must be a key feature in academic work and research. During this journey, I benefited from many people's expertise, knowledge, and comments. I owe recognition for insights about my research and this project to Bridget Anderson, Mike Collyer, Julien Brachet, Elena Fiddian-Qasmiyeh, Ruben Andersson, Carlos Vargas-Silva, Sabina Alkire, Mihika Chatterjee, Sabina Barone, Noelle Brigden, Amalia Campos-Delgado, Rafael Alonso Hernández López, Priscilla Solano, Felipe Roa-Clavijo, and Richard Nolan. I thank those scholars with whom I have shared panels at different conferences, especially at LASA, ISA, and conferences on migration and theology held in Oxford. In the later stages of the project, I received significant feedback at the workshop on migration, religion, and the environment sponsored by the American University's Center for Latin American and Latino Studies (CLALS) and from my colleagues during my fellowship at the Center for US-Mexican Studies at the University of California San Diego. I genuinely appreciate these opportunities. I am also grateful to the anonymous reviewers of this book; their observations and comments helped me improve the book and recognize blind spots. I thank my colleagues at the Boston College School of Social Work for their accompaniment and support during these past years.

Thanks to Jennifer Hammer at New York University Press for believing in this project and for her patience, guidance, and helpful editing. Thanks to Maria Soriano for her watchful eye as she proofread early versions of my work. Thanks also to Jorge Picasso, who has been responsible for most of the graphic work in this book.

Conducting fieldwork along migration routes is a challenging endeavor. During my fieldwork, I benefited from the unconditional support of many who facilitated conversations, visits, volunteer opportunities, interviews, and observations. Special recognition and gratitude go to Arturo González, SJ, Conrado Zepeda, SJ, and the Servicio Jesuita a Migrantes (SJM) and Servicio Jesuita a Refugiados (SJR) teams for their support. Thanks to the Friars of the Franciscan Order (OFM), the Scalabrini Fathers and Brothers, and the many *casas de migrantes* at different Catholic dioceses in Mexico for their invaluable work for migrants, asylum seekers, and refugees. Thanks to Sister Leticia Gutiérrez Valderrama, Sor María Nidelvia Ávila, Sor María Luisa Fuentes, Sor Ligia Cámara, Sor María del Carmen Rivera, Sor Maricarmen Ramírez, Sister María de los Dolores Palencia, Sister Diana Muñoz, Sister Daryl de Guzmán, Alberto Xicoténcatl Carrasco, Father Rubén Pérez Ortíz, and Father Francisco Javier Calvillo Salazar for their commitment and support.

I am deeply grateful to the Jesuits West, who gave me the freedom, support, and encouragement to pursue my interest in migration. Ministry among migrants has become a special call within my vocation as a Jesuit Catholic priest. Thanks also to the Jesuits of the Mexican Province and the Jesuit Province in the United Kingdom for their generosity and support. Through the years, I have been blessed to live in nurturing and supportive Jesuit communities that allowed me to work on this book. Thanks to the community at Campion Hall in Oxford, the Jesuit community in Nogales, Arizona, the Jesuit community at Sacred Heart in El Paso, Texas, the Jesuit community in Brownsville, Texas, the Jesuit community in San Diego, California, and the Jesuit community at Boston College. I am genuinely grateful for your care and support. Also, many Jesuits and friends responded to requests for help and supported me during my highs and lows. Thanks to the late Brad Schaeffer, James Hanvey, James Gartland, Pat Lee, Jack Butler, and Greg Kalscheur, who have become mentors and role models in my Jesuit life. I am grateful to Adrian Danker, Jayme Stayer, Rob Marsh, Gustavo Morello, Peter Neely, Victor Yañez, Jaret Ornelas, and the late Joe Munitiz and Gerard Hughes for patiently and generously commenting or reading my work at different moments. I am also grateful to my Jesuit brothers who are my community in diaspora: Arturo Araujo, Fernando Álvarez-Lara, Christopher Duffy, Matthew Kunkel, Craig Hightower, Alberto Ares, and Victor Hugo Miranda. Also, thank you to my very close friends Peggy Haun-McEwen, Sister Immaculata Atienza, Tobias León, Guadalupe Morales, and Rogaciano Soto, whose unconditional love, support, and prayers have been invaluable all these past years.

Thank you to my family for their support during all these years. I especially thank my nieces and nephews, Adolfo, Ceci, Rebeca, Fernanda, Paola, and Andrea, for your support and encouragement. Thank you, Cecybon, for all your unconditional love and support for my mother, myself, and my family; I have no doubt that I will forever grateful to you. Thanks to my dad, Dr. Jaime Arturo Olayo Guadarrama, for his support, example, generous heart, and deep love. I am grateful to you for being a role model in my life. Te amo. Namasté.

Finally, I dedicate this book to the three most important women in my life: Li, Lina, and Mamá Chanita (La Bonita). I have no words to express how much you mean to me and how much I love each of you. I will forever be grateful to you for the freedom you gave me to live my vocation. Because of your love and example, I have become who I am today.

ABBREVIATIONS

CBP US Customs and Border Protection

CEPMH Comisión Episcopal para la Pastoral de la Movilidad Humana (Episcopal Commission for Human Mobility Ministries)

CGCSEV Coordinación General de Comunicación Social del Estado de Veracruz (Social Communication Office of the State of Veracruz)

CIDH Comisión Interamericana de Derechos Humanos (Interamerican Commission for Human Rights)

CNDH Comisión Nacional de Los Derechos Humanos México (Mexican National Commission for Human Rights)

DPMH Dimensión Pastoral de la Movilidad Humana (Pastoral Ministry of Human Mobility)

INM Instituto Nacional de Migración (National Migration Institute)

IOM International Organization for Migration

MSF Médecins Sans Frontières (Doctors Without Borders)

REDODEM Red de Documentación de las Organizaciones Defensoras de Migrantes (Documentation Network of Organizations for the Defense of Migrants)

SEGOB Secretaría de Gobernación (Mexico Department of State)

UNHCR United Nations High Commissioner for Refugees

NOTES

INTRODUCTION

1 I have changed the names of migrants and shelter directors to protect their identities. Only when the reference to a particular event is in the public domain are the
original names mentioned.

2 I have also changed the names of *casas de migrantes* to protect their privacy and
identities.

3 The terms "migrant," "refugee," and "asylum seeker" are used to describe people
who are on the move, who have left their countries and have crossed international
borders. *Migrants* are people who, for different reasons, move outside their regular place of residence across an international border, temporarily or permanently.
People considered *irregular migrants* are those who do not have the documentation required by the receiving state to remain legally within their territory, as
indicated in Article 5.b of the International Convention on the Protection of the
Rights of All Migrant Workers and Members of Their Families 1990 (UN 1990).
According to the Refugee Convention of 1951, a *refugee* is a person who has fled
their own country because they are at risk of and fear serious persecution and
human rights violations there. The risks to their safety and life were so great that
they felt they had no choice but to leave and seek safety outside their country
because their own government cannot or will not protect them. Refugees have a
right to international protection. According to the United Nations High Commissioner for Refugees (UNHCR), an *asylum seeker* is a person who has left their
country and is seeking protection from persecution and serious human rights
violations in another country, but who hasn't yet been legally recognized as a refugee and is waiting to receive a decision on their asylum claim. *Internally displaced
persons (IDPs)*, similar to refugees, are people forced to leave their hometown and
habitual place of residence due to armed conflict, generalized violence, human
rights violations, or natural or human-made disasters, and who have not crossed
an international border. See IOM, "Key Migration Terms," n.d., www.iom.int;
UNHCR, "Master Glossary of Terms," n.d., www.unhcr.org.

4 Rodríguez Chávez 2016; Pederzini et al. 2015; IOM 2012a; CNDH 2011, 5; Imaz
2011, 454; Amnesty International 2010, 5; Casillas 2008, 141–42.

5 Pederzini et al. 2015; Cave 2013; Durand 2011, 459; SEGOB 2011.

6 CONAPO, Fundación BBVA, and BBVA Research 2022; Rodríguez Chávez 2016;
IOM 2012b; CNDH 2011, 3–5; Casillas 2008, 143.

7 US Department of Homeland Security 2020.

8 On October 13, 2018, a group of Honduran migrants left San Pedro Sula in a "caravan" headed toward the United States. Traveling mostly by foot, they were fleeing violence and seeking a better life for themselves and their families. On October 19, the caravan reached Mexican territory and the group grew from hundreds to thousands, with rough estimates of between 3,000 to 7,000 migrants. Days later, a second group of approximately 1,800 Central Americans arrived at the southern Mexican border, and a third group of around 500 migrants from El Salvador also reached the Mexican border on October 30. By November 2, 2018, three groups of migrants, which included children, women, and families mostly from Central American countries, were moving through Mexico with the intention of reaching the US-Mexico border. However, the evolution of migrant caravans has taken place in conjunction with the shifting migration enforcement and political landscapes in Mexico. Movements of big number of migrants have occurred before in what was called the Viacrucis Migrante and other forms of protest against migration policies. The Viacrucis Migrantes of 2014 and 2015 were of political significance for the large mobilization of people and the tensions generated with local and federal authorities. See also Vargas Carrasco 2018; Frank-Vitale 2023; and Contreras Delgado, París Pombo, and Velasco Ortiz 2021.

9 The Migrant Protection Protocols (MPP), or "Remain in Mexico" program, was a US government program initiated in January 2019 in accordance with Section 235(b)(2)(C) of the Immigration and Nationality Act. Under MPP, the United States returned to Mexico certain citizens and nationals of countries other than Mexico seeking admission to the United States. The program stated that the Mexican government would provide them with all appropriate humanitarian protections during their stay and for the duration of their immigration proceedings. MPP applied to those migrants who arrived from Mexico by land. On June 1, 2021, during the Biden administration, the secretary of homeland security determined that the Migrant Protection Protocols should be terminated and issued a memorandum to that effect. After several legal battles and an order to reinstate the program, MPP finally came to an end on August 2022. See US Department of Homeland Security for detailed and historical information, www.dhs.gov.

10 Title 42 is an order under sections 362 and 365 of the Public Health Service Act (42 U.S.C. §§ 265, 268) issued by the US Department of Health and Human Services Centers for Disease Control and Prevention (CDC). The order suspends the introduction of certain persons from countries where a communicable disease exists. In practice, the policy effectively closed the US borders, as it explicitly banned people from entering the United States from the borders between Mexico and Canada and with the potential to be held in congregate settings by US authorities. Title 42 applied only to asylum seekers and other irregular migrants. It did not apply to US citizens, visa holders, or anyone else crossing the border from Mexico or Canada who was deemed essential. The policy prevented exercising the right to seek asylum in the United States. On May 23, 2022, the Title 42 policy

was set to end; legal battles allowed its continuous implementation. In December 2022, the order was expected to be rescinded once again. However, the Supreme Court allowed Title 42 to continue while it considered a bid by Republican state officials to keep the rules in place. Finally, after continuous legal battles, the policy came to an end on May 11, 2023.

11 According to UNHCR, the term "stranded migrant" refers to a migrant who is unable to return to their country of origin, cannot regularize their status in the country where they reside, and does not have access to legal migration opportunities that would enable them to move on to another state. The term may also refer to migrants who are stranded because of practical, humanitarian, or security reasons in the country of destination, transit, or origin preventing them from returning home while leaving them unable to go elsewhere. See UNHCR, "Master Glossary of Terms," n.d., www.unhcr.org.

12 US Customs and Border Protection 2022.

13 UNHCR 2022. See also IDMC 2021.

14 Kimball 2007; CNDH 2009, 2011; Rosales Sandoval 2013, 216–17; Sørensen 2013, 238–40; Ortega Ramírez and Morales Gámez 2021.

15 SEGOB 2013; Kimball 2007, 42–45.

16 SEGOB 2013, 2011; Solano and Massey 2022; Leutert et al. 2020; Ortega Ramírez and Morales Gámez 2021.

17 Arias and Goldstein 2010b; Ríos 2013; Zepeda Gil 2018; Perez Esparza, Johnson, and Gill 2020.

18 Casillas 2008, 143–46; Casillas 2006; CNDH 2009; Rosales Sandoval 2013, 216–17; Sørensen 2013, 238–40, 250–54.

19 Trevino-Rangel 2021.

20 Olayo-Méndez 2013, 27.

21 IOM 2012a.

22 DPMH 2012, 54–55.

23 Giorguli-Saucedo, García-Guerrero, and Masferrer 2016; Castles, de Haas, and Miller 2014; de Haas 2010; Massey et al. 2008; Skeldon 1997; Singer and Massey 1998.

24 Faist 1997, 196–203.

25 Castles, de Haas, and Miller 2014, 235; Hernández-León 2008, 24, 154; Gammeltoft-Hansen and Sørensen 2013, 3–7.

26 Gammeltoft-Hansen and Sørensen 2013; Sezgin and Dijkzeul 2013.

27 See Manenti 2012; Basok et al. 2015; Solano 2024; Doering-White 2018; and Merlín-Escorza, Davids, and Schapendonk 2020.

28 There are several monographs and edited works that have become the backbone of humanitarian literature. Barnett's *Empire of Humanity*; Didier's *Humanitarian Reason*; Wilson and Brown's *Humanitarianism and Suffering*; Barnett and Weiss's *Humanitarianism in Question*; Forsythe's *The Humanitarians*; Bornstein and Rendfield's *Forces of Compassion*; and Slim's *Humanitarian Ethics*, among others, discuss the history of humanitarianism, its philosophical and moral underpin-

nings and the inherent tensions of humanitarian assistance, as well as the notion of humanitarian governance.

29 Moorehead 1998.

30 Dunant 1939, 41, 55, 62–63.

31 Moorehead 1998; Dunant 1939.

32 Barnett and Stein 2012, 11–12.

33 Barnett 2011, 9.

34 Barnett 2011, 10; Scott-Smith 2014, 10; Forsythe 2009, 58.

35 Barnett 2011, 8.

36 Wilson and Brown 2009, 2.

37 Barnett 2011, 13.

38 For safety reasons, I used public transportation to move along migration routes. I observed migrants jump onto the train known as "La Bestia" and I saw them disembarking at other points along the route. While traveling on public transportation, I observed several times abuses from authorities against migrants, and I observed how migrants found their way to migrant shelters.

39 I formally interviewed 228 migrants (140 were in-depth interviews) and had many informal conversations with them. I also interviewed 32 shelter directors, several staff members and volunteers, and stakeholders (mostly migration authorities). While living in or visiting shelters, I conducted over four thousand hours of participant observation and took multiple field notes.

40 According to the US Customs and Border Protection website, "CBP One™ is a mobile application that serves as a single portal to a variety of CBP services. Through a series of guided questions, the app will direct each user to the appropriate travel or trade services based on their needs." See www.cbp.gov. In January 2023, aside from other services, CBP One started to facilitate the safe and orderly arrival of noncitizens seeking an exception from the Title 42 public health order based on an individualized assessment of vulnerability. In May 2023, once the Title 42 public health order was no longer in place, the scheduling mechanism has been available for those people who seek to make asylum claims. Through the CBP One app, people are able to schedule a time to present themselves at a port of entry for inspection and processing. Those who use this process will generally be eligible for work authorization during their period of authorized stay. After changes, adjustments, and many updates to the app, by August 2023, the app facilitated the allocation of 1,450 appointments per day for people to present themselves at one of the eight ports of entry along the US-Mexico border.

41 Paerregaard 2008, 22; Gupta and Ferguson 1997, 8–11; Olwig 2003, 796–98; Urry 2007; Schapendonk 2009; Brachet 2012b.

42 Collyer 2007, 670–71; de Haas 2010; Brachet 2012a, 92.

43 Marcus 1995, 97.

44 Khosravi 2010.

45 Carling 2010; Werbner 1999.

46 Xiang 2007; Olwig 2003.

47 Brachet 2012b, 94.
48 Paerregaard 2008, 22.
49 Salazar, Elliot, and Norum 2017; Urry 2007.
50 Schapendonk and Steel 2014, 296–300; Andersson 2017, 90.
51 Hein, Evans, and Jones 2008, 1266; Brachet 2012b, 92–98.
52 Andersson 2017.

CHAPTER 1. THE CHANGING PATTERNS OF MIGRATION IN MEXICO AND ITS VIOLENT CONTEXT

1 UPM (Unidad de Política Migratoria) 2019, 2020, 2021, 2022.
2 In this book, I use interchangeably the terms "irregular," "undocumented," and "unauthorized" to refer to those migrants who have not entered the country through an authorized port of entry. Following Kubal (2013) and others, I avoid using the term "illegal" because I side with scholars and humanitarian organizations stating that acts can be "illegal," but not people.
3 These statistics are a compilation of those available from 2016 to 2018 through the UPM in Mexico.
4 Olayo-Méndez 2018.
5 UPM 2023. According to Mexican government officials from the Instituto Nacional de Migration (INM) and researchers (see Yates 2019 and Yates and Bolter 2021), in the last decade, migration patterns in Mexico have continued diversifying to include more than one hundred nationalities. See also CONAPO, Fundación BBVA, and BBVA Research 2022.
6 COMAR 2023. See also CONAPO, Fundación BBVA, and BBVA 2017, 2022.
7 CONAPO, Fundación BBVA, and BBVA Research 2022; UPM 2021, 2022.
8 IOM 2017.
9 UNHCR 2022.
10 Casillas 2008.
11 Rodríguez Chávez 2014; Sørensen 2013, 238–39.
12 Hagan 2006, 1554–61; Sørensen 2013, 246–47.
13 CNDH 2009; Rosales Sandoval 2013, 216–17; Sørensen 2013, 238–40; Rodríguez Chávez, 2016; Vogt 2017.
14 Morton 2012; H. Rodríguez 2016.
15 Amnesty International 2017, 250–54; H. Rodríguez 2016; CIDH 2015.
16 Wurtz 2020; Chávez 2019.
17 Casillas 2008.
18 Brigden 2018; Nevins 2018.
19 Casillas 2008, 148.
20 Hamilton and Chinchilla 1991; Sørensen 2014, 46.
21 Sørensen 2014, 46–47; Casillas 1992, 8.
22 Hamilton and Chinchilla 1991; Casillas 1992, 11–15; Sørensen 2014, 46; Alba and Castillo 2012, 8–9.
23 Sørensen 2014, 47.

24 Babich and Batalova 2021.

25 Stoney and Batalova 2013; Sørensen 2014, 47; Casillas 1992, 12–13.

26 Castillo 2003, 2008; Sørensen 2014, 53–56.

27 Pons 2021.

28 Rodríguez Chávez 2014; Sørensen 2013, 239–43.

29 Casillas 2008, 141.

30 Rodríguez Chávez 2014, 4–6.

31 See the monthly bulletins from the Instituto Nacional de Migración (INM), www
.politicamigratoria.gob.mx.

32 US Department of Homeland Security 2019.

33 Montoya Ortiz and González Becerril 2015.

34 Casillas 2008, 143; CNDH 2009, 2011; Rodríguez Chávez 2016; US Department of
Homeland Security 2019, 2022. Also see the CBP "Nationwide Encounters" page
in its Newsroom section, www.cbp.gov.

35 Rosenblum et al. 2014; Gandini, Lozano-Ascencio, and Gaspar Olvera 2015.

36 Stumpf 2006, 10; Hartry 2012, 6.

37 Menjívar and Abrego 2012.

38 Isacson, Meyer, and Davis 2014; Martínez, Slack, and Martínez-Schuldt 2018.

39 Sládková 2016.

40 REDODEM 2015, 2016, 2017, 2018, 2019.

41 Cornelius 2018; Faret, Téllez, and Rodríguez-Tapia 2021; Solano and Massey 2022.

42 See Torre Cantalapiedra and Mariscal 2020; Gandini, Fernández de la Reguera,
and Narváez 2020; Torre Cantalapiedra 2021; and Correa-Cabrera and Koizumi
2021.

43 US Department of Homeland Security 2023. Also see the CBP "Nationwide Encounters" page in its Newsroom section, www.cbp.gov.

44 IOM explains that "mixed migration" is a relatively new term seeking to capture
the intertwined and multifaceted drivers of movement of all people, regardless of
status. It refers to "cross-border movements of people, including refugees fleeing
persecution and conflict, victims of trafficking and people seeking better lives and
opportunities." See IOM, "Mixed Migration," last updated February 21, 2022, www
.migrationdataportal.org.

45 Salazar and Álvarez Lobato 2018; Cazabat and O'Connor 2021, 93; UNHCR 2022.
See also IDMC 2022.

46 INEGI 2022; see also UNHCR 2022.

47 Menjívar 2014; Campos-Delgado 2021a.

48 REDODEM 2016, 69–72; Díaz Prieto 2016.

49 Herrera-Lasso and Artola 2011, 11; Olayo-Méndez 2017.

50 Sin Fronteras IAP 2013.

51 Casillas 2008, 145–46.

52 INM 2016a.

53 Ruiz Soto 2020.

54 SEGOB 2019.

55 Ortega Ramírez and Morales Gámez 2021.
56 Ortega Ramírez and Morales Gámez 2021; de la Fernández de la Reguera Ahedo 2023.
57 Ruiz Soto 2020. See UNHCR, "Master Glossary of Terms," n.d., www.unhcr.org.
58 Koulish and van der Woude 2020.
59 SEGOB 2016.
60 INM 2022.
61 A port of entry is a place where one may lawfully enter a country. International airports are usually ports of entry, as are road and rail crossings on a land border, and major seaports.
62 INM 2016b.
63 INM 2016b.
64 Schuster and Majidi 2015; Martínez-Saldaña 2003.
65 Campos-Delgado 2021a.
66 Casillas 2008, 143–46; Casillas 2006; CNDH 2009; Rosales Sandoval 2013, 216–17; Sørensen 2013, 238–40, 250–54.
67 Kerwin and Martínez 2024.
68 Sanchez 2017, 18–19.
69 Sanchez 2017, 19; see also Boyce, Banister, and Slack 2015; Rivera Sánchez 2015.
70 Bourgois 2001, 2004.
71 Scholars have used the term "violent pluralities" to indicate that the increase of violence in Mexico is due to different groups, including organized crime, drug cartels, and criminal gangs, striving to preserve their particular agendas. Their goal is not to overtake the state, but rather to constrain its intervention so the groups can continue their illicit operations. Often these groups collude with government officials and local police. See Arias and Goldstein 2010b; Santamaría 2015.
72 Skeldon 1997, 8.
73 DPMH 2012.
74 Castillo 2003; Hagan 2008, 162.
75 Manenti 2012, 42; DPMH 2012, 39.
76 Peters 2016; Semple 2016; Tourliere 2016.
77 Hagan 2006; DPMH 2012.
78 Vogt 2018, 113; DPMH 2012, 91.
79 Balaguera 2018; DPMH 2012, 34.
80 DPMH 2012, 34–35.
81 DPMH 2012, 35.
82 Wilson and Brown 2009, 2.
83 US Department of Homeland Security 2022.
84 Without a doubt, US immigration policies play a key role in the migration processes in Mexico. Two books offering deep accounts regarding the evolution of US immigration policies and their effects are *Impossible Subjects*, by Mae M. Ngai (2014), and *The Deportation Machine*, by Adam Goodman (2020). *The Shadow of*

the Wall, edited by Jeremy Slack, Daniel E. Martínez, and Scott Whiteford (2018), offers an in-depth overview of the interplay between cross-border migration and the migration policies at the US-Mexico border.

85 Rigoni 2007, 1; Anguiano and Trejo Peña 2007, 51; Meyer and Brewer 2010, 5.

86 Taylor 2022; Miraglia 2016.

CHAPTER 2. HUMANITARIANISM FROM BELOW

1 On March 28, 2023, a fire broke out at a detention center in Ciudad Juárez, a Mexican northern border city. At least thirty-eight migrants from Central and South America died due to the lack of safety procedures and negligence of migration authorities. To honor the victims in the fire, I have changed migrant shelters' names using some of the last names of migrants who died in the event.

2 Olayo-Méndez 2013; Coubès, Velasco, and Contreras 2020.

3 DPMH 2012, 54–55.

4 DPMH 2012, 87-88.

5 Gutiérrez 2016.

6 CEPMH 2003, 1.

7 See Portes and Rumbaut 2014, 20–21.

8 CEPMH 2003, 2–3.

9 DPMH 2012, 54.

10 DPMH 2012, 54.

11 DPMH 2012, 52–60; CEPMH 2004.

12 The DPMH (Dimensión Pastoral de la Movilidad Humana) is an organizational branch of the Mexican Bishops' Conference. Its name has had different iterations, including DEPMH (Dimensión Episcopal de la Pastoral de la Movilidad Humana), and CEPMH (Comisión Episcopal de la Pastoral de la Movilidad Humana). The branch is led by a bishop who is elected every three years, with the possibility of reelection for a second term. See also DEPMH, "¿Quiénes Somos?," n.d., https://depmh.org; and CEPMH 2004, 5.

13 CEPMH 2004, 5–6.

14 DPMH 2012, 43.

15 DPMH 2012, 55.

16 DPMH 2012.

17 DPMH 2012, 55–56.

18 DPMH 2012.

19 Guzmán Elizalde 2014.

20 Goodman 2020, 179–80.

21 CNDH 2009, 5–6.

22 Meyer and Brewer 2010, 2.

23 DPMH 2012, 55–56.

24 DPMH 2012, 55–56.

25 Arias Muñoz and Carmona Arellano 2012; Imaz 2011; SEGOB 2011.

26 SEGOB 2011, 25.

27 Coubès, Velasco, and Contreras 2020.

28 Vogt (2018) and Brigden (2018) stress the importance of considering the interactions between migrants and shelters within the larger migration process in Mexico. Migration processes encompass not only migrants' experiences and decision making (agency), but also the formal and informal organizations (structures) that they interact with during their migration trajectories, as well as the migration policies that aim to manage migration movements. See Emirbayer and Mische 1998; and Bakewell 2010.

29 Casillas 2011, 528.

30 DPMH 2012.

31 Adapted from Rincón Gabourel 2018, 196–99.

32 IOM 2022.

33 Diamond et al. 2020; Soria-Escalante et al. 2022.

34 DPMH 2012, 34.

35 Slim 2015, 12.

36 Martin, Weerasinghe, and Taylor in their edited volume *Humanitarian Crises and Migration* (2014, 5–7) state that a "'humanitarian crisis' refers to those situations in which there is a widespread threat to life, physical safety, health or basic subsistence that is beyond the coping capacity of individuals and the communities in which the reside. Humanitarian crises may be triggered by events or processes, and can unfold naturally, in combination with anthropogenic factors and/or through human accident or ill will. Hurricanes, cyclones, tsunamis, earthquakes, epidemics and pandemics, nuclear and industrial accidents, 'acts of terrorism', armed conflict, environmental degradation, drought, famine, other climate change impacts, and situations of generalized violence and political instability are all potential triggers." Furthermore, they emphasize that generally there are underlying structural factors or stressors like weak local and national governance, emergency preparedness, poverty, human rights violations, inadequate access to basic services, among others, which may contribute to or perpetuate such crises.

37 Many INGOs involved in migration issues in Mexico (Red Cross, UNHCR, HIAS, Save the Children, MSF, and others) have specific agendas (protection of minors or women, attention to asylum seekers, mental health services) and regional foci. Often their interventions are outsourced with local agencies or through projects at particular institutions. Also, as when the context presents difficulties or challenges that may seem unsurmountable, INGO staff will leave and occasionally provide material support. See also Bakewell 2000, 105.

38 Linde 2009, 572–77; see Scott-Smith 2016, 19.

39 See Barnett and Stein 2012.

40 OCHA 2022.

41 Calhoun 2010, 48; see also Barnett 2005, 726.

42 McAdam 2014b, 2014a.

43 Wilson and Brown 2009, 3–4.

44 See UNHCR 2021, 2022.

45 Barnett 2005, 727, 733–34.
46 Horst, Lubkemann, and Pailey 2016.
47 Barnett 2005, 727.
48 Calhoun 2010, 54.
49 Rieff 2002, 88.
50 Barnett and Weiss 2008b, 4.
51 Calhoun 2008, 73; Bornstein and Redfield 2010, 5.
52 Barnett 2011, 10.
53 Wilson and Brown 2009, 1–28; Donini 2010; Ticktin 2011; Barnett 2011.
54 Pallister-Wilkins 2022; Carruth 2021; Refugee Hosts, n.d.; Vandevoordt 2019; Sandri 2018; Hilhorst 2018; Rozakou 2017. See also Bakewell 2000.
55 Pallister-Wilkins 2022, 112–13.
56 Carruth 2021, 29.
57 Carruth 2021, 30.
58 Refugee Hosts is an interdisciplinary AHRC-ESRC funded research project, which aims to improve our understanding of the challenges and opportunities that arise in local responses to displacement, both for refugees from Syria and for the members of the communities that are hosting them in Lebanon, Jordan, and Turkey. See https://refugeehosts.org. See also Fiddian-Qasmiyeh, Ager, and Greatrick 2021.
59 Hilhorst 2002, 199. See also Prakash et al. 2020; Larson and Foropon 2018; and Jones and Ryan 2002.
60 Angulo-Pasel 2022a, 731–32.
61 Parker and Vaughan-Williams 2012, 729; Yuval-Davis, Wemyss, and Cassidy 2017; Angulo-Pasel 2022b.
62 Bornstein and Redfield 2010, 17; Fiddian-Qasmiyeh, Rowlands, and Greatrick 2021.
63 Bornstein and Redfield 2010, 17; Fiddian-Qasmiyeh, Rowlands, and Greatrick 2021.
64 Laqueur 2009, 39.
65 Fiddian-Qasmiyeh, Rowlands, and Greatrick 2021; Carpi and Fiddian-Qasmiyeh 2020; Ager and Ager 2015.
66 Barnett and Stein 2012, 12.
67 Rieff 2002, 57; Barnett and Stein 2012, 12.
68 Christoplos 1998.
69 Christoplos 1998, 1. See also Donini 2010; and Ager and Ager 2015.
70 Barnett 2012, 202; Fiddian-Qasmiyeh, Rowlands, and Greatrick 2021; Carpi and Fiddian-Qasmiyeh 2020; Ager and Ager 2015.
71 Wurtz and Wilkinson 2020.
72 Castro 2015.
73 Calderón Chelius 2006, 2016.

CHAPTER 3. FERTILE GROUND

1 Lunn 2009, 937.
2 Wilkinson 2018.
3 Casillas 2011; M. T. Rodríguez 2016.

4 Casillas 2011.

5 Forment 2013.

6 For an overview of the Reformation period, see Lira and Staples 2010; and Hamnett 2022.

7 Forment 2013, 100.

8 Forment 2013, 101–4.

9 Forment 2013, xvi.

10 For more information on these periods of Mexican history, see Velásquez García et al. 2010.

11 Forment 2013, 99–106.

12 Forment 2013, 119.

13 Forment 2013, xii.

14 Cornelius 2018; Delgado Wise and Márquez Covarrubias 2007.

15 Hernández 2010, 151–90.

16 Orozco and Lapointe 2004; Bada 2014.

17 Baggio 2008. See also Pontifical Council, *Instruction: Erga Migrantes Caritas Christi*.

18 Pontifical Council, *Instruction: Erga Migrantes Caritas Christi*, 20.

19 Second Vatican Council, *Gaudium et Spes*, 63–66; 84.

20 Second Vatican Council, *Gaudium et Spes*, 87.

21 Pontifical Council, *Instruction: Erga Migrantes Caritas Christi*, 21.

22 More information on these messages up to 2022 can be found at the website of the Holy See Press Office, "World Day for Migrants and Refugees," n.d., https://press .vatican.va.

23 The idea of "irruption of the poor" has its roots in the 1940s and 1950s, when industrialization and the consolidation of urbanization in Latin American cities created a movement (migration) from rural areas to the cities. The cities' inability to respond to the demands of newcomers created belts of poverty around them. That is when the poor "irrupt" into the consciousness of the communities in the city and challenge their way of life.

24 Campese 2012.

25 Kevin F. Burke, as cited in Campese 2012, 6.

26 Robert J. Schreiter, as cited in Campese 2012, 18–19.

27 Campese 2012, 20.

28 Rieff 2002, 67.

29 Davey 2012, 4.

30 Fiddian-Qasmiyeh and Pacitto 2016, 2.

31 Guterres 2012.

32 Ager and Ager 2015, 3.

33 Ager and Ager 2015, 3.

34 Ager and Ager 2015, 9.

35 Slim 2003.

36 Pacitto 2012.

37 Fiddian-Qasmiyeh 2015.
38 Ager and Ager 2011.
39 Ferris 2011, 610; Ager, Fiddian-Qasmiyeh, and Ager, 208; Fiddian-Qasmiyeh and Ager 2013, 9.
40 Fiddian-Qasmiyeh and Pacitto 2016.
41 Agier 2010, 29; Fiddian-Qasmiyeh and Pacitto 2016.
42 Ferris 2005, 325.
43 Haynes 2019; Carpi 2018; Ager, Fiddian-Qasmiyeh, and Ager 2015; Calderón Chelius 2016.
44 Fiddian-Qasmiyeh and Ager 2013.
45 Fiddian-Qasmiyeh and Pacitto 2016.
46 Fiddian-Qasmiyeh and Ager 2013; Pacitto 2012.
47 Ager and Ager 2015, 13.
48 Fiddian-Qasmiyeh and Pacitto 2016.
49 Ager and Ager 2015, 23; see also Hagan 2008.
50 Barnett 2011, 17–18.
51 Wilson and Brown 2009, 1.
52 Barnett and Stein 2012, 4–5.
53 Basok et al. 2015; Calderón Chelius 2016. Casillas (2011) offered a short analysis of the faith dimension of shelters operating in Mexico and explained the role it plays in the migration process.
54 Ferris 2011, 607. See also Occhipinti 2015.
55 Scott 2003, 3; see also Fiddian-Qasmiyeh 2011; Bielefeld and Cleveland 2013; and Ehrkamp and Nagel 2012.
56 Clarke and Jennings 2008, 6.
57 Scott 2003, 1–2.
58 Wilkinson 2018.
59 Occhipinti 2015; Clarke and Ware 2015; Bielefeld and Cleveland 2013; Clarke 2006.
60 Occhipinti 2015, 335–36; Bielefeld and Cleveland 2013, 446–47.
61 Fiddian-Qasmiyeh 2011.
62 Ferris 2011, 607.
63 See Ager, Fiddian-Qasmiyeh, and Ager 2015.
64 Fray Rubén, former shelter director of Casa Rojche.
65 Barnett and Stein 2012, 21.
66 Hopgood and Vinjamuri 2012, 43.
67 See Bobes 2017.
68 Aboites and Loyo 2010.
69 See Bobes 2017; París Pombo and Müller 2016; and Casillas 2021.

CHAPTER 4. AN INFORMAL WELFARE SYSTEM ALONG MIGRATION ROUTES

1 Skeldon 1997, 8; de Haas 2007, 10; Sørensen 2013, 246; Andersson 2014, 20; Van Hear 2014; see also de Haan and Yaqub 2010.

2 Skeldon 1997, 164.
3 Skeldon 1997, 8.
4 Andersson 2014; Kastner 2013; Sutter 2013.
5 Sládková 2016; Sørensen 2013; Basok et al. 2015; Solano 2024.
6 My sample size consisted of 160 individuals who responded to the MPI question-naire.
7 Quang and Thu 2015; UNDP 2014, 2–3; Alkire and Shen 2017.
8 Skeldon 2002.
9 Skeldon 2002, 71.
10 During the time I spent along migrant trails, I found that migrants left their coun-tries with a median of USD 114 for the whole journey.
11 Literature on poverty and livelihood strategies has discussed the ample dexterity of women as they find ways to make ends meet, especially with little savings or other sources of income. See Edin and Lein 1997; González de la Rocha 1994.
12 Hagan 2008; Basok et al. 2015; Mainwaring and Brigden 2016.
13 Hufton 1974, 15.
14 See B. Anderson 2013.
15 King and Tomkins 2003.
16 Anderson and Walker 2016, 11.
17 Anderson and Walker 2016.
18 Innes, King, and Winter 2013, 1–28.
19 Castles, de Haas, and Miller 2014, 40; de Haas 2010, 1590; Faist 2000.
20 Barrett 2003, 200; Innes 1996, 142.
21 Portes 1998; Faist 2000.
22 Casillas 2006; Vogt 2018, 198–200.
23 Mauss 1973, 70.
24 See De León 2013.
25 Mountz 2004, 328.
26 Hansen and Stepputat 2005, 13.
27 H. Johnson 2012, 118–19.
28 Wurtz 2020.
29 Lees 1998.
30 Van Leeuwen 1994, 606, 611.
31 Lees 1998, 2.
32 Lees 1998, 6–7.
33 See Carney 2021; Della Porta and Steinhilper 2021; Pallister-Wilkins 2022; and Solano 2024.
34 See King and Tomkins 2003; Hufton 1974; Innes 1996; van Leeuwen 1994, 2013; and Lees 1998, 6.
35 King and Tomkins 2003, 6; van Leeuwen 2013, 180; Jones 1996, 57; Lees 1998, 11.
36 King and Tomkins 2003, 16; Hufton 1974, 201; van Leeuwen 2013, 178; Head-König 2013, 153.
37 King and Tomkins 2003, 2.

38 Innes 1996, 142; B. Anderson 2013, 14.
39 Innes 1996, 142–43.
40 King and Tomkins 2003, 2, 6.
41 Van Leeuwen 1994; Jones 1996; King and Tomkins 2003.
42 Baldock et al. 2012, 20–21.
43 Greve 2008; Baldock et al. 2012, 20–21.
44 Baldock et al. 2012, 20–21.
45 N. Johnson 1999, 22; Baldock et al. 2012, 28; Powell 2007, 2–3; Dobbs and Levitt 2017.
46 Sabates-Wheeler and Feldman 2011; Faist 2013; Faist et al. 2015; Bilecen and Barglowski 2015; Levitt et al. 2016; Dobbs and Levitt 2017, 3.
47 MacAuslan and Sabates-Wheeler 2011, 62.
48 MacAuslan and Sabates-Wheeler 2011, 62.
49 Faist et al. 2015, 194–95; Levitt et al. 2016, 2–6; Bilecen and Barglowski 2015, 204.
50 Sabates-Wheeler and Devereux 2008, 70. Stephen Devereux is a development economist at the Institute of Development Studies in the United Kingdom.
51 Levitt et al. 2016; Boccagni 2017.
52 Martínez-Schuldt 2020.
53 Ryndyk, Suter, and Odden 2021.
54 Levitt et al. 2016, 2; see also Dobbs and Levitt 2017.
55 Levitt et al. 2016.
56 Faist 2013.
57 Bilecen and Barglowski 2015, 207; Faist 2013.
58 Arskey and Glendinning 2007, 108; Bilecen and Bargloswki 2015, 207.
59 Sabates-Wheeler and Feldman 2011, 22; Faist et al. 2015, 196.
60 Sabates-Wheeler and Feldman 2011; see also Levitt et al. 2016.
61 Faist et al. 2015.
62 Faist et al. 2015, 201.

CHAPTER 5. BROKERS OF AID

1 Castles, de Haas, and Miller 2014, 235.
2 Hernández-León 2008, 28, 154; see also Hernández-León 2013, 25.
3 Hernández-León 2008, 154. See also Harney 1977, 45; and Massey et al. 2008, 44.
4 Hernández-León 2013, 24–44.
5 Spener 2009.
6 Gammeltoft-Hansen and Sørensen 2013, 6–7.
7 Merlín-Escorza, Davids, and Schapendonk 2020.
8 Gammeltoft-Hansen and Sørensen 2013; Andersson 2014; Cuttitta 2017; Schapendonk 2018.
9 Gammeltoft-Hansen and Sørensen 2013.
10 Marchand 2021; Magallanes-Gonzalez 2020; Merlín-Escorza, Davids, and Schapendonk 2020; Newell, Vannini, and Gomez 2020; Schapendonk 2018.
11 Gammeltoft-Hansen and Sørensen 2013, 10; see also Hernández-León 2013.
12 Spener 2009, 10.

13 Spener 2009, 9; Spaan and Hillmann 2013, 68–69; Cranston, Schapendonk, and Spaan 2017.
14 Faist 2014a, 3.
15 Stovel and Shaw 2012, 141.
16 Gould and Fernandez 1989, 91.
17 Faist 2014b, 39; Alpes 2017, 265.
18 Faist 2014b, 41.
19 Alpes 2017, 265.
20 McAdam, Tarrow, and Tilly 2001, 26.
21 McAdam, Tarrow, and Tilly 2001, 26.
22 Faist 2014a.
23 Faist 2014b, 40.
24 Spiro, Acton, and Butts 2013, 131–32.
25 Stovel and Shaw 2012, 142–43; see also Gould and Fernandez 1989, 92–93.
26 Gould and Fernandez 1989, 93–94.
27 For an analysis of the intermediary role of faith-based organizations in a different context, see Kraft and Smith 2019. They offer an analysis of the delivery of aid to Syrian refugees in Jordan and Lebanon by FBOs.
28 Brachet 2005.
29 Ager, Fiddian-Qasmiyeh, and Ager 2015; Horst 2006; Koizumi and Hoffstaedter 2015.
30 Doering-White 2018; see also Mol 2008.
31 Fassin 2010.
32 Cooley and Ron 2002.
33 Harrell-Bond, Voutira, and Leopold 1992.
34 James 2022.
35 Bakewell, Kubal, and Pereira 2016, 7–8.
36 Christoplos 1998, 2–3.

CHAPTER 6. BETWEEN WELFARE AND CONTAINMENT
1 Fassin 2012; İşleyen 2018.
2 Scott-Smith 2016; Agier 2011; Pallister-Wilkins 2020, 2018, 116–17.
3 Harrell-Bond, Voutira, and Leopold 1992.
4 Hilhorst 2002, 205.
5 Hilhorst 2002, 205; Angulo-Pasel 2022a.
6 Harrell-Bond, Voutira, and Leopold 1992.
7 See Balaguera 2018.
8 Barnett 2011, 12; see also Hernández-León 2013, 34.
9 Pallister-Wilkins 2015, 64; De Genova 2010; Nyers 2003; Willen 2007.
10 INM 2014a, 2014b.
11 See Chapter VII, Articles 114–125 in the Migration Law (SEGOB 2011). Campos-Delgado (2023) offers a deeper discussion on the use of euphemistic rhetoric in Mexican migration politics.

12 Coutin 2010.

13 See Slack 2019; J. Anderson 2015; Rocha Romero and Ocegueda Hernández 2013; and Rivera Sánchez 2015.

14 Susan Bibler Coutin, a sociocultural anthropologist, has described the restrictions of movement and activities that deported Salvadorans experience in El Salvador. She explains how Salvadoreans become foreigners in their own land. This echoes the reality of deportees in Mexico. See Coutin 2010, 206.

15 Casillas 2008.

16 Isacson, Meyer, and Davis 2014.

17 Fan 2008; Cornelius and Salehyan 2007.

18 See also McNevin 2010.

19 Agier 2011, 4.

20 Barnett and Weiss 2008a, 38–40; Barnett 2005, 734.

21 Barnett and Weiss 2008a, 39.

22 Titterton 1992, 5.

23 Sabates-Wheeler and Devereux 2008, 70.

24 B. Anderson 2013, 13.

25 Innes, King, and Winter 2013, 1–3.

26 Lees 1998, 29; Landau 1988, 409; van Leeuwen 2013, 186–89.

27 Pallister-Wilkins 2015; see also Chkam 2016.

28 US Customs and Border Protection 2023.

29 During several months in 2023 and 2024, as part of a research project exploring migrants' digital practices, I visited the Mexican cities of Tijuana, Mexicali, Nogales, Ciudad Juárez, Nuevo Laredo, Piedras Negras, Reynosa, and Matamoros, all located along the Mexico-US border. During these visits, I observed the most recent developments in migration patterns in Mexico and the ways *casas de migrantes* and other humanitarian actors have dealt with the most recent surge of migrants.

30 Coubès, Velasco, and Contreras 2020; Bermudez Tapia 2023.

31 Bermudez Tapia 2023; Minca 2015.

32 Davies, Isakjee, and Dhesi 2017.

33 París Pombo 2021.

34 Candiz and Bélanger 2018; Jasso Vargas 2021; Gil Everaert 2020.

35 REDODEM 2020.

36 Cwerner 2001; Schapendonk et al. 2020; Fee 2022.

37 Gil Everaert 2020.

38 Auyero 2012; see also Gil Everaert 2020.

39 Auyero 2011.

40 Schewel 2020.

41 Fee 2022.

42 Gil Everaert 2020, 4335.

43 Barnett 2011, 11–12.

44 See Donini 2010, S223; Barnett 2011.

CHAPTER 7. CONTESTATION, ALLIANCE, AND INSTITUTIONALIZATION

1　Tim Cresswell (2014) offers a good, short introduction to the role of place in social processes. Also, Deborah Martin (2013) explores the role of space in the practice and construction of politics.

2　I present these ways of engagement as a typology and in relation to geography. However, this should not limit the analysis of *casas de migrantes'* relationships across Mexico. *Casas de migrantes* in different regions may have a different way of engagement to the ones I offer to guide the analysis. Some shelters may even have a mix of styles to engage with different actors.

3　See Martínez and Camacho 2014.

4　Tyler and Marciniak (2013); McNevin (2006); De Genova and Borcila (2011); and Sigona (2015) offer analyses of these particular movements.

5　See Vargas Carrasco 2018 for a deeper analysis of the Viacrucis Migrante as a social movement.

6　Gandini, Fernández de la Reguera, and Narváez 2020. The Colegio de la Frontera Norte in Mexico has additional publications regarding the development and outcomes of the migrant caravans in Mexico.

7　Slack et al. 2016.

8　Nail 2015.

9　De Genova (2017), Kron (2016), and Gandini, Fernández de la Reguera, and Narváez (2020) offer different accounts of migrants' experiences and expressions of resistance in the United States and in Mexico.

10　See Larrauri Olguín and Solano Sánchez 2013; Moguel and Córdova 2012.

11　Olayo-Méndez 2018.

12　Deeper discussion of humanitarian assistance as containment can be found in Merlín-Escorza, Davids, and Schapendonk 2020; see also Chimni 2002.

13　Durand Arp-Nisen 2019; Marchand 2021; Gandini, Fernández de la Reguera, and Narváez 2020.

14　I visited and collected data for a different research project at the eight US southwest border land ports of entry where asylum seekers can submit information in advance and schedule an appointment, through the CBP One app, with the hopes of filing for asylum. The ports of entry are Brownsville, Hidalgo, Laredo, Eagle Pass, and El Paso in Texas, Nogales in Arizona, and Calexico and San Ysidro in California.

15　Scanlon et al. 2016; Omilusi 2018, 113.

16　See Valarezo 2015.

17　Diamond et al. 2020.

18　Olayo-Méndez 2018.

19　Barnett and Weiss 2008a, 39.

20　See Barnett and Stein 2012; Barnett 2013; Fassin 2012, 2007; Agier 2011; Ticktin 2011; and Betts 2013.

21 Barnett 2013, 379; see also Fassin 2007, 151.

22 Fassin 2007, 151; Agier 2011.

23 Ticktin 2011, 61.

24 Barnett 2013, 382.

25 Fassin 2012, 4.

26 Campos-Delgado 2023.

27 Fassin 2007, 150.

28 See Barnett 2005.

29 See Fassin 2010.

30 Campos-Delgado 2023, 75; Vogt 2018; Faret, Téllez, and Rodríguez-Tapia 2021.

31 Ortega Ramírez and Morales Gámez 2021.

32 Angulo-Pasel 2022b; Campos-Delgado 2021a.

CONCLUSION

1 McAuliffe and Triandafyllidou 2021; Horwood and Frouws 2021; Heyman, Slack, and Guerra 2018; Bush-Joseph 2024.

2 Zepeda Gil 2018.

3 See McAuliffe and Triandafyllidou 2021; and IOM 2015.

4 See Barnett 2005, 733–34; Manenti 2012; Vogt 2018; Brigden 2018; Basok et al. 2015; Candiz and Bélanger 2018.

5 Barnett 2011, 10.

6 Cuttitta 2017; Pallister-Wilkins 2017, 2022.

7 Boltanski 1999, xv; Wilson and Brown 2009, 1–28; Bornstein and Redfield 2010, 6; Donini 2010, S220; Ticktin 2011; Barnett 2011, 14–15; Slim 2015, 1.

8 Barnett 2013, 379.

9 Czaika and de Haas 2013.

10 See Barnett 2013, 394; Fassin 2012.

11 Hernández-León 2008, 24, 154; Gammeltoft-Hansen and Sørensen 2013.

12 Schapendonk 2018, 665.

13 See also Turkewitz 2023.

14 Faist 2014a.

15 Schapendonk describes the relationships of migration intermediaries as a "force field of relationalities." See Schapendonk 2018; and Ingold 2011, 93.

16 Faist 2014b; Gross 2009.

17 Castles, de Haas, and Miller 2014, 235; Hernández-León 2008.

REFERENCES

Aboites, Luis, and Engracia Loyo. 2010. "La Construcción del Nuevo Estado, 1920–1945." In *Nueva Historia General de México*, edited by Erik Velásquez García et al., 357–86. Ciudad de Mexico: Colegio de México. Digitalia, https://www.digitalia publishing.com/a/105680.

Ager, Alastair, and Joey Ager. 2011. "Faith and the Discourse of Secular Humanitarianism." *Journal of Refugee Studies* 24 (3): 456–72. https://doi.org/10.1093/jrs/fer030.

———. 2015. "Why Humanitarianism Doesn't Get Religion . . . and Why It Needs To." In *Faith, Secularism, and Humanitarian Engagement: Finding the Place of Religion in the Support of Displaced Communities*, edited by Alastair Ager and Joey Ager, 1–30. New York: Palgrave Macmillan.

Ager, Joey, Elena Fiddian-Qasmiyeh, and Alastair Ager. 2015. "Local Faith Communities and the Promotion of Resilience in Contexts of Humanitarian Crisis." *Journal of Refugee Studies* 28 (2): 202–21. https://doi.org/10.1093/jrs/fev001.

Agier, Michel. 2010. "Humanity as an Identity and Its Political Effects (a Note on Camps and Humanitarian Government)." *Humanity: An International Journal of Human Rights, Humanitarianism, and Development* 1: 29–45. https://doi.org/10.1353/hum.2010.0005.

———. 2011. *Managing the Undesirables*. Cambridge: Polity.

Alba, Francisco, and Manuel Ángel Castillo. 2012. "New Approaches to Migration Management in Mexico and Central America." Migration Policy Institute. www.migrationpolicy.org.

Alkire, Sabina, and Yangyang Shen. 2017. "Exploring Multidimensional Poverty in China: 2010 to 2014." OPHI Research in Progress 47a. University of Oxford.

Alpes, Maybritt Jill, 2017. "Papers That Work: Migration Brokers, State/Market Boundaries, and the Place of Law." *Political and Legal Anthropology Review* 40 (2): 262–77.

Alvarez, Lisette, and Mario Moreno. 2020. "Beyond the Wall: Seeking Shelter in the Age of COVID-19." *Latin America Today* (podcast), April 6, 2020. www.wola.org.

Amnesty International. 2010. "Invisible Victims: Migrants on the Move in Mexico." Amnesty International. www.amnesty.org.

———. 2017. "Amnesty International Report 2016/2017: The State of the World's Human Rights." Amnesty International. www.amnesty.org.

Anderson, Bridget. 2013. *Us and Them? The Dangerous Politics of Immigration Control*. Oxford: Oxford University Press.

Anderson, Bridget, et al. 2016. *Citizenship and Work: Case Studies of Differential Inclusion/Exclusion*. bEUcitizen Project Deliverable 10. www.uu.nl.

Anderson, Bridget, and Sarah Walker. 2016. "Beggars and Begging (UK & Croatia)." Appendix 6 in *Citizenship and Work: Case Studies of Differential Inclusion/Exclusion*, edited by Bridget Anderson et al., 82–100. beUcitizen Project Deliverable 10. www.uu.nl.

Anderson, Jill. 2015. "'Tagged as a Criminal': Narratives of Deportation and Return Migration in a Mexico City Call Center." *Latino Studies* 13 (1): 8–27. https://doi.org/10.1057/lst.2014.72.

Andersson, Ruben. 2014. *Illegality, Inc.: Clandestine Migration and the Business of Bordering Europe*. Berkeley: University of California Press.

———. 2017. "From Radar Systems to Rickety Boats." In *Methodologies of Mobility: Ethnography and Experiment*, edited by Alice Elliot, Roger Norum, and Noel B. Salazar, 88–108. New York: Berghahn Books.

Anguiano, María Eugenia, and Alma Trejo Peña. 2007. "Políticas de Seguridad Fronteriza y Nuevas Rutas de Movilidad de Migrantes Mexicanos y Guatemaltecos." *LiminaR. Estudios Sociales y Humanísticos* 2: 47–65. https://doi.org/10.29043/liminar.v5i2.250.

Angulo-Pasel, Carla. 2022a. "Rethinking the Space of the Migrant Shelter in Mexico: Humanitarian and Security Implications in the Practices of Bordering." *Identities* 29 (6): 730–47. https://doi.org/10.1080/1070289X.2022.2029068.

———. 2022b. "The More Things Change, the More They Stay the Same: Border Governance and Resistance along Mexico's Southern Border with Guatemala." *Borders in Globalization Review* 3 (2): 26–37. https://doi.org/10.18357/bigr32202220400.

Arias, Enrique Desmond, and Daniel M. Goldstein (eds.). 2010a. *Violent Democracies in Latin America*. Durham: Duke University Press.

———. 2010b. "Violent Pluralism: Understanding the New Democracies of Latin America." In *Violent Democracies in Latin America*, edited by Enrique Desmond Arias and Daniel M. Goldstein, 1–34. Durham: Duke University Press.

Arias Muñoz, Karina, and Nancy Carmona Arellano. 2012. *Evolución y Retos del Marco Normativo Migratorio en México: Una Perspectiva Histórica*. Sin Fronteras IAP. https://sinfronteras.org.mx.

Arskey, Hilary, and Caroline Glendinning. 2007. "Informal Welfare." In *Understanding the Mixed Economy of Welfare*, edited by Martin Powel, 107–28. Bristol: Bristol University Press, 2007. https://doi.org/10.2307/j.ctt1t89b4m.11.

Ataç, Ilker, Kim Rygiel, and Maurice Stierl. 2016. "Introduction: The Contentious Politics of Refugee and Migrant Protest and Solidarity Movements: Remaking Citizenship from the Margins." *Citizenship Studies* 20 (5): 527–44. https://doi.org/10.1080/13621025.2016.1182681.

Auyero, Javier. 2011. "Patients of the State: An Ethnographic Account of Poor People's Waiting." *Latin American Research Review* 46 (1): 5–29. https://doi.org/doi:10.1353/lar.2011.0014.

———. 2012. *Patients of the State: The Politics of Waiting in Argentina*. Durham: Duke University Press.

Babich, Erin, and Jeanne Batalova. 2021. "Central American Immigrants in the United States." Migration Policy Institute, August 11, 2021. www.migrationpolicy.org.

Bada, Xóchitl. 2014. *Mexican Hometown Associations in Chicagoacán*. New Brunswick: Rutgers University Press. https://doi.org/doi:10.36019/9780813564944.

Baggio, Fabio. 2008. Introduction to *Faith on the Move: Toward a Theology of Migration in Asia*, edited by Fabio Baggio and Agnes M. Brazal, vii–xx. Quezon City: Ateneo de Manila University Press.

Bakewell, Oliver. 2000. "Uncovering Local Perspectives on Humanitarian Assistance and Its Outcomes." *Disasters* 24 (2): 103–16. https://doi.org/10.1111/1467-7717.00136.

———. 2010. "Some Reflections on Structure and Agency in Migration Theory." *Journal of Ethnic and Migration Studies* 36 (10): 1689–1708. https://doi.org/10.1080/1369183X.2010.489382.

Bakewell, Oliver, Agnieszka Kubal, and Sónia Pereira. 2016. "Introduction: Feedback in Migration Processes." In *Beyond Networks: Feedback in International Migration*, edited by Oliver Bakewell, Godfried Engbersen, Maria Lucinda Fonseca, and Cindy Horst, 1–17. Basingstoke: Palgrave Macmillan.

Balaguera, Martha. 2018. "Trans-migrations: Agency and Confinement at the Limits of Sovereignty." *Signs: Journal of Women in Culture and Society* 43 (3): 641–64. https://doi.org/10.1086/695302.

Baldock, John, Lavinia Mitton, Nick Manning, and Sarah Vickerstaff. 2012. *Social Policy*. 4th ed. New York: Oxford University Press.

Barnett, Michael. 2005. "Humanitarianism Transformed." *Perspectives on Politics* 3 (4): 723–40.

———. 2011. *Empire of Humanity: A History of Humanitarianism*. Ithaca: Cornell University Press.

———. 2013. "Humanitarian Governance." *Annual Review of Political Science* 16: 379–98. https://doi.org/10.1146/annurev-polisci-012512-083711.

Barnett, Michael, and Janice Gross Stein. 2012. *Sacred Aid: Faith and Humanitarianism*. Oxford: Oxford University Press.

Barnett, Michael, and Thomas George Weiss. 2008a. "Humanitarianism: A Brief History of the Present." In *Humanitarianism in Question: Politics, Power, Ethics*, edited by Michael Barnett and Thomas George Weiss, 1–48. Ithaca: Cornell University Press.

——— (eds.). 2008b. *Humanitarianism in Question: Politics, Power, Ethics*. Ithaca: Cornell University Press.

Barrett, Sam. 2003. "Kinship, Poor Relief, and the Welfare Process in Early Modern England." In *The Poor in England, 1700–1850: An Economy of Makeshifts*, edited by Steven King and Alannah Tomkins, 199–227. Manchester: Manchester University Press.

Basok, Tanya, Danièle Bélanger, Martha Luz Rojas Wiesner, and Guillermo Candiz. 2015. *Rethinking Transit Migration: Precarity, Mobility, and Self-Making in Mexico*. Basingstoke: Palgrave Macmillan.

Bermudez Tapia, Bertha Alicia. 2023. "From Matamoros to Reynosa: Migrant Camps on the US-Mexico Border." *Contexts* 22 (1): 30–37. https://doi.org/10.1177/15365042221142833.

Betts, Alexander. 2013. "The Migration Industry in Global Migration Governance." In *The Migration Industry and the Commercialization of International Migration*, edited by Thomas Gammeltoft-Hansen and Ninna Nyberg Sørensen, 45–63. London: Routledge.

Bielefeld, Wolfgang, and William Suhs Cleveland. 2013. "Defining Faith-Based Organizations and Understanding Them through Research." *Nonprofit and Voluntary Sector Quarterly* 42 (3): 442–67. https://doi.org/10.1177/0899764013484090.

Bilecen, Başak, and Karolina Barglowski. 2015. "On the Assemblages of Informal and Formal Transnational Social Protection." *Population, Space and Place* 21 (3): 203–14. https://doi.org/10.1002/psp.1897.

Blue, Sarah A., Jennifer A. Devine, Matthew P. Ruiz, Kathryn McDaniel, Alisa R. Hartsell, Christopher J. Pierce, Makayla Johnson et al. 2021. "Im/Mobility at the US–Mexico Border during the COVID-19 Pandemic." *Social Sciences* 10 (2): 47. https://doi.org/10.3390/socsci10020047.

Bobes, Velia Cecilia. 2017. "ONG de Migración como Actores de un Campo de Acción Solidaria." *Migración y Desarrollo* 15 (28): 125–46.

Boccagni, Paolo. 2017. "Addressing Transnational Needs through Migration? An Inquiry into the Reach and Consequences of Migrants' Social Protection across Borders." *Global Social Policy* 17 (2): 168–87. https://doi.org/10.1177/1468018116678523.

Boltanski, Luc. 1999. *Distant Suffering: Morality, Media and Politics*. Cambridge: Cambridge University Press.

Bornstein, Erica, and Peter Redfield. 2010. *Forces of Compassion: Humanitarianism between Ethics and Politics*. Santa Fe, NM: School for Advanced Research Press.

Bourgois, Philippe. 2001. "The Power of Violence in War and Peace: Post–Cold War Lessons from El Salvador." *Ethnography* 2 (1): 5–34. https://doi.org/10.1177/14661380122230803.

———. 2004. "The Continuum of Violence in War and Peace: Post–Cold War Lessons from El Salvador." In *Violence in War and Peace: An Anthology*, edited by Nancy Scheper-Hughes and Philippe Bourgois, 425–34. Oxford: Blackwell.

Boyce, Geoffrey A., Jeffrey M. Banister, and Jeremy Slack. 2015. "You and What Army? Violence, the State, and Mexico's War on Drugs." *Territory, Politics, Governance* 3 (4): 446–68. https://doi.org/10.1080/21622671.2015.1058723.

Brachet, Julien. 2005. "Migrants, Transporteurs et Agents de l'État: Rencontre sur l'Axe Agadez-Sebha." *Autrepart* 4 (36): 43–62. https://doi.org/10.3917/autr.036.0043.

———. 2012a. "From One Stage to the Next: Transit and Transport in (Trans) Saharan Migrations." In *African Migrations Research: Innovative Methods and Methodologies*, edited by Mohamed Berriane and Hein de Haas, 91–113. Trenton: Africa World Press.

———. 2012b. "Geography of Movement, Geography in Movement: Mobility as a Dimension of Fieldwork in Migration Research." *Annales de Géographie* 5: 543–560.

Brigden, Noelle K. 2018. *The Migrant Passage: Clandestine Journeys from Central America*. Ithaca: Cornell University Press.

Bush-Joseph, Kathleen. 2024. *Outmatched: The US Asylum System Faces Record Demands*. Washington, DC: Migration Policy Institute. www.migrationpolicy.org.

Calderón Chelius, Leticia. 2006. "El Estudio de la Dimensión Política dentro del Proceso Migratorio." *Sociológica* 21 (60): 43–73.

———. 2016. "Organized Civil Society in Response to Transit Migration through Mexico." CANAMID Policy Brief Series, 13. CIESAS.

Calhoun, Craig. 2008. "The Imperative to Reduce Suffering: Charity, Progress, and Emergencies in the Field of Humanitarian Action." In *Humanitarianism in Question: Politics, Power, Ethics*, edited by Michael Barnett and Thomas George Weiss, 73–97. Ithaca: Cornell University Press.

———. 2010. "The Idea of Emergency: Humanitarian Action and Global (Dis)Order." In *Contemporary States of Emergency: The Politics of Military and Humanitarian Interventions*, edited by Didier Fassin and Mariella Pandolfi, 29–58. New York: Zone Books.

Campese, Gioacchino. 2012. "The Irruption of Migrants: Theology of Migration in the 21st Century." *Theological Studies* 73 (1): 3–32. https://doi.org/10.1177/004056391207300101.

Campos-Delgado, Amalia. 2021a. "Abnormal Bordering: Control, Punishment, and Deterrence in Mexico's Migrant Detention Centres." *British Journal of Criminology* 61 (2): 476–96. https://doi.org/10.1093/bjc/azaa071.

———. 2021b. "Bordering through Exemption: Extracontinental Migration Flows in Mexico." *International Journal for Crime, Justice and Social Democracy* 10 (3): 30–40. https://doi.org/10.5204/ijcjsd.2039.

———. 2023. "Euphemistic Rhetoric and Dysphemistic Practices: Governing Migration in Mexico." *Geopolitics* 29 (1): 64–89. https://doi.org/10.1080/14650045.2023.2185513.

Candiz, Guillermo, and Danièle Bélanger. 2018. "Del Tránsito a la Espera: El Rol de las Casas del Migrante en México en las Trayectorias de los Migrantes Centroamericanos." *Canadian Journal of Latin American and Caribbean Studies/Revue Canadienne Des Études Latino-Américaines et Caraïbes* 43 (8): 277–97. https://doi.org/10.1080/08263663.2018.1467533.

Carling, Jørgen. 2010. "Migration Corridors: Conceptual and Methodological Issues." THEMIS Project Paper. Peace Research Institute Oslo. www.prio.org.

Carney, Megan A. 2021. *Island of Hope: Migration and Solidarity in the Mediterranean*. Berkeley: University of California Press.

Carpi, Estella. 2018. "The 'Need to Be There': North-South Encounters and Imaginations in the Humanitarian Economy." In *Routledge Handbook of South-South Relations*, edited by Elena Fiddian-Qasmiyeh and Patricia Daley. London: Routledge.

Carpi, Estella, and Elena Fiddian-Qasmiyeh. 2020. "Keeping the Faith? Examining the Roles of Faith and Secularism in Syrian Diaspora Organisations in Lebanon." In *Diaspora Organizations in International Affairs*, edited by Dennis Dijkzeul and Margit Fauser, 129–49. London: Routledge.

Carruth, Lauren. 2021. *Love and Liberation : Humanitarian Work in Ethiopia's Somali Region*. Ithaca: Cornell University Press.

Casillas, Rodolfo. 1992. *Los Procesos Migratorios Centroamericanos y Sus Efectos Regionales.* Vol. 1. Mexico: FLACSO.

———. 2006. "Una Vida Discreta, Fugaz y Anónima: Los Centroamericanos Transmigrantes en México." FLACSO. www.elfaro.net.

———. 2008. "The Routes of Central Americans through Mexico: Characterization, Principal Agents and Complexities." *Migración y Desarrollo* 6 (10): 141zxperiencia de los Albergues y las Casas de Migrantes, Realidades y Desafíos." In *Las Políticas Públicas sobre Migraciones y la Sociedad Civil en América Latina: Los Casos de Argentina, Brasil, Colombia y México,* edited by Mario Chiarello, 524–59. New York: Scalabrinian International Migration Network.

———. 2021. "Migración Internacional y Solidaridad: Los Albergues y las Casas de Migrantes en México." *Migración y Desarrollo* 19 (37): 65–92. https://doi.org/10.35533/myd.1937.rcr.

Castillo, Manuel Ángel. 2003. "Los Desafíos de la Emigración Centroamericana en el Siglo XXI." *Amérique Latine Histoire et Mémoire. Les Cahiers ALHIM* 7. https://doi.org/10.4000/alhim.369.

Castles, Stephen, Hein de Haas, and Mark J. Miller. 2014. *The Age of Migration: International Population Movements in the Modern World.* 5th ed. Basingstoke: Palgrave Macmillan.

Castro, Elizabeth Mariana. 2015. "Experiencias Comunitarias de Protección a Migrantes en Tránsito en México." PNUD (Programa de las Naciones Unidas para el Desarrollo). www.mx.undp.org.

Cave, Damien. 2013. "For Migrants, New Land of Opportunity Is Mexico." *New York Times,* September 21, 2013. www.nytimes.com.

Cazabat, Christelle, and Alesia O'Connor. 2021. *Internal Displacement Index Report.* Geneva, Switzerland: Internal Displacement Monitoring Centre (iDMC). www.internal-displacement.org.

CEPMH (Comisión Episcopal para la Pastoral de la Movilidad Humana). 2003. *La Comisión Episcopal para la Pastoral de la Movilidad Humana: Su Historia, Identidad y Trayectoria (1957–2003).* Mexico: CEPMH.

———. 2004. *V Taller Nacional: Seguimos Juntos en el Camino de la Esperanza. Fortaleciendo la Pastoral de Migrantes.* Mexico: CEPMH.

Chávez, Karma R. 2019. "Understanding Migrant Caravans from the Place of Place Privilege." *Departures in Critical Qualitative Research* 8 (1): 9–16. https://doi.org/10.1525/dcqr.2019.8.1.9.

Chimni, Bhuppindir S. 2002. "Aid, Relief, and Containment: The First Asylum Country and Beyond." *International Migration* 40 (5): 75–94. https://doi.org/10.1111/1468-2435.00212.

Chkam, Hakim. 2016. "Aid and the Perpetuation of Refugee Camps: The Case of Dadaab in Kenya, 1991–2011." *Refugee Survey Quarterly* 35 (2): 79–97. https://doi.org/10.1093/rsq/hdw005.

Christoplos, Ian. 1998. "Humanitarianism and Local Service Institutions in Angola." *Disasters* 22 (1): 1–20. https://doi.org/10.1111/1467-7717.00072.

CIDH (Comisión Interamericana de Derechos Humanos). 2015. *Situación de los Derechos Humanos en México*. Comisión Interamericana de Derechos Humanos. www.oas.org.

Clarke, Gerard. 2006. "Faith Matters: Faith-Based Organisations, Civil Society and International Development." *Journal of International Development: The Journal of the Development Studies Association* 18 (6): 835–48. https://doi.org/10.1002/jid.1317.

Clarke, Gerard, and Michael Jennings. 2008. *Development, Civil Society and Faith-Based Organizations: Bridging the Sacred and the Secular*. New York: Palgrave Macmillan.

Clarke, Matthew, and Vicki-Anne Ware. 2015. "Understanding Faith-Based Organizations: How FBOs Are Contrasted with NGOs in International Development Literature." *Progress in Development Studies* 15 (1): 37–48. https://doi.org/10.1177/1464993414546979.

CNDH (Comisión Nacional de los Derechos Humanos México). 2009. *Informe Especial de la Comisión Nacional de Derechos Humanos sobre los Casos de Secuestro en contra de Migrantes*. Mexico: Comisión Nacional de los Derechos Humanos México.

———. 2011. "Informe Especial sobre Secuestro de Migrantes en México." Comisión Nacional de Los Derechos Humanos México. www.cndh.org.mx.

Collyer, Michael. 2007. "In-Between Places: Trans-Saharan Transit Migrants in Morocco and the Fragmented Journey to Europe." *Antipode* 39 (4): 668–90. https://doi.org/10.1111/j.1467-8330.2007.00546.x.

COMAR (Comisión Mexicana de Ayuda a Refugiados). 2023. "Estadística Enero 2023." *La COMAR en Números*. Secretaría de Gobernación. www.gob.mx.

Combinido, Pamela, and Jonathan Corpus Ong. 2017. "Silenced in the Aid Interface: Responsible Brokerage and Its Obstacles in Humanitarian Interventions." *Philippine Sociological Review* 65: 39–64. http://www.jstor.org/stable/45014298.

CONAPO (Consejo Nacional de Población), Fundación BBVA Bancomer, and BBVA Research. 2017. *Anuario de Migración y Remesas, México 2017*. Mexico: CONAPO, Fundación BBVA Bancomer, BBVA Research.

———. 2022. *Anuario de Migración y Remesas, México 2022*. Mexico: CONAPO, Fundación BBVA, BBVA Research.

Contreras Delgado, Camilo, María Dolores París Pombo, and Laura Velasco Ortiz (eds.). 2021. *Caravanas Migrantes y Desplazamientos Colectivos en la Frontera México-Estados Unidos*. Tijuana: El Colegio de la Frontera Norte.

Cooley, Alexander, and James Ron. 2002. "The NGO Scramble: Organizational Insecurity and the Political Economy of Transnational Action." *International Security* 27 (1): 5–39. http://www.jstor.org/stable/3092151.

Cornelius, Wayne. 2018. "Mexico: From Country of Mass Emigration to Transit State." Discussion Paper No. IDB-DP-006300. Inter-American Development Bank. http://dx.doi.org/10.18235/0001415.

Cornelius, Wayne A., and Idean Salehyan. 2007. "Does Border Enforcement Deter Unauthorized Immigration? The Case of Mexican

Migration to the United States of America." *Regulation & Governance* 1 (2): 139–53. https://doi.org/10.1111/j.1748-5991.2007.00007.x.

Correa-Cabrera, Guadalupe, and Naoru Koizumi. 2021. "Explicando las Caravanas Migrantes: ¿Hipótesis de Trabajo, Activismo Académico o Teorías Conspirativas?" *Frontera Norte* 33. https://doi.org/10.33679/rfn.v1i1.2197.

Coubès, Marie Laure, Laura Velasco, and Oscar Contreras. 2020. "Migrantes en Albergues en las Ciudades Fronterizas del Norte de México." In *Documentos de Contingencia 2: Poblaciones Vulnerables ante COVID-19*. Tijuana: El Colegio de la Frontera Norte. www.colef.mx.

Coutin, Susan Bibler. 2010. "Confined Within: National Territories as Zones of Confinement." *Political Geography* 29 (4): 200–208. https://doi.org/10.1016/j.polgeo.2010.03.005.

Cranston, Sophie, Joris Schapendonk, and Ernst Spaan. 2017. "New Directions in Exploring the Migration Industries: Introduction to Special Issue." *Journal of Ethnic and Migration Studies* 44 (4): 543–57. doi:10.1080/1369183X.2017.1315504.

Cresswell, Tim. 2014. *Place: An Introduction*. West Sussex: John Wiley.

Cuttitta, Paolo. 2017. "Repoliticization through Search and Rescue? Humanitarian NGOs and Migration Management in the Central Mediterranean." *Geopolitics* 23 (3): 632–60. https://doi.org/10.1080/14650045.2017.1344834.

Cwerner, Saulo B. 2001. "The Times of Migration." *Journal of Ethnic and Migration Studies* 27 (1): 7–36. https://doi.org/10.1080/13691830125283.

Czaika, Mathias, and Hein de Haas. 2013. "The Effectiveness of Immigration Policies." *Population and Development Review* 39 (2): 487–508.

Davey, Eleanor. 2012. "New Players through Old Lenses: Why History Matters in Engaging with Southern Actors." Overseas Development Institute.

Davies, Thom, Arshad Isakjee, and Surindar Dhesi. 2017. "Violent Inaction: The Necropolitical Experience of Refugees in Europe." *Antipode* 49: 1263–84. https://doi: 10.1111/anti.12325.

De Genova, Nicholas. 2010. "The Deportation Regime: Sovereignty, Space, and the Freedom of Movement." In *The Deportation Regime: Sovereignty, Space, and the Freedom of Movement*, edited by Nicholas De Genova and Nathalie Peutz, 33–65. Durham: Duke University Press.

———. 2017. "The Incorrigible Subject: Mobilizing a Critical Geography of (Latin) America through the Autonomy of Migration." *Journal of Latin American Geography* 16 (1): 17–42. https://doi:10.1353/lag.2017.0007.

De Genova, Nicholas, and Rozalinda Borcila. 2011. "An Image of Our Future: On the Making of Migrant 'Illegality.'" AREA Chicago. www.areachicago.org.

de Haan, Arjan, and Shahin Yaqub. 2010. "Migration and Poverty: Linkages, Knowledge Gaps and Policy Implications." In *South-South Migration: Implications for Social Policy and Development*, edited by Katja Hujo and Nicola Piper, 190–219. London: Palgrave Macmillan. https://doi.org/10.1057/9780230283374_6.

de Haas, Hein. 2007. "Remittances, Migration and Social Development: A Conceptual Review of the Literature." Social Policy and Development Programme Paper 34. United Nations Research Institute for Social Development.

———. 2010. "The Internal Dynamics of Migration Processes: A Theoretical Inquiry." *Journal of Ethnic and Migration Studies* 36 (10): 1587–1617. https://doi.org/10.1080/1369183X.2010.489361.

De León, Jason. 2013. "Undocumented Migration, Use Wear, and the Materiality of Habitual Suffering in the Sonoran Desert." *Journal of Material Culture* 18 (4): 321–45. https://doi.org/10.1177/1359183513496489.

———. 2015. *The Land of Open Graves: Living and Dying on the Migrant Trail.* Oakland: University of California Press.

Delgado Wise, Raúl, and Humberto Márquez Covarrubias. 2007. "Teoría y Práctica de la Relación Dialéctica entre Desarrollo y Migración." *Migración y Desarrollo*, no. 9: 5–25. www.redalyc.org.

Della Porta, Donatella, and Elias Steinhilper (eds.). 2021. *Contentious Migrant Solidarity: Shrinking Spaces and Civil Society Contestation.* London: Routledge.

Diamond, Megan, Luke Testa, Carissa Novak, Kathryn Kempton-Amaral, Thalia Porteny, and Alejandro Olayo-Méndez. 2020. "A Population in Peril: A Health Crisis among Asylum Seekers on the Northern Border of Mexico." Harvard Global Health Institute. www.bc.edu.

Díaz Prieto, Gabriela. 2016. *Operativos Móviles de Revisión Migratoria en las Carreteras de México: Una Práctica Discriminatoria e Ilegal.* Tijuana: El Colegio de la Frontera Norte.

Dobbs, Erica, and Peggy Levitt. 2017. "The Missing Link? The Role of Sub-National Governance in Transnational Social Protections." *Oxford Development Studies* 45(1): 47–63. https://doi.org/10.1080/13600818.2016.1271867.

Doering-White, John. 2018. "Evidencing Violence and Care along the Central American Migrant Trail through Mexico." *Social Service Review* 92 (3): 432–69. https://doi.org/10.1086/699196.

Donini, Antonio. 2010. "The Far Side: The Meta Functions of Humanitarianism in a Globalised World." *Disasters* 34 (S2): S220–37. https://doi.org/10.1111/j.1467-7717.2010.01155.x.

DPMH (Dimensión Pastoral de la Movilidad Humana). 2012. "Informe de Actividades de la Dimensión Pastoral de la Movilidad Humana, en el Periodo 2006–2012." Comisión Episcopal para La Pastoral Social, Conferencia del Episcopado Mexicano.

Dunant, Henry. 1939. *A Memory of Solferino.* Geneva: International Committee of the Red Cross.

Durand, Jorge. 2011. "La Dinámica Migratoria en México." In *Las Políticas Públicas sobre Migraciones y la Sociedad Civil en América Latina: Los Casos de Argentina, Brasil, Colombia y México*, edited by Mario Chiarello, 458–82. New York: Scalabrinian International Migration Network.

Durand Arp-Nisen, Jorge. 2019. "Immigration Policy: Between Discourse, Practice and Reality." *Foro Internacional* 59 (3–4): 1021–47. https://doi.org/10.24201/fi.v59i3-4.2650.

Duvall, Raymond, and Michael Barnett. 2005. "Power in Global Governance." In *Power in Global Governance*, edited by Michael Barnett and Raymond Duvall, 1–32. Cambridge: Cambridge University Press. https://doi.org/10.1017/CBO9780511491207.

Edin, Kathryn, and Laura Lein. 1997. *Making Ends Meet: How Single Mothers Survive Welfare and Low-Wage Work*. New York: Russell Sage.

Ehrkamp, Patricia, and Caroline Nagel. 2012. "Immigration, Places of Worship and the Politics of Citizenship in the US South." *Transactions of the Institute of British Geographers* 37 (4): 624–38. https://doi.org/10.1111/j.1475-5661.2012.00499.x.

El País. 2019. "La Casa del Migrante de Saltillo denuncia acoso de la Guardia Nacional." July 24, 2019 https://elpais.com.

Emirbayer, Mustafa, and Ann Mische. 1998. "What Is Agency?" *American Journal of Sociology* 103 (4): 962–1023. https://doi.org/10.1086/231294.

Faist, Thomas. 1997. "The Crucial Meso-Level." In *International Migration, Mobility, and Development*, edited by Tomas Hammer, Grete Brochmann, Kristof Tamas, and Thomas Faist, 187–217. New York: Berg.

———. 2000. *The Volume and Dynamics of International Migration and Transnational Social Spaces*. Oxford: Clarendon.

———. 2013. "Transnational Social Protection: An Emerging Field of Study." COMCAD Working Papers 113. Bielefeld: Universität Bielefeld, Centre on Migration, Citizenship and Development (COMCAD). https://nbn-resolving.org.

———. 2014a. "Brokerage in Cross-Border Migration: From Networks to Social Mechanisms." COMCAD Working Papers 121. Bielefeld: Universität Bielefeld, Centre on Migration, Citizenship and Development (COMCAD). http://nbn-resolving.de/urn:nbn:de:0168-ssoar-50965-7.

———. 2014b. "Brokerage in Cross-Border Mobility: Social Mechanisms and the (Re)Production of Social Inequalities." *Social Inclusion* 2 (4): 38–52. https://doi.org/10.17645/si.v2i4.29.

Faist, Thomas, Başak Bilecen, Karolina Barglowski, and Joanna Jadwiga Sienkiewicz. 2015. "Transnational Social Protection: Migrants' Strategies and Patterns of Inequalities." *Population, Space and Place* 21 (3): 193–202. https://doi.org/10.1002/psp.1903.

Fan, Mary D. 2008. "When Deterrence and Death Mitigation Fall Short: Fantasy and Fetishes as Gap-Fillers in Border Regulation." *Law & Society Review* 42 (4): 701–34. https://doi.org/10.1111/j.1540-5893.2008.00356.x.

Faret, Laurent, María Eugenia Téllez, and Luz Helena Rodríguez-Tapia. 2021. "Migration Management and Changes in Mobility Patterns in the North and Central American Region." *Journal on Migration and Human Security* 9 (2): 63–79. https://doi.org/10.1177/23315024211008096.

Fassin, Didier. 2007. "Humanitarianism: A Nongovernmental Government." In *Nongovernmental Politics*, edited by Michel Feher, Gaëlle Krikorian, and Yates McKee, 149–60. New York: Zone Books.

———. 2010. "Heart of Humaneness: The Moral Economy of Humanitarian Intervention." In *Contemporary States of Emergency: The Politics of Military and Humanitarian Interventions*, edited by Didier Fassin and Mariella Pandolfi, 269–94. New York: Zone Books.

———. 2012. *Humanitarian Reason*. Berkeley: University of California Press.

Fearon, James D. 2008. "The Rise of Emergency Relief." In *Humanitarianism in Question: Politics, Power, Ethics*, edited by Michael Barnett and Thomas George Weiss, 49–72. Ithaca: Cornell University Press.

Fee, Molly. 2022. "Lives Stalled: The Costs of Waiting for Refugee Resettlement." *Journal of Ethnic and Migration Studies* 48 (11): 2659–77. https://doi.org/10.1080/1369183X.2021.1876554.

Fernández de la Reguera Ahedo, Alethia. 2023. "The Gender Effects of the Militarization of Migratory Controls in Mexico Violence against Migrant Women Perpetrated by the State." In *Gender-Based Violence in Mexico: Narratives, the State and Emancipations*, edited by Ana Luisa Sánchez Hernández, Miguel Angel Martínez Martínez, and Francisco Díaz Estrada. London: Routledge. https://doi:10.4324/9781003385844.

Ferris, Elizabeth. 2005. "Faith-Based and Secular Humanitarian Organizations." *International Review of the Red Cross* 87 (858): 311–25.

———. 2011. "Faith and Humanitarianism: It's Complicated." *Journal of Refugee Studies* 24 (3): 606–25. https://doi.org/10.1093/jrs/fer028.

Fiddian-Qasmiyeh, Elena. 2011. "Introduction: Faith-Based Humanitarianism in Contexts of Forced Displacement." *Journal of Refugee Studies* 24 (3): 429–39. https://doi.org/10.1093/jrs/fer033.

———. 2015. "Engendering Understandings of Faith-Based Organizations: Intersections between Religion and Gender in Development and Humanitarian Interventions." In *The Routledge Handbook of Gender and Development*, edited by Anne Coles, Leslie Gray, and Janet Momsen, 560–70. https://doi.org/10.4324/9780203383117.

Fiddian-Qasmiyeh, Elena, and Alastair Ager. 2013. "Local Faith Communities and the Promotion of Resilience in Humanitarian Situations: A Scoping Study." Working Paper Series 90. Refugee Studies Centre, University of Oxford.

Fiddian-Qasmiyeh, Elena, Alastair Ager, and Aydan Greatrick. 2021. *Understanding Local Responses to Displacement*. Refugee Hosts Project Recommendation for Research and Practice 1. October 2021. https://refugeehosts.org.

Fiddian-Qasmiyeh, Elena, and Julia Pacitto. 2016. "Writing the Other into Humanitarianism: A Conversation between 'South-South' and 'Faith-Based' Humanitarianisms." In *The New Humanitarians in International Practice*, edited by Zeynep Sezgin and Dennis Dijkzeul, 282–300. London: Routledge.

Fiddian-Qasmiyeh, Elena, Anna Rowlands, and Aydan Greatrick. 2021. *Local Faith Community Responses to Displacement*. Refugee Hosts Project Recommendation for Research and Practice 4. October 2021. https://refugeehosts.org.

Forment, Carlos A. 2013. *Democracy in Latin America, 1760–1900*. Vol. 1, *Civic Selfhood and Public Life in Mexico and Peru*. Chicago: University of Chicago Press.

Forsythe, David P. 2005. *The Humanitarians: The International Committee of the Red Cross*. Cambridge: Cambridge University Press.

———. 2009. "Contemporary Humanitarianism: The Global and the Local." In *Humanitarianism and Suffering: The Mobilization of Empathy*, edited by Richard Ashby Wilson and Richard D. Brown, 58–87. Cambridge: Cambridge University Press.

Frank-Vitale, Amelia. 2023. "Coyotes, Caravans, and the Central American Migrant Smuggling Continuum." *Trends in Organized Crime* 26: 64–79. https://doi.org/10.1007/s12117-022-09480-z.

Gammeltoft-Hansen, Thomas, and Ninna Nyberg Sørensen (eds.). 2013. *The Migration Industry and the Commercialization of International Migration*. London: Routledge.

Gandini, Luciana, Alethia Fernández de la Reguera, and Juan Carlos Narváez Gutiérrez. 2020. *Caravanas*. Mexico: UNAM, Secretaría de Desarrollo Institucional.

Gandini, Luciana, Fernando Lozano-Ascencio, and Selene Gaspar Olvera. 2015. "El Retorno en el Nuevo Escenario de la Migración entre México y Estados Unidos." CONAPO. www.conapo.gob.mx.

Gil Everaert, Isabel. 2020. "Inhabiting the Meanwhile: Rebuilding Home and Restoring Predictability in a Space of Waiting." *Journal of Ethnic and Migration Studies* 47 (19): 4327–43. https://doi.org/10.1080/1369183X.2020.1798747.

Giorguli-Saucedo, Silvia E., Víctor M. García-Guerrero, and Claudia Masferrer. 2016. *A Migration System in the Making*. Center for Demographic, Urban and Environmental Studies (CEDUA), El Colegio de México. https://cedua.colmex.mx.

Godoy, Margaret, and Harald Bauder. 2021. "Ciudades Santuario y Solidarias en América Latina: Una Revisión de Literatura." *Migración y Desarrollo* 19 (36): 89–113. www.redalyc.org.

González de la Rocha, Mercedes. 1994. *The Resources of Poverty: Women and Survival in Mexican Cities*. Oxford: Blackwell.

Goodman, Adam. 2020. *The Deportation Machine: America's Long History of Expelling Immigrants*. Princeton: Princeton University Press.

Gould, Roger V., and Roberto M. Fernandez. 1989. "Structures of Mediation: A Formal Approach to Brokerage in Transaction Networks." *Sociological Methodology* 19 (19): 89–126. https://doi.org/10.2307/270949.

Greve, Bent. 2008. "What Is Welfare?" *Central European Journal of Public Policy* 2 (1): 50–73.

Gross, Neil. 2009. "A Pragmatist Theory of Social Mechanisms." *American Sociological Review* 74 (3): 358–79. https://doi.org/10.1177/000312240907400302.

Gupta, Akhil, and James Ferguson. 1997. *Culture, Power, Place: Explorations in Critical Anthropology*. Durham: Duke University Press.

Guterres, António. 2012. "High Commissioner's Dialogue on Protection Challenges, Theme: Faith and Protection; Chairman's Summary by António Guterres, United Nations High Commissioner for Refugees." United Nations High Commissioner for Refugees.

Gutiérrez, Oscar. 2016. "Iglesia Aumenta Apoyo a Migrantes en Chiapas." *El Universal*, November 13, 2016. www.eluniversal.com.mx.

Guzmán Elizalde, Lorena. 2014. *Estudio Regional sobre Políticas Públicas de Integración de Migrantes en Centroamérica y México*. Sin Fronteras, IAP. https://sinfronteras.org.mx.

Hagan, Jacqueline. 2006. "Making Theological Sense of the Migration Journey from Latin America: Catholic, Protestant, and Interfaith Perspectives." *American Behavioral Scientist* 49 (11): 1554–73. https://doi.org/10.1177/0002764206289361.

———. 2008. *Migration Miracle: Faith, Hope, and Meaning on the Undocumented Journey*. Cambridge: Harvard University Press.

Hamilton, Nora, and Norma Stoltz Chinchilla. 1991. "Central American Migration: A Framework for Analysis." *Latin American Research Review* 26 (1): 75–110. https://www.jstor.org/stable/2503765.

Hamnett, Brian R. 2022. *Reform, Rebellion and Party in Mexico, 1836–1861*. Cardiff: University of Wales Press.

Hansen, Thomas Blom, and Finn Stepputat. 2005. *Sovereign Bodies: Citizens, Migrants, and States in the Postcolonial World*. Princeton: Princeton University Press.

Harney, Robert F. 1977. "The Commerce of Migration." *Canadian Ethnic Studies / Etudes Ethniques au Canada* 9: 42–53.

Harrell-Bond, Barbara, Eftihia Voutira, and Mark Leopold. 1992. "Counting the Refugees: Gifts, Givers, Patrons and Clients." *Journal of Refugee Studies* 5 (3–4): 205–25. https://doi.org/10.1093/jrs/5.3-4.205.

Hartry, Allison S. 2012. "Gendering Crimmigration: The Intersection of Gender, Immigration, and the Criminal Justice System." *Berkeley Journal of Gender, Law & Justice* 27 (1): 1–27. https://doi.org/10.15779/Z38TM72082.

Haynes, Jeffrey. 2019. "Faith-Based Organizations in Europe." In *Religion and European Society: A Primer*, edited by Benjamin Schewel and Erin K. Wilson, 99–109. Hoboken, NJ: Wiley Blackwell. https://doi.org/10.1002/9781119162766.ch6.

Head-König, Anne-Lise. 2013. "Citizens but Not Belonging: Migrants' Difficulties in Obtaining Entitlement to Relief in Switzerland from the 1550s to the Early Twentieth Century." In *Migration, Settlement and Belonging in Europe, 1500–1930s: Comparative Perspectives*, edited by Stephen King and Anne Winter. New York: Berghahn.

Hein, Jane Ricketts, James Evans, and Phil Jones. 2008. "Mobile Methodologies: Theory, Technology and Practice." *Geography Compass* 2 (5): 1266–85. https://doi.org/10.1111/j.1749-8198.2008.00139.x.

Hernández, Kelly Lytle. 2010. *Migra! A History of the US Border Patrol*. Berkeley: University of California Press.

Hernández-León, Rubén. 2008. *Metropolitan Migrants: The Migration of Urban Mexicans to the United States*. Berkeley: University of California Press.

———. 2013. "Conceptualizing the Migration Industry." In *The Migration Industry and the Commercialization of International Migration*, edited by Thomas Gammeltoft-Hansen and Ninna Nyberg Sørensen, 24–44. London: Routledge.

Herrera-Lasso, Luis, and Juan Artola. 2011. "Migración y Seguridad: Dilemas e Interrogantes." In *Migración y Seguridad: Nuevo Desafío en México*, edited by Natalia Armijo Canto, 11–34. Mexico: Colectivo de Análisis de la Seguridad con Democracia, A.C. (CASEDE).

Heyman, Josiah. 2018. Foreword to *The Shadow of the Wall: Violence and Migration on the US-Mexico Border*, edited by Jeremy Slack, Daniel E. Martínez, and Scott Whiteford. Tucson: University of Arizona Press.

Heyman, Josiah, Jeremy Slack, and Emily Guerra. 2018. "Bordering a 'Crisis': Central American Asylum Seekers and the Reproduction of Dominant Border Enforcement Practices." *Journal of the Southwest* 60: 754–86.

Hilhorst, Dorothea. 2002. "Being Good at Doing Good? Quality and Accountability of Humanitarian NGOs." *Disasters* 26 (3): 193–212.

———. 2018. "Classical Humanitarianism and Resilience Humanitarianism: Making Sense of Two Brands of Humanitarian Action." *Journal of International Humanitarian Action* 3 (1): 1–12. https://doi.org/10.1186/s41018-018-0043-6.

Hopgood, Stephen, and Leslie Vinjamuri. 2012. "Faith in Markets." In *Sacred Aid: Faith and Humanitarianism*, edited by Michael Barnett and Janice Gross Stein, 37–64. New York: Oxford University Press.

Horst, Cindy. 2006. "Buufis amongst Somalis in Dadaab: The Transnational and Historical Logics behind Resettlement Dreams." *Journal of Refugee Studies* 19 (2): 143–57. https://doi.org/10.1093/jrs/fej017.

Horst, Cindy, Stephen Lubkemann, and Robtel Neajai Pailey. 2016. "Diaspora Humanitarianism: The Invisibility of a Third Humanitarian Domain." In *The New Humanitarians in International Practice: Emerging Actors and Contested Principles*, edited by Zeynep Sezgin and Dennis Dijkzeul. London: Routledge.

Horwood, C., and B. Frouws (eds.). 2021. *Mixed Migration Review 2021. Highlights. Interviews. Essays. Data.* Mixed Migration Centre. https://mixedmigration.org.

Hufton, Olwen H. 1974. *The Poor of Eighteenth-Century France, 1750–1789*. Oxford: Clarendon.

IDMC (Internal Displacement Monitoring Centre). 2021. *Figures Analysis: Mexico, 2021*. https://internal-displacement.org.

———. 2022. *Country Profile: Mexico*. www.internal-displacement.org.

Imaz, Cecilia. 2011. "Políticas Públicas sobre Migración y Sociedad Civil en México." In *Las Políticas Públicas sobre Migraciones y la Sociedad Civil en América Latina: Los Casos de Argentina, Brasil, Colombia y México*, edited by Mario Chiarello, 483–522. New York: Scalabrinian International Migration Network.

INEGI (Instituto Nacional de Estadística, Geografía e Informática). 2022. "Tabulados Predefinidos. VII. Caracterización del Delito en los Hogares." *Encuesta Nacional de Victimización y Percepción sobre Seguridad Pública (ENVIPE)*. www.inegi.org.mx.

Ingold, Tim. 2011. *Being Alive: Essays on Movement, Knowledge and Description*. London: Routledge.

INM (Instituto Nacional de Migración). 2014a. "Rescata el INM a 12 Hondure-
ños Secuestrados por Una Banda Delictiva en Tabasco." SEGOB (Secretaría de
Gobernación). www.gob.mx.

———. 2014b. "Rescata INM a 61 Migrantes en Chiapas y Coahuila." SEGOB (Secretaría de Gobernación). www.gob.mx.

———. 2016a. "Folio Infomex No. 0411100087716: Solicitud de Información." Edited
by Acceso a la Información y Protección de Datos Personales Instituto Nacional
de Transparencia.

———. 2016b. "Programa Paisano del INM." Edited by Acceso a la Información y Protección de Datos Personales Instituto Nacional de Transparencia. SEGOB (Secretaría de Gobernación). www.gob.mx.

———. 2022. "Dirección de Repatriación Digna." www.gob.mx.

Innes, Joanna. 1996. "The 'Mixed Economy of Welfare' in Early Modern England: Assessments of the Options, from Hale to Malthus (c. 1683–1803)." In *Charity, Self-Interest and
Welfare in the English Past*, edited by Martin Daunton, 139–80. London: UCL Press.

Innes, Joanna, Stephen King, and Anne Winter. 2013. "Settlement and Belonging
in Europe, 1500–1930s: Structures, Negotiations and Experiences." In *Migration,
Settlement and Belonging in Europe, 1500–1930s: Comparative Perspectives*, edited by
Stephen King and Anne Winter, 1–28. New York: Berghahn.

IOM (International Organization for Migration). 2012a. "IOM Launches Migrant Mass
Information Campaign in Mexico and Guatemala." www.iom.int.

———. 2012b. "Migration Trends. Mexico." www.iom.int.

———. 2015. "The World's Congested Human Migration Routes in 5 Maps." IOM
blog. https://weblog.iom.int.

———. 2017. "Marco Operacional para las Situaciones de Crisis Migratoria (MOCM):
Plan Estratégico México." www.iom.int.

———. 2022. "Latest Migrant Tragedy in Texas Highlights Crisis along Deadliest Migration Land Route." www.iom.int.

Isacson, Adam, Maureen Meyer, and Ashley Davis. 2014. "Border Security and
Migration: A Report from Arizona." Washington Office on Latin America
(WOLA). www.wola.org.

İşleyen, Beste. 2018. "Turkey's Governance of Irregular Migration at European Union
Borders: Emerging Geographies of Care and Control." *Environment and Planning
D: Society and Space* 36 (5): 849–66. https://doi.org/10.1177/0263775818762132.

James, Myfanwy. 2022. "Humanitarian Shapeshifting: Navigation, Brokerage and
Access in Eastern DR Congo." *Journal of Intervention and Statebuilding* 16 (3):
349–67. https://doi.org/10.1080/17502977.2021.2002591.

Jasso Vargas, Rosalba. 2021. "Espacios de Estancia Prolongada para la Población
Migrante Centroamericana en Tránsito por México." *Frontera Norte* 33
(Febrero). https://doi.org/10.33679/rfn.v1i1.2075.

Johnson, Heather. 2012. "Moments of Solidarity, Migrant Activism and (Non) Citizens
at Global Borders: Political Agency at Tanzanian Refugee Camps, Australian

Detention Centres and European Borders." In *Citizenship, Migrant Activism and the Politics of Movement*, edited by Peter Nyers and Kim Rygiel, 109–28. London: Routledge.

Johnson, Norman. 1999. *Mixed Economies Welfare: A Comparative Perspective*. Hemel Hempstead: Prentice Hall Europe.

Jones, Colin. 1996. "Some Recent Trends in the History of Charity." In *Charity, Self-Interest and Welfare in the English Past*, edited by Martin Daunton, 51–64. London: UCL Press.

Jones, Robert T., and Chuck Ryan. 2002. "Matching Process Choice and Uncertainty: Modeling Quality Management." *Business Process Management Journal* 8 (2): 161–68. https://doi.org/10.1108/14637150210425117.

Kastner, Kristin. 2013. "Nigerian Border Crossers: Women Travelling to Europe by Land." In *Long Journeys: African Migrants on the Road*, edited by Alessandro Triulzi and Robert McKenzie, 25–44. Leiden: Brill.

Kerwin, Donald, and Daniel E. Martínez. 2024. "Forced Migration, Deterrence, and Solutions to the Non-Natural Disaster of Migrant Deaths along the US-Mexico Border and Beyond." *Journal on Migration and Human Security* 12 (3): 127–59. https://doi.org/10.1177/23315024241277532.

Khosravi, Shahram. 2010. *"Illegal" Traveller: An Auto-Ethnography of Borders*. New York: Palgrave Macmillan.

Kimball, Ann. 2007. "The Transit State: A Comparative Analysis of Mexico and Morocco Immigration Policies." Working Paper 150. Center for Comparative Immigration Studies, University of California San Diego. http://ccis.ucsd.edu/_files/wp150.pdf.

King, Stephen, and Alannah Tomkins (eds.). 2003. *The Poor in England, 1700–1850: An Economy of Makeshifts*. Manchester: Manchester University Press.

Koizumi, Koichi, and Gerhard Hoffstaedter (eds.). 2015. *Urban Refugees: Challenges in Protection, Services and Policy*. London: Routledge.

Koulish, Robert, and Martje van der Woude (eds.). 2020. *Crimmigrant Nations: Resurgent Nationalism and the Closing of Borders*. New York: Fordham University Press.

Kraft, Kathryn, and Jonathan D. Smith. 2019. "Between International Donors and Local Faith Communities: Intermediaries in Humanitarian Assistance to Syrian Refugees in Jordan and Lebanon." *Disasters* 43 (1): 24–45. https://doi.org/10.1111/disa.12301.

Kron, Stefanie. 2016. "'Nacimos de la Nada': Border Struggles and Maternal Politics in Mexico." *Citizenship Studies* 20 (5): 579–94. https://doi.org/10.1080/13621025.2016.1182684.

Kubal, Agnieszka. 2013. "Conceptualizing Semi-Legality in Migration Research." *Law & Society Review* 47 (3): 555–87. https://doi.org/10.1111/lasr.12031.

Landau, Norma. 1988. "The Laws of Settlement and the Surveillance of Immigration in Eighteenth-Century Kent." *Continuity and Change* 3 (3): 391–420. https://doi.org/10.1017/S026841600000429X.

Laqueur, Thomas. 2009. "Mourning, Pity, and the Work of Narrative in the Making of 'Humanity.'" In *Humanitarianism and Suffering: The Mobilization of Empathy*, edited by Richard Ashby Wilson and Richard D. Brown, 31–57. Cambridge: Cambridge University Press.

Larrauri Olguín, Gibran, and Edwing Solano Sánchez. 2013. "Segregación y Violencia: Migrantes Transitando por México." *Desde el Jardín de Freud: Revista de Psicoanálisis*, no. 13: 305–21. https://repositorio.unal.edu.co.

Larson, Paul D., and Cyril Foropon. 2018. "Process Improvement in Humanitarian Operations: An Organisational Theory Perspective." *International Journal of Production Research* 56 (21): 6828–41. https://doi.org/10.1080/00207543.2018.1424374.

Lees, Lynn Hollen. 1998. *The Solidarities of Strangers: The English Poor Laws and the People, 1700–1948*. Cambridge: Cambridge University Press.

Leutert, Stephanie, Ana Ruiz, Ethan Tenison, and Raymond Weyandt. 2020. *Las Políticas Migratorias de Andrés Manuel López Obrador en México*. Austin: Strauss Center for International Security and Law, University of Texas.

Levitt, Peggy, Jocelyn Viterna, Armin Mueller, and Charlotte Lloyd. 2016. "Transnational Social Protection: Setting the Agenda." *Oxford Development Studies* 45 (1): 2–19. https://doi.org/10.1080/13600818.2016.1239702.

Linde, Thomas. 2009. "Humanitarian Assistance to Migrants Irrespective of Their Status: Towards a Non-Categorical Approach." *International Review of the Red Cross* 91 (875): 567–78. https://doi.org/10.1017/S1816383109990439.

Li Ng, Juan José. 2020. "Map 2020 of Migrant Houses, Shelters and Soup Kitchens for Migrants in Mexico." BBVA Research. www.bbvaresearch.com.

Lira, Andrés, and Anne Staples. 2010. "Del Desastre a la Reconstrucción Republicana, 1848–1876." In *Nueva Historia General de México*, edited by Erik Velásquez García et al., 443–86. Mexico: Colegio de Mexico. http://www.jstor.org/stable/j.ctt14jxnr2.

Lunn, Jenny. 2009. "The Role of Religion, Spirituality and Faith in Development: A Critical Theory Approach." *Third World Quarterly* 30 (5): 937–51. https://doi.org/10.1080/01436590902959180.

MacAuslan, Ian, and Rachel Sabates-Wheeler. 2011. "Structures of Access to Social Provision for Migrants." In *Migration and Social Protection: Claiming Social Rights beyond Borders*, edited by Rachel Sabates-Wheeler and Rayah Feldman, 61–87. London: Palgrave Macmillan.

Magallanes-Gonzalez, Cynthia. 2020. "Sub-Saharan Leaders in Morocco's Migration Industry: Activism, Integration, and Smuggling. *Journal of North African Studies* 26 (5): 993–1012. https://doi.org/10.1080/13629387.2020.1800213.

Mainwaring, Ċetta, and Noelle Brigden. 2016. "Matryoshka Journeys: Im/Mobility during Migration." *Geopolitics* 21 (2): 407–34. https://doi.org/10.1080/14650045.2015.1122592.

Manenti, Rene. 2012. "Migration and Borders: The 'Casas del Migrante' and the Flow of Unauthorized Migrants." PhD diss., Fordham University. http://search.proquest.com/docview/1399597266.

Marchand, Marianne H. 2021. "The Caravanas de Migrantes Making Their Way North: Problematising the Biopolitics of Mobilities in Mexico." *Third World Quarterly* 42 (1): 141–61. https://doi.org/10.1080/01436597.2020.1824579.

Marcus, George E. 1995. "Ethnography in/of the World System: The Emergence of Multi-Sited Ethnography." *Annual Review of Anthropology* 24 (1): 95–117.

Martin, Deborah G. 2013. "Place Frames: Analysing Practice and Production of Place in Contentious Politics." In *Spaces of Contention: Spatialities and Social Movements*, edited by Walter Nicholls, Byron Miller, and Justin Beaumont, 85–103. Farnham: Ashgate.

Martin, Susan F., Sanjula Weerasinghe, and Abbie Taylor (eds.). 2014. *Humanitarian Crises and Migration: Causes, Consequences, and Responses*. London: Routledge.

Martínez, Daniel E. 2013. "The Crossing Experience: Unauthorized Migration along the Arizona-Sonora Border." PhD diss., University of Arizona. http://hdl.handle.net/10150/293415.

Martínez, Daniel E., Jeremy Slack, and Ricardo D. Martínez-Schuldt. 2018. "Repeat Migration in the Age of the 'Unauthorized Permanent Resident': A Quantitative Assessment of Migration Intentions Postdeportation." *International Migration Review* 52 (4): 1186–1217. https://doi.org/10.1177/0197918318767921.

Martínez, Fernando, and Fabiola Camacho. 2014. "Recibe Caravana del Migrante Permisos de Tránsito por México." *La Jornada*, April 26, 2014, 11. www.jornada.com.mx.

Martínez-Saldaña, Jesús. 2003. "Los Olvidados Become Heroes: The Evolution of Mexico's Policies towards Citizens Abroad." In *International Migration and Sending Countries: Perceptions, Policies and Transnational Relations*, edited by Eva Østergaard-Nielsen, 33–56. Basingstoke: Palgrave Macmillan.

Martínez-Schuldt, Ricardo D. 2020. "Mexican Consular Protection Services across the United States: How Local Social, Economic, and Political Conditions Structure the Sociolegal Support of Emigrants." *International Migration Review* 54 (4): 1016–44. https://doi.org/10.1177/0197918319901264.

Massey, Douglas S., Joaquín Arango, Graeme Hugo, Ali Kouaouci, Adela Pellegrino, and J. Edward Taylor. 2008. *Worlds in Motion: Understanding International Migration at the End of the Millennium*. Oxford: Oxford University Press.

Mauss, Marcel. 1973. "Techniques of the Body." *Economy and Society* 2 (1): 70–88. https://doi.org/10.1080/03085147300000003.

McAdam, Doug, Sidney G. Tarrow, and Charles Tilly. 2001. *Dynamics of Contention*. Cambridge: Cambridge University Press.

McAdam, Jane. 2014a. "Conceptualizing 'Crisis Migration': A Theoretical Perspective." In *Humanitarian Crises and Migration: Causes, Consequences, and Responses*, edited by Susan F. Martin, Sanjula Weerasinghe, and Abbie Taylor, 28–49. London: Routledge.

———. 2014b. "The Concept of Crisis Migration." *Forced Migration Review*, no. 45: 10. www.fmreview.org.

McAuliffe, Marie, and Anna Triandafyllidou (eds.). 2021. *World Migration Report, 2022*. Geneva: International Organization for Migration.

McNevin, Anne. 2006. "Political Belonging in a Neoliberal Era: The Struggle of the Sans-Papiers." *Citizenship Studies* 10 (2): 135–51. https://doi.org/10.1080/13621020600633051.

———. 2010. "Border Policing and Sovereign Terrain: The Spatial Framing of Unwanted Migration in Melbourne and Australia." *Globalizations* 7 (3): 407–19. https://doi.org/10.1080/14747731003669834.

Menjívar, Cecilia. 2014. "Immigration Law beyond Borders: Externalizing and Internalizing Border Controls in an Era of Securitization." *Annual Review of Law and Social Science* 10 (November): 353–69.

Menjívar, Cecilia, and Leisy Abrego. 2012. "Legal Violence in the Lives of Immigrants: How Immigration Enforcement Affects Families, Schools, and Workplaces." Center for American Progress. www.americanprogress.org.

Merlín-Escorza, Cesar E., Tine Davids, and Joris Schapendonk. 2020. "Sheltering as a Destabilising and Perpetuating Practice in the Migration Management Architecture in Mexico." *Third World Quarterly* 42 (1): 105–22. https://doi.org/10.1080/01436597.2020.1794806.

Meyer, Maureen, and Stephanie Brewer. 2010. "A Dangerous Journey through Mexico: Human Rights Violations against Migrants in Transit." Washington Office on Latin America (WOLA) and Centro de Derechos Humanos Pro. www.wola.org.

Minca, Claudio. 2015. "Geographies of the Camp." *Political Geography* 49: 74–83. https://doi.org/10.1016/j.polgeo.2014.12.005.

Miraglia, Peter. 2016. "The Invisible Migrants of the Darién Gap: Evolving Immigration Routes in the Americas." *Council on Hemispheric Affairs*. www.coha.org.

Moguel, Miguel, and Rodolfo Córdova. 2012. "El Drama de Lechería." Animal Político, August 25, 2012. https://animalpolitico.com.

Mol, Annemarie. 2008. *The Logic of Care: Health and the Problem of Patient Choice.* New York: Routledge.

Montoya Ortiz, Merari Stephanie, and Juan Gabino González Becerril. 2015. "Evolución de la Migración de Retorno en México: Migrantes Procedentes de Estados Unidos en 1995 y de 1999 a 2014." *Papeles de Población* 21: 47–78.

Moorehead, Caroline. 1998. *Dunant's Dream: War, Switzerland and the History of the Red Cross.* London: HarperCollins.

Morello, Gustavo. 2021. *Lived Religion in Latin America: An Enchanted Modernity.* Oxford: Oxford University Press.

Morton, Adam David. 2012. "The War on Drugs in Mexico: A Failed State?" *Third World Quarterly* 33 (9): 1631–45. https://doi.org/10.1080/01436597.2012.720837.

Mountz, Alison. 2004. "Embodying the Nation-State: Canada's Response to Human Smuggling." *Political Geography* 23 (3): 323–45. https://doi.org/10.1016/j.polgeo.2003.12.017.

Nail, Thomas. 2015. *The Figure of the Migrant.* Stanford: Stanford University Press.

Nevins, Joseph. 2018. "The Speed of Life and Death: Migrant Fatalities, Territorial Boundaries, and Energy Consumption." *Mobilities* 13 (1): 29–44. https://doi.org/10.1080/17450101.2017.1349392.

Newell, Bryce Clayton, Sara Vannini, and Ricardo Gomez. 2020. "The Information Practices and Politics of Migrant-Aid Work in the US-Mexico

Borderlands." *Information Society* 36 (4): 199–213. https://doi.org/10.1080
/01972243.2020.1761918.

Ngai, Mae M. 2014. *Impossible Subjects: Illegal Aliens and the Making of Modern America*. Updated ed. Princeton: Princeton University Press.

Nyers, Peter. 2003. "Abject Cosmopolitanism: The Politics of Protection in the Anti-Deportation Movement." *Third World Quarterly* 24 (6): 1069–93. https://doi.org/10.1080/01436590310001630071.

Occhipinti, Laurie A. 2015. "Faith-Based Organizations and Development." In *The Routledge Handbook of Religions and Global Development*, edited by Emma Tomalin, 331–45. London: Routledge.

OCHA (Office for the Coordination of Humanitarian Affairs). 2022. "OCHA on Message: Humanitarian Principles." www.unocha.org.

Olayo-Méndez, Alejandro. 2013. "Refining the Concept of the Migration Industry: The Emergence of a Humanitarian Aid Network in the Mexican Migration Corridor." University of Oxford. Unpublished manuscript.

———. 2017. "Programa de la Frontera Sur and Interdiction." *Peace Review* 29 (1): 24–30. https://doi.org/10.1080/10402659.2017.1272287.

———. 2018. "Migration, Poverty, and Violence in Mexico: The Role of Casas de Migrantes." PhD diss., University of Oxford.

Olwig, Karen Fog. 2003. "'Transnational' Socio-Cultural Systems and Ethnographic Research: Views from an Extended Field Site." *International Migration Review* 37 (3): 787–811.

Omilusi, Mike. 2018. "Investigando o Significado Decrescente de Governo e Filantropia na Nigéria: Religião Como Refúgio?" *Revista Brasileira de Estudos Africanos* 3 (5). https://doi.org/http://dx.doi.org/10.22456/2448-3923.80821.

Orozco, Manuel, and Michelle Lapointe. 2004. "Mexican Hometown Associations and Development Opportunities." *Journal of International Affairs* 57 (2): 31–51. https://www.jstor.org/stable/24357864.

Ortega Ramírez, Adriana Sletza, and Luis Miguel Morales Gámez. 2021. "(In) Seguridad, Derechos y Migración: La Guardia Nacional en Operativos Migratorios en México." *REVISTA IUS* 15 (47). https://doi.org/10.35487/rius.v15i47.2021.699.

Pacitto, Julia. 2012. "Workshop Report: South-South Humanitarianism in Contexts of Forced Displacement." Refugee Studies Centre, University of Oxford. www.rsc.ox.ac.uk.

Paerregaard, Karsten. 2008. *Peruvians Dispersed: A Global Ethnography of Migration*. Lanham, MD: Lexington Books.

Pallister-Wilkins, Polly. 2015. "The Humanitarian Politics of European Border Policing: Frontex and Border Police in Evros." *International Political Sociology* 9 (1): 53–69. https://doi.org/10.1111/ips.12076.

———. 2017. "Humanitarian Rescue/Sovereign Capture and the Policing of Possible Responses to Violent Borders." *Global Policy* 8 (S1): 19–24. https://doi.org/10.1111/1758-5899.12401.

———. 2018. Médecins Avec Frontières and the Making of a Humanitarian Borderscape. *Environment and Planning D: Society and Space* 36 (1): 114–38. https://doi.org/10.1177/0263775817740588.

———. 2020. "Hotspots and the Geographies of Humanitarianism." *Environment and Planning D: Society and Space* 38 (6): 991–1008. https://doi.org/10.1177/0263775818754884.

———. 2022. *Humanitarian Borders: Unequal Mobility and Saving Lives*. New York: Verso.

París Pombo, María Dolores. 2021. "Movilidades e Inmovilidades Humanas ante el Cierre Parcial de la Frontera México-Estados Unidos." In *Ciencias Sociales en Acción: Respuesta frente al COVID-19 desde el Norte de México*, edited by Oscar Contreras. Tijuana: El Colegio de la Frontera Norte.

París Pombo, María Dolores, and Peter Müller. 2016. "La Incidencia Política de las Organizaciones Promigrantes en México." In *Asociaciones Inmigrantes y Fronteras Internacionales*, edited by Luis Escala Rabadán, 255–82. Tijuana: El Colegio de la Frontera Norte; San Luis Potosí, SLP: El Colegio de San Luis.

Parker, Noel, and Nick Vaughan-Williams. 2012. "Critical Border Studies: Broadening and Deepening the 'Lines in the Sand' Agenda." *Geopolitics* 17 (4): 727–33. https://doi.org/10.1080/14650045.2012.706111.

Parrini Roses, Rodrigo, and Luis Alquisiras Terrones. 2019. "Discursive Displacements and Institutional Transformations in the Practices of Solidarity for Central American Migrants in Mexico." *Migraciones Internacionales* 10 (36). https://doi.org/10.33679/rmi.v1i1.2181.

Pederzini, Carla, Fernando Riosmena, Claudia Masferrer, and Noemy Molina. 2015. "Three Decades of Migration from the Northern Triangle of Central America: A Historical and Demographic Outlook." CANAMID Policy Brief Series, 1. CIESAS. www.canamid.org.

Perez Esparza, David, Shane Johnson, and Paul Gill. 2020. "Why Did Mexico Become a Violent Country?" *Security Journal* 33: 179–209. https://doi.org/10.1057/s41284-019-00178-6.

Peters, María de Jesús. 2016. "La Ruta de la Migración Africana: Congo-Brasil-México." *El Universal*, September 1, 2016. www.eluniversal.com.mx.

Pons, Diego. 2021. "Climate Extremes, Food Insecurity, and Migration in Central America: A Complicated Nexus." Migration Policy Institute. www.migrationpolicy.org.

Pontifical Council for the Pastoral Care of Migrants and Itinerant People. 2004. *Instruction: Erga Migrantes Caritas Christi (The Love of Christ towards Migrants)*. Holy See. www.vatican.va.

Portes, Alejandro. 1998. "Social Capital: Its Origins and Applications in Modern Sociology." *Annual Review of Sociology*, no. 24: 1–24.

Portes, Alejandro, and Rubén G. Rumbaut. 2014. *Immigrant America: A Portrait*. 4th ed. Berkeley: University of California Press.

Powell, Martin A. 2007. "The Mixed Economy of Welfare and the Social Division of Welfare." In *Understanding the Mixed Economy of Welfare*, edited by Martin A. Powell, 1–21. Bristol, UK: Policy Press/Social Policy Association.

Prakash, Chandra, Maria Besiou, Parikshit Charan, and Sumeet Gupta. 2020. "Organization Theory in Humanitarian Operations: A Review and Suggested Research Agenda." *Journal of Humanitarian Logistics and Supply Chain Management* 10 (2): 261–84. https://doi.org/10.1108/JHLSCM-08-2019-0051.

Quang, Pham, and Anh Thu. 2015. "Multidimensional Poverty and Migrant Households: A Case Study of Vietnam." Macquarie University. https://doi.org/10.25949/19435610.v1.

REDODEM (Red de Documentación de las Organizaciones Defensoras de Migrantes). 2015. "Migración en Tránsito por México: Rostro de Una Crisis Humanitaria Internacional." REDODEM.

———. 2016. "Migrantes en México: Recorriendo un Camino de Violencia." REDODEM.

———. 2017. "El Estado Indolente: Recuento de la Violencia en las Rutas Migratorias y Perfiles de Movilidad en México." REDODEM.

———. 2018. "Procesos Migratorios en México: Nuevos Rostros, Mismas Dinámicas." REDODEM.

———. 2019. "Migraciones en México: Fronteras, Omisiones y Transgresiones." REDODEM.

———. 2020. "Movilidad Humana en Confinamiento: Contención, Vulneración de Derechos y Desprotección en México." REDODEM.

———. 2021. "Fronteras, Omisiones y Trasgresiones." REDODEM.

Refugee Hosts. n.d. "Our Work." https://refugeehosts.org/.

Rieff, David. 2002. *A Bed for the Night: Humanitarianism in Crisis.* London: Vintage.

Rigoni, Flor María. 2007. "La Última Frontera del Crimen: El Secuestro del Migrante Indocumentado." *Migrantes. Revista de Información y Pastoral Migratoria* XIII (3): 3. http://casadelmigrantetijuana.com.

Rincón Gabourel, Elvira. 2018. "La Sociedad Civil Organizada Responde al Impacto de Políticas Públicas." *Gestión y Política Pública* 27 (1): 181–209.

Ríos, Viridiana. 2013. "Why Did Mexico Become So Violent? A Self-Reinforcing Violent Equilibrium Caused by Competition and Enforcement." *Trends in Organized Crime* 16: 138–55. https://doi.org/10.1007/s12117-012-9175-z.

Rivera Sánchez, Liliana. 2015. "Narratives of Return Migration and Mobility: Between Practices of Engagement and Multiple Spatialities in the City." *Estudios Políticos*, no. 47: 243–64. https://doi.org/10.17533/udea.espo.n47a14.

Rocha Romero, David, and Marco Tulio Ocegueda Hernández. 2013. "After Many Years, I Was Deported: Identifying and Deportation Process of Non-Criminal Immigrant Women." *Estudios Fronterizos* 14 (28): 9–34.

Rodríguez, Hipólito. 2016. "Governmentality and Violence towards Central American Migrants in the Gulf of Mexico." CANAMID Policy Brief Series, 12. CANAMID. www.canamid.org.

Rodríguez, María Teresa. 2016. "Migración en Tránsito y Prácticas de Ayuda Solidaria en el Centro de Veracruz, México." *Encuentro* 103: 47–58. https://doi.org/10.5377/encuentro.v0i103.2693.

Rodríguez Chávez, Ernesto (ed.) 2014. *Central American Transit Migration through Mexico to the United States: Diagnosis and Recommendations*. Mexico: ITAM. www.migracionentransito.org.

———. 2016. "Migración Centroamericana en Tránsito Irregular por México: Nuevas Cifras y Tendencias." CANAMID Policy Brief Series, 14. CANAMID. www.canamid.org.

Rosales Sandoval, Isabel. 2013. "Public Officials and the Migration Industry in Guatemala: Greasing the Wheels of a Corrupt Machine." In *The Migration Industry and the Commercialization of International Migration*, edited by Thomas Gammeltoft-Hansen and Ninna Nyberg Sørensen, 215–37. London: Routledge.

Rosenblum, Marc R., Doris Meissner, Claire Bergeron, and Faye Hipsman. 2014. "The Deportation Dilemma: Reconciling Tough and Humane Enforcement." Migration Policy Institute. www.migrationpolicy.org.

Rozakou, Katerina. 2017. "Solidarity #Humanitarianism: The Blurred Boundaries of Humanitarianism in Greece." *Etnofoor* 29 (2): 99–104. https://www.jstor.org/stable/26296172.

Ruiz Soto, Ariel. 2020. "One Year after the US-Mexico Agreement Reshaping Mexico's Migration Policies." Migration Policy Institute. www.migrationpolicy.org.

Ryndyk, Oleksandr, Brigitte Suter, and Gunhild Odden (eds.). 2021. *Migration to and from Welfare States: Lived Experiences of the Welfare-Migration Nexus in a Globalised World*. Cham, Switzerland: Springer Nature. https://doi.org/10.1007/978-3-030-67615-5.

Sabates-Wheeler, Rachel, and Stephen Devereux. 2008. "Transformative Social Protection: The Currency of Social Justice." In *Social Protection for the Poor and Poorest*, edited by Armando Barrientos and David Hulme, 64–84. Basingstoke: Palgrave Macmillan.

Sabates-Wheeler, Rachel, and Rayah Feldman (eds.). 2011. *Migration and Social Protection: Claiming Social Rights beyond Borders*. New York: Palgrave Macmillan. https://doi.org/10.1057/9780230306554.

Salazar, Noel B., Alice Elliot, and Roger Norum. 2017. "Studying Mobilities Theoretical Notes and Methodological Queries." In *Methodologies of Mobility: Ethnography and Experiment Responsibility*, edited by Alice Elliot, Roger Norum, and Noel B. Salazar. New York: Berghahn.

Salazar C., Luz María, and José Antonio Álvarez Lobato. 2018. "Violencia y Desplazamientos Forzados en México." *Cuicuilco: Revista de Ciencias Antropológicas* 25 (73): 19–37. www.scielo.org.mx.

Sanchez, Gabriella. 2014. *Human Smuggling and Border Crossings*. London: Routledge.

———. 2017. "Critical Perspectives on Clandestine Migration Facilitation: An Overview of Migrant Smuggling." *Journal on Migration and Human Security* 5 (1): 9–27 https://doi.org/10.1177/233150241700500102.

Sanchez, Gabriella, and Sheldon Zhang. 2018. "Rumors, Encounters, Collaborations, Survival: The Migrant Smuggling-Drug Trafficking Nexus in the US Southwest." *Annals of the American Academy of Political Sciences* 676 (1): 135–51. https://doi.org/10.1177/0002716217752331.

Sandri, Elisa. 2018. "'Volunteer Humanitarianism': Volunteers and Humanitarian Aid in the Jungle Refugee Camp of Calais." *Journal of Ethnic and Migration Studies* 44 (1): 65–80. https://doi.org/10.1080/1369183X.2017.1352467.

Santamaría, Gema. 2015. "Drugs, Gangs and Vigilantes: How to Tackle the New Breeds of Mexican Armed Violence." *Estudios Internacionales* (Santiago) 47 (181): 115–34. http://dx.doi.org/10.5354/0719-3769.2015.36841.

Scanlon, Ted, Obinna Paul Uguru, Tahseen Jafry, Blessings Chinsinga, Peter Mvula, Joseph Chunga, Lilian Mukuka Zimba, et al. 2016. "The Role of Social Actors in Water Access in Sub-Saharan Africa: Evidence from Malawi and Zambia." *Water Resources and Rural Development* 8: 25–36. https://doi.org/10.1016/j.wrr.2016.08.001.

Schapendonk, Joris. 2009. "Moving and Mediating: A Mobile View on Sub-Saharan African Migration towards Europe." In *Communication Technologies in Latin America and Africa: A Multidisciplinary Perspective*, edited by M. Fernández-Ardèvol and A. Ros, 293–318. Barcelona: Universitat Oberta de Catalunya.

———. 2018. "Navigating the Migration Industry: Migrants Moving through an African-European Web of Facilitation/Control." *Journal of Ethnic and Migration Studies* 44 (4): 663–79. https://doi.org/10.1080/1369183X.2017.1315522.

Schapendonk, Joris, and Griet Steel. 2014. "Following Migrant Trajectories: The Im/Mobility of Sub-Saharan Africans en Route to the European Union." *Annals of the Association of American Geographers* 104 (2): 262–70.

Schapendonk, Joris, Ilse van Liempt, Inga Schwarz, and Griet Steel. 2020. "Re-routing Migration Geographies: Migrants, Trajectories and Mobility Regimes." *Geoforum* 116: 211–16. https://doi.org/10.1016/j.geoforum.2018.06.007.

Schewel, Kerilyn. 2020. "Understanding Immobility: Moving beyond the Mobility Bias in Migration Studies." *International Migration Review* 54 (2): 328–55. https://doi.org/10.1177/0197918319831952.

Schuster, Liza, and Nassim Majidi. 2015. "Deportation Stigma and Re-Migration." *Journal of Ethnic and Migration Studies* 41 (4): 635–52. https://doi.org/10.1080/1369183X.2014.957174.

Scott, Jason D. 2003. "The Scope and Scale of Faith-Based Social Services: A Review of the Research Literature Focusing on the Activities of Faith-Based Organizations in the Delivery of Social Services." Roundtable on Religion and Social Welfare Policy. Albany, NY: Rockefeller Institute of Government.

Scott-Smith, Tom. 2014. "Defining Hunger, Redefining Food: Humanitarianism in the Twentieth Century." PhD diss., University of Oxford. https://ora.ox.ac.uk.

———. 2016. "Humanitarian Dilemmas in a Mobile World." *Refugee Survey Quarterly* 35 (2): 1–21. https://doi.org/10.1093/rsq/hdw001.

Second Vatican Council. 1965. *Pastoral Constitution Gaudium et Spes* [Church in the Modern World]. Holy See. www.vatican.va.

SEGOB (Secretaría de Gobernación). 2011. *Ley de Migración*. Edited by Diario Oficial de la Federación. Mexico: Diario Oficial de la Federación.

———. 2013. "Síntesis 2013: Estadística Migratoria." Edited by Unidad de Política Migratoria. www.politicamigratoria.gob.mx.

———. 2016. "Programa Somos Mexicanos." Instituto Nacional de Migración blog. www.gob.mx.

———. 2019. *DECRETO por el Que se Reforman, Adicionan y Derogan Diversas Disposiciones de la Constitución Política de los Estados Unidos Mexicanos, en Materia de Guardia Nacional*. Mexico: Diario Oficial de la Federación.

Semple, Kirk. 2016. "Haitians, after Perilous Journey, Find Door to US Abruptly Shut." *New York Times*, September 23, 2016. www.nytimes.com.

Sezgin, Zeynep, and Dennis Dijkzeul. 2013. "Migrant Organisations in Humanitarian Action." *International Migration and Integration* 15: 159–77. https://doi.org/10.1007/s12134-013-0273-9.

——— (eds.). 2016. *The New Humanitarians in International Practice: Emerging Actors and Contested Principles*. London: Routledge.

Shutes, Isabel, and Armine Ishkanian. 2022. "Transnational Welfare within and beyond the Nation-State: Civil Society Responses to the Migration Crisis in Greece." *Journal of Ethnic and Migration Studies* 48 (3): 524–41. https://doi.org/10.1080/1369183X.2021.1892479.

Sigona, Nando. 2015. "Campzenship: Reimagining the Camp as a Social and Political Space." *Citizenship Studies* 19 (1): 1–15. https://doi.org/10.1080/13621025.2014.937643.

Silva Quiroz, Yolanda. 2014. "Transmigración de Centroamericanos por México: Su Vulnerabilidad y Sus Derechos Humanos." PhD diss., El Colegio de la Frontera Norte. *http://colef.repositorioinstitucional.mx*.

Sin Fronteras IAP. 2013. "La Ruta del Encierro: Situación de las Personas en Detención en Estaciones Migratorias y Estancias Provisionales." Sin Fronteras IAP. https://sinfronteras.org.mx.

Singer, Audrey, and Douglas S. Massey. 1998. "The Social Process of Undocumented Border Crossing among Mexican Migrants." *International Migration Review* 32 (3): 561–92. https://www.jstor.org/stable/2547764.

Skeldon, Ronald. 1997. *Migration and Development: A Global Perspective*. Essex: Addison Wesley Longman.

———. 2002. "Migration and Poverty: Ambivalent Relationships." *Asia-Pacific Population Journal* 17 (4): 67–82. https://doi.org/10.18356/7c0e3452-en.

Slack, Jeremy. 2016. "Captive Bodies: Migrant Kidnapping and Deportation in Mexico." *Area* 48 (3): 271–77. https://doi.org/10.1111/area.12151.

———. 2019. *Deported to Death: How Drug Violence Is Changing Migration on the US–Mexico Border*. Berkeley: University of California Press.

Slack, Jeremy, Daniel E. Martínez, Alison Elizabeth Lee, and Scott Whiteford. 2016. "The Geography of Border Militarization: Violence, Death and Health in Mexico and the United States." *Journal of Latin American Geography* 15 (1): 7–32. https://doi.org/10.1353/lag.2016.0009.

Slack, Jeremy, Daniel E. Martínez, Scott Whiteford, and Emily Peiffer. 2013. "In the Shadow of the Wall: Family Separation, Immigration Enforcement and Security." Center for Latin American Studies, University of Arizona. https://ssrn.com/abstract=2633204.

Sládková, Jana. 2010. *Journeys of Undocumented Honduran Migrants to the United States*. El Paso: LFB Scholarly Publishing.

———. 2016. "Stratification of Undocumented Migrant Journeys: Honduran Case." *International Migration* 54 (1): 84–99. https://doi.org/10.1111/imig.12141.

Slim, Hugo. 2003. "Humanitarianism with Borders? NGOs, Belligerent Military Forces and Humanitarian Action." In *Conference Report: Conference on NGOs in a Changing World Order: Dilemmas and Challenges*. Geneva: International Council of Voluntary Agencies.

———. 2015. *Humanitarian Ethics: A Guide to the Morality of Aid in War and Disaster*. London: Hurst.

Solano, Priscilla. 2024. *Shelter on the Journey: Humanitarianism, Human Rights, and Migration*. Philadelphia: Temple University Press.

Solano, Priscilla, and Douglas S. Massey. 2022. "Migrating through the Corridor of Death: The Making of a Complex Humanitarian Crisis." *Journal on Migration and Human Security* 10 (3): 147–72. https://doi.org/10.1177/23315024221119784.

Sørensen, Ninna Nyberg. 2013. "Migration between Social and Criminal Networks: Jumping the Remains of the Honduran Migration Train." In *The Migration Industry and the Commercialization of International Migration*, edited by Thomas Gammeltoft-Hansen and Ninna Nyberg Sørensen, 238–61. London: Routledge.

———. 2014. "Central American Migration, Remittances and Transnational Development." In *Handbook of Central American Governance*, edited by Diego Sánchez-Ancochea and Salvador Martí i Puig, 45–58. London: Routledge, Taylor & Francis.

Soria-Escalante, Hada, Alejandra Alday-Santiago, Erika Alday-Santiago, Natalia Limón-Rodríguez, Pamela Manzanares-Melendres, and Adriana Tena-Castro. 2022. "'We All Get Raped': Sexual Violence against Latin American Women in Migratory Transit in Mexico." *Violence Against Women* 28 (5): 1259–81. https://doi.org/10.1177/10778012211013909.

Spaan, Ernst, and Felicitas Hillmann. 2013. "Migration Trajectories and the Migration Industry: Theoretical Reflections and Empirical Examples from Asia." In *The Migration Industry and the Commercialization of International Migration*, edited by Thomas Gammeltoft-Hansen and Ninna Nyberg Sørensen, 64–86. London: Routledge.

Spener, David. 2009. "Some Critical Reflections on the Migration Industry Concept." Migration in the Pacific Rim Workshop, University of California at Los Angeles.

Spiro, Emma S., Ryan M. Acton, and Carter T. Butts. 2013. "Extended Structures of Mediation: Re-Examining Brokerage in Dynamic Networks." *Social Networks* 35 (1): 130–43. https://doi.org/10.1016/j.socnet.2013.02.001.

Stoney, Sierra, and Jeanne Batalova. 2013. "Mexican Immigrants in the United States." *Migration Information Source*, February 28, 2013. www.migrationpolicy.org.

Stovel, Katherine, and Lynette Shaw. 2012. "Brokerage." *Annual Review of Sociology* 38 (7): 139–58.

Stumpf, Juliet P. 2006. "The Crimmigration Crisis: Immigrants, Crime, and Sovereign Power." *American University Law Review* 56 (2): 367–419. http://law.bepress.com/expresso/eps/1635.

Sutter, Brigitte. 2013. "Untangling Immobility in Transit: Sub-Saharan Migrants in Istanbul." In *Long Journeys: African Migrants on the Road*, edited by Alessandro Triulzi and Robert Lawrence McKenzie, 93–112. Leiden: Brill.

Taylor, Luke. 2022. "The Growing Health Crisis on the World's Most Perilous Migrant Crossing." *BMJ* 2022; 376. https://doi.org/10.1136/bmj.o419.

Ticktin, Miriam I. 2011. *Casualties of Care: Immigration and the Politics of Humanitarianism in France*. Berkeley: University of California Press.

Titterton, Michael. 1992. "Managing Threats to Welfare: The Search for a New Paradigm of Welfare." *Journal of Social Policy* 21 (1): 1–23. https://doi.org/10.1017/S0047279400020638.

Torre Cantalapiedra, Eduardo. 2021. *Caravanas: Sus Protagonistas ante las Políticas Migratorias*. Tijuana: El Colegio de la Frontera Norte.

Torre Cantalapiedra, Eduardo, and Dulce María Mariscal. 2020. "Batallando con Fronteras: Estrategias Migratorias en Tránsito de Participantes en Caravanas de Migrantes." *Estudios Fronterizos* 21. https://doi.org/10.21670/ref.2005047.

Tourliere, Mathieu. 2016. "Más de 5 Mil Haitianos y Africanos, Varados en Baja California." *Revista Proceso*, October 6, 2016. www.proceso.com.mx.

Trevino-Rangel, Javier. 2021. "'Cheap Merchandise': Atrocity and Undocumented Migrants in Transit in Mexico's War on Drugs." *Critical Sociology* 47 (4–5): 777–93. https://doi.org/10.1177/0896920520961815.

Turkewitz, Julie. 2023. "'A Ticket to Disney'? Politicians Charge Millions to Send Migrants to US." *New York Times*, September 14, 2023. www.nytimes.com.

Tyler, Imogen, and Katarzyna Marciniak. 2013. "Immigrant Protest: An Introduction." *Citizenship Studies* 17 (2): 143–56. https://doi.org/10.1080/13621025.2013.780728.

UNDP (United Nations Development Programme). 2014. "Migration, Resettlement and Climate Change in Viet Nam: Reducing Exposure and Vulnerabilities to Climatic Extremes and Stresses through Spontaneous and Guided Migration." United Nations Vietnam.

UNHCR (United Nations High Commissioner for Refugees). 2021. *Global Report, 2021: The Stories behind the Numbers*. Geneva, Switzerland: UNHCR. https://reporting.unhcr.org.

———. 2022. *Internal Displacement in Mexico, July–December 2022*. Geneva, Switzerland: UNHCR. https://reporting.unhcr.org.

———. 2023. *Global Trends: Forced Displacement in 2022*. Geneva, Switzerland: UNHCR. www.unhcr.org.

United States Customs and Border Protection. 2022. "CBP Enforcement Statistics, Fiscal Year 2022." www.cbp.gov.

———. 2023. "Nationwide Enforcement Encounters: Title 8 Enforcement Actions and Title 42 Expulsions, Fiscal Year 2023." www.cbp.gov.

United States Department of Homeland Security. 2017. *Yearbook of Immigration Statistics, 2016*. Washington, DC: US Department of Homeland Security, Office of Immigration Statistics.

———. 2019. *Yearbook of Immigration Statistics, 2018*. Washington, DC: US Department of Homeland Security, Office of Immigration Statistics.

———. 2020. *Yearbook of Immigration Statistics, 2019*. Washington, DC: US Department of Homeland Security, Office of Immigration Statistics.

———. 2022. "DHS Statement on US District Court's Decision Regarding MPP." August 8, 2022. www.dhs.gov.

———. 2023. "Fact Sheet: Notice of Proposed Rulemaking 'Circumvention of Lawful Pathways.'" February 2023. www.dhs.gov.

UPM (Unidad de Política Migratoria). 2016. *Boletín Mensual de Estadísticas Migratorias. Registro e Identidad de Personas*. Mexico: Secretaría de Gobernación. www.politicamigratoria.gob.mx.

———. 2017. *Boletín Mensual de Estadísticas Migratorias. Registro e Identidad de Personas*. Mexico: Secretaría de Gobernación. www.politicamigratoria.gob.mx.

———. 2018. *Boletín Mensual de Estadísticas Migratorias. Registro e Identidad de Personas*. Mexico: Secretaría de Gobernación. www.politicamigratoria.gob.mx.

———. 2019. *Boletín Mensual de Estadísticas Migratorias. Registro e Identidad de Personas*. Mexico: Secretaría de Gobernación. www.politicamigratoria.gob.mx.

———. 2020. *Boletín Mensual de Estadísticas Migratorias. Registro e Identidad de Personas*. Mexico: Secretaría de Gobernación. www.politicamigratoria.gob.mx.

———. 2021. *Boletín Mensual de Estadísticas Migratorias. Registro e Identidad de Personas*. Mexico: Secretaría de Gobernación. www.politicamigratoria.gob.mx.

———. 2022. *Boletín Mensual de Estadísticas Migratorias. Registro e Identidad de Personas*. Mexico: Secretaría de Gobernación. www.politicamigratoria.gob.mx.

———. 2023. *Boletín Mensual de Estadísticas Migratorias. Registro e Identidad de Personas*. Mexico: Secretaría de Gobernación. www.politicamigratoria.gob.mx.

Urry, John. 2007. *Mobilities*. Cambridge: Polity.

Valarezo, Giselle. 2015. "Offloading Migration Management: The Institutionalized Authority of Non-State Agencies over the Guatemalan Temporary Agricultural Worker to Canada Project." *Journal of International Migration and Integration* 16 (3): 661–77. https://doi.org/10.1007/s12134-014-0351-7.

Vandevoordt, Robin. 2019. "Subversive Humanitarianism: Rethinking Refugee Solidarity through Grass-Roots Initiatives." *Refugee Survey Quarterly* 38 (3): 245–65. https://doi.org/10.1093/rsq/hdz008.

Van Hear, Nicholas. 2014. "Reconsidering Migration and Class." *International Migration Review* 48 (s1): S100–121.

van Leeuwen, Marco H. D. 1994. "Logic of Charity: Poor Relief in Pre-industrial Europe." *Journal of Interdisciplinary History* 24 (4): 589–613. https://doi.org/10.2307/205627.

———. 2013. "Overrun by Hungry Hordes? Migration and Poor Relief in the Netherlands, Sixteenth to Twentieth Centuries." In *Migration, Settlement and Belonging in Europe, 1500–1930s: Comparative Perspectives*, edited by Stephen King and Anne Winter, 173–203. New York: Berghahn.

Vargas Carrasco, Felipe de Jesús. 2018. "El Vía Crucis del Migrante: Demandas y Membresía." *Trace* 73: 117–33. www.scielo.org.mx.

Velásquez García, Erik, Enrique Nalda, Pablo Escalanate Gozalbo, Bernardo García Martínez, Bernd Heusberger, Óscar Mazín, Dorothy Tanck de Estrada, et al. 2010. *Nueva Historia General de México*. Mexico: El Colegio de México.

Vogt, Wendy A. 2017. "The Arterial Border: Negotiating Economies of Risk and Violence in Mexico's Security Regime." *International Journal of Migration and Border Studies* 3 (203): 192–207. https://doi.org/10.1504/IJMBS.2017.10001443.

———. 2018. *Lives in Transit: Violence and Intimacy on the Migrant Journey*. Berkeley: University of California Press.

Werbner, Pnina. 1999. "Global Pathways: Working Class Cosmopolitans and the Creation of Transnational Ethnic Worlds." *Social Anthropology* 7 (1): 17–35. https:// doi:10.1017/S0964028299000026.

Wilkinson, Olivia J. 2018. "'It's Being, Not Doing': Hospitality and Hostility between Local Faith Actors and International Humanitarian Organizations in Refugee Response." *Migration and Society* 1 (1): 111–26. https://doi.org/10.3167/arms.2018.010110.

Willen, Sarah S. 2007. "Toward a Critical Phenomenology of 'Illegality': State Power, Criminalization, and Abjectivity among Undocumented Migrant Workers in Tel Aviv, Israel." *International Migration* 45 (3): 8–38. https://doi.org/10.1111/j.1468-2435.2007.00409.x.

Wilson, Richard Ashby, and Richard D. Brown (eds.). 2009. *Humanitarianism and Suffering: The Mobilization of Empathy*. Cambridge: Cambridge University Press.

Wurtz, Heather M. 2020. "A Movement in Motion: Collective Mobility and Embodied Practice in the Central American Migrant Caravan." *Mobilities* 15 (6): 930–44. https://doi.org/10.1080/17450101.2020.1806511.

Wurtz, Heather, and Olivia Wilkinson. 2020. "Local Faith Actors and the Global Compact on Refugees." *Migration and Society* 3 (1): 145–61. https://doi.org/10.3167/arms.2020.030112.

Xiang, Biao. 2007. *Global "Body Shopping": An Indian Labor System in the Information Technology Industry*. Princeton: Princeton University Press.

Yates, Caitlyn. 2019. "As More Migrants from Africa and Asia Arrive in Latin America, Governments Seek Orderly and Controlled Pathways." *Migration Information Source*, October 22, 2019. www.migrationpolicy.org.

Yates, Caitlyn, and Jessica Bolter. 2021. *African Migration through the Americas: Drivers, Routes, and Policy Responses*. Washington, DC: Migration Policy Institute.

Yuval-Davis, Nira, George Wemyss, and Kathryn Cassidy. 2017. "Everyday Bordering, Belonging and the Reorientation of British Immigration Legislation." *Sociology* 52 (2): 1–17. https://doi.org/10.1177/0038038517702599.

Zepeda Gil, Raúl. 2018. "Seven Explanatory Approaches about the Increasing of Violence in Mexico." *Política y Gobierno* 25 (1): 185–211.

INDEX

ABOUT THE AUTHOR

Alejandro Olayo-Méndez is Assistant Professor at the Boston College School of Social Work. His research focuses on migrants' and refugees' livelihoods and the role of humanitarian organizations in contexts of migration and forced displacement. He is the author of *Navigating the US-Mexico Border: Digital Practices of Migrants and Their Psychosocial Needs*. Dr. Olayo-Méndez is a Jesuit Catholic priest.

www.ingramcontent.com/pod-product-compliance
Lightning Source LLC
Chambersburg PA
CBHW031142020426
42333CB00013B/484